HANCOCK'S

Half-Hour

HANCOCK'S

Half-Hour

RADIO SCRIPTS BY

RAY GALTON &

ALAN SIMPSON

COMPILED BY CHRIS BUMSTEAD

BBC BOOKS

THE·CLASSIC·YEARS

Published by BBC Books
A division of BBC Enterprises Ltd
Woodlands, 80 Wood Lane, London W12 0TT

First published 1987
Scripts © Ray Galton and Alan Simpson
Additional material © Chris Bumstead 1987

ISBN 0 563 20610 1

Typeset in Linotron Times by
Phoenix Photosetting, Chatham, Kent
Printed in Great Britain by
Mackays of Chatham Ltd, Kent
Jacket printed by Belmont Press, Northampton

CONTENTS

Yes please. See what you can develop. We could pay say 15 gns for a script treatment. M.S. 15/7.

From: PE

To: Mr. Peter Eton

Subject: PROGRAMME SUGGESTION

8th July 1952

Copy to: D.H.V.; A.H.V.(P)

interim script treatment — agreed, good.

To: H.V.

Here is an Tony Hancock and Larry Stephens have suggested an idea for a new "Hancock" series. As Tony is genuinely enthusiastic about Larry's idea, I thought it might be a good thing to tell you about it, even while discussions are at a preliminary stage. Here is an outline:

Tony Hancock plays the part of an estate-agent-cum-bachelor-town-councillor, who lives with his old aunt in one of those frightful semi-detached villas in a small South Coast town. Our hero is an unimaginative, unenterprising, charming idiot who has a lot of trouble with his eccentric aunt because of her ambition for him to marry into the County 'set'. Tony, on the other hand, prefers the local girls and is, of course, considered an eligible and reliable bachelor by their mothers. The villain of the piece is a local garage proprietor, a loud-mouthed, witless, back-slapping oaf, always ready with a clumsy, unfunny leg-pull and a raucous laugh.

Apart from the fact that each of the six or more half-hour programmes would consist of a complete story about Tony's pompous, yet likeable, blundering, there would be no set formula.

No audience - no orchestra - and no singers would be required. Recorded music would be used for opening, closing and links.

Shall I encourage them to go further?

(Peter Eton)

PE/DBL.

N.B. Recently Tony took part in a sketch in "Hullo There". I gather, everyone connected with the programme advised him that his metier was non-audience comedy, hence the above idea.

Please turn o[ver]

A historic document – the BBC internal memo, written in 1952, that was to lead to a radio series that gripped the attention of the nation.

D.q.v.

Possible, I'd say.
What do you think?

T 17/7

A.H.V.(P)

I think we should include
this in the Programme offer.

21/7

Home reading
23 July

INTRODUCTION

by Chris Bumstead

THE RADIO FUN

'Ladies and Gentlemen, I have been asked to address you, prior to the commencement of this publication, on the subject of *Hancock's Half-Hour* radio shows, and I have been given 6,000 words from the time I said "Ladies and Gentlemen . . ."'

That paragraph, for the uninitiated among you, was vintage Galton and Simpson. Not from the scripts, but from a specially-written introduction to preface the very first album of radio excerpts, entitled *Pieces of Hancock*, which has since become a much sought-after collector's item. That album, incidentally, included a sketch called 'The Secret Life of Anthony Aloysius Hancock', better known as 'The Test Pilot', which itself was extracted from a show called 'The Diary', and was most probably, as I recall, my first introduction to Tony Hancock, since it was a frequently requested piece on *Children's Favourites*, with 'Uncle Mac'.

Having said that, and before I go any further, you are perhaps wondering why I, a mere mortal, should suddenly be given the great honour and marvellous opportunity of selecting these scripts, and, moreover, what credentials I have that enable me to talk about them; so, without more ado, allow me to introduce myself.

'Chris Bumstead, a plump, balding and eccentric individual with a ridiculous name!' That was how I was described in an article from the Australian daily newspaper, *The Age*, and whilst I don't disagree with the journalistic gentleman on most of his assessments, I might take exception to the term 'plump'. Portly, perhaps, but never plump! No matter – what is criticism to intellectuals? At least he spelt the name right!

However, I first declared my public interest in the works of Tony Hancock by joining the newly-formed Tony Hancock Appreciation Society in 1976, and whilst I had trouble in keeping up the payments of fifty pence a year, I was still there in 1980, when some fool asked me to 'take things over'. Well, having been President of this august body of intellectuals for seven years now, it has been my tremendous pleasure to meet and talk with many of the wonderful people who were involved in the making of the *Hancock's Half-Hour* radio shows, none more so than the writers, Alan Simpson and Ray Galton.

As you probably know, Alan and Ray first met in the Milford Sanatorium in 1948, whilst undergoing treatment for tuberculosis.

'There was a chap there,' said Alan, 'who had set up an internal radio circuit and, after joining in with all sorts of weird and wonderful programmes, Ray and I got together, wrote some comedy scripts and then broadcast them ourselves over this hospital network.'

As Alan was speaking, I couldn't help but think back to a time when a friend and I used to sneak off early from school to his dad's shed, where we would hectically write and record some material, and then expect his parents to enjoy the playbacks! But then we were committed Galton and Simpson fans from the outset and as I was now,

twenty-five years on, talking to 'my heroes' I had to ask, 'What influenced Galton and Simpson?'

'Phil Harris, Braden, *Life with the Lyons*,' said Ray, 'and people like Stephen Leacock and Thorne Smith.'

'Our real heroes of the day,' added Alan, 'were almost definitely Frank Muir and Dennis Norden, and we even wrote to them, asking how we might become scriptwriters!'

The reply gave them the name of Gale Pedrick, Script Editor at the BBC, and it wasn't long before they were writing, albeit mainly 'gags' and one-liners, for Derek Roy, at the rate of five shillings a joke. The show was *Happy Go Lucky* and co-starred Tony Hancock.

Tony was, by then, already well established in radio through his appearances as the schoolmaster in *Educating Archie*, but was a long way yet from the character of Anthony Aloysius.

His radio career had begun in 1941, in a light entertainment show called *A La Carte*, but was interrupted by the war years and his own National Service. In the opening years of the 1950s Hancock appeared in numerous variety broadcasts.

George Fairweather, Tony's life-long friend and mentor, recalled one particular show from the *Workers' Playtime* series, in which 'there were no laughs at all'. 'In explanation,' George said, 'Tony told me that he was trying something new, building up a character within a situation. I told him to cut it out and stick to making people laugh!'

But the laughs which greeted Hancock in *Educating Archie* were beginning to fade in *Happy Go Lucky*, running concurrently, and for the last three shows in that latter series the new producer, Dennis Main Wilson, brought in two new writers to do the whole show. Thus, for the first time, Tony Hancock was using material written by Alan Simpson and Ray Galton.

'After that,' recalled Alan, 'we went back to writing short sketches for various comedians . . .' 'Music-hall stuff really,' added Ray, 'and then we were asked to write for the last six shows of a series called *Calling All Forces* and that was the real breakthrough.' 'Hancock shared the billing with Charlie Chester,' said Alan, 'but most of our material was for Tony.'

At this time Tony's radio character was not very far removed from his schoolmaster act in *Educating Archie*, and the shows were a great success, gathering audiences of about 30 million a week, progressing onwards as *Forces All Star Bill*, *All Star Bill* and finally *Star Bill*, with Alan and Ray writing all of Hancock's material.

With the Hancock character gradually developing, the team was ready for its own show, with Dennis Main Wilson as producer, Galton and Simpson the writers and starring Tony Hancock, in *Hancock's Half-Hour*.

Hancock, in a *TV Times* article, much later, recalled: 'Some time earlier I had made a film with Sid James and we hit it off rather well. He went absolutely white when I asked him to join the show.' Ray Galton remembered Sid's early fears of performing before an audience: 'He was scared stiff of looking at the studio audience, and actually came out with a hat pulled down over his eyes!'

Bill Kerr, already an established comedian, was drafted in to play the swift-talking Australian and it was the inspiration of Dennis Main Wilson that enticed Kenneth Williams to join the crew, whilst Moira Lister was carried over from the *Star Bill* series to play the 'girlfriend' role.

That very first *Hancock's Half-Hour* was broadcast on 2 November 1954 and involved Anthony Aloysius St John Hancock renting some rooms from Sid James (setting the pattern of con-man and conned!) so that he might throw a 'First Night Party' to launch the new series – the catch being that Sid had not informed the people who were living there!

Tony's voice was still set in the character of the dummy's tutor, a little 'plummy', and seems, now, to be high-pitched and forced with a tendency to rush the lines as if uncertain of their laughter value – the Hancockian pauses were to come much later. Whilst Sid's semi-criminal character varied little through the years, the very buoyant, Americanised character played by Bill Kerr in the early days could hardly be recognised as the lovable innocent who was to emerge in the later series.

Hancock himself admitted that 'those first shows were received rather coolly really, but we survived.'

From survival to success took time and that first series was really a testing ground for cast and writers alike, and for that reason I have not included any of the scripts from that particular era but cannot allow myself to pass directly on to the second series without some mention of a few important factors, especially the music.

Those opening bars of 'H-H-*Hancock's Half-Hour*' are now as instantly recognisable as the signature tune to *The Archers* or *EastEnders*, and the person responsible was Wally Stott, now known as Angela Morley.

In a recent interview for our society's magazine (*Railway Cuttings*), Angela Morley recalled: 'In the early fifties, Stanley Black was so successful that he could not handle all the assignments that were offered to him, and I was lucky enough to take over several from him, including *Hancock's Half-Hour*. Dennis Main Wilson spent a lot of time describing the style of Hancock and it took me about a week to think about it and five minutes to write. I just had this vision of a tubby, rather pompous character and wrote the snatch of tuba music to suit!'

Wally Stott's music, played by Harry Rabinowitz and his orchestra, was only used to change scenes or mood, or to denote the passage of time, and rarely exceeded a few bars. This was quite a breakthrough in situation comedy (or any comedy show) in this country, because Galton and Simpson were following leads laid down by some of the American comedy shows which they had listened to on AFN (American Forces Network) whilst in the Sanatorium. Whereas other British comedy shows were clinging to the old 'variety' approach, with a five- or ten-minute break for a musical interlude, they, with Hancock's approval and encouragement, were writing the first British situation comedy show to run the full half hour without interruption.

Keeping the whole plot simmering for that time, however, sometimes proved a little difficult in those early shows where the individual characters had not fully developed themselves, so a little 'bit of business' was introduced wherein Tony would side-step from the plot and spend five minutes or so talking to a complete stranger. The budget for the shows being very small (as a BBC memo at the time revealed, one episode of *Hancock's Half-Hour* cost only £260 in December 1954), they couldn't afford to bring in another member for the cast, so it was Alan Simpson who stepped up to the microphone to play the part of the stranger. Amazingly, wherever the cast was in the plot, that same stranger would turn up and Tony would approach him with 'Of course, this isn't the first time I've done this . . .', and Alan's replies would usually consist of a 'yes' or 'no'.

This sequence between Alan and Tony was most effectively used in 'The Monte Carlo Rally' (from the first series), where the two met halfway up a mountain, with Hancock recalling the time when he used to run up and down Mount Everest before breakfast!

Other noteworthy episodes from that first series include 'The New Car', with Kenneth Williams as the AA man who had never completed a successful repair, and 'A House on the Cliff' which allowed Sid some double-double-dealing in a plot resembling a French farce.

At the end of the first series Moira Lister left the cast to return to South Africa, and the second series opened on 19 March 1955 with Andrée Melly taking the role of Tony's new, and French, girlfriend.

'I was a little nervous about joining an already established cast,' admitted Andrée, 'but they all made me feel very welcome; Sid, Ken, sweet Bill Kerr, and Tony too, of course, though I got the feeling that he was closest to Ken. Tony seemed to be on the defensive when introduced to women, children and dogs – a bit like W. C. Fields!'

As it happened, Harry Secombe replaced Tony Hancock for the opening three shows of that second series, guesting, on Hancock's return to good health, in the fourth.

The fifth show took them, metaphorically, to a holiday camp which turned out to be an army barrack in the middle of an artillery firing range. Although most of the show is absorbed in the plot and careful exploitation of the situation, there is a marvellous sequence in which Hancock and Kerr run through a dreadful Holiday Camp Variety Show in under five minutes and end up congratulating themselves!

Tony's voice was still a little high (although slowing down some) and Andrée's French accent a slight handicap, but the writers and cast were settling now and becoming more relaxed. Relaxed enough, it seemed, to divert from the usual pattern in the sixth show, 'The Chef that Died of Shame', which told the story of 'Iggins. This was a character often referred to by Hancock in *Star Bill* and the early 'H.H.H.' shows, but who, until then, had never appeared. The fact that 'Iggins isn't mentioned at all after this show makes one wonder if Galton and Simpson didn't make that the opportunity to exorcise him completely; anyway, for other reasons this show makes uncomfortable listening today.

Not that comfort was the uppermost factor in the railway service offered by Messrs Hancock, Kerr and James during 'The Rail Strike', and eighth show of the second series, which had a plot as fantastical as that of *The Titfield Thunderbolt*.

Other shows of note included 'The Marrow Contest', with a typically Hancock line:

TONY No, the dustmen came yesterday.
BILL How can you tell?
TONY There's the trail of rubbish up the garden path!

However, my own choice from this second series is 'The Television Set' because this episode, perhaps even more than the classic 'Sunday Afternoon at Home', displays the character of 'Snide', played by Kenneth Williams, to the absolute full. 'Snide', referring to the nasal tone in which Ken delivered the character's lines, was never intended to be included. Alan Simpson recalled that 'our original idea was to have no musical interludes, no funny voices and no catchphrases, but then Kenneth Williams walked on, said "Good Evening" and the whole audience fell about!'

It was the audience that initially disconcerted Andrée Melly, as with Sid James earlier, but far more hair-raising for her was the occasional instance of the script not being ready for recordings. 'I remember Galton and Simpson writing frantically away,' she recalled, 'while we were actually recording! But it was great fun, very relaxed and friendly, and I'm very proud to have worked with Tony. He contributed so much to the world of British humour.'

The third series, carrying over an unchanged team from the second, differed little in style from its predecessor. There was still that urgency to get the punch line across to the audience, something not unique to the *Hancock's Half-Hour* team but which was symptomatic of all the comedy programmes of that time; as if there were a general fear that studio audiences would rise up in unison to catch the last bus home before the laughs came, but was more probably due to the continued trend of imitating the quick-fire American shows. This was most discernible in the fast-talking Bill Kerr character. But there was a small concession made in the third series by the sudden disappearance of the French accent in Andrée Melly's portrayal of the girlfriend.

This series built upon the success of the second, however, but was to remain firmly dominated by plot, parody or situation, instead of character-development to any great degree.

The fact that the characters' circumstances changed from week to week didn't seem to matter – one week Hancock would own his house and the next week it would be rented; poor one minute, rich the next – it gave the writers a certain freedom to expand and to experiment. Sometimes the continuity within a single show would be suspect, but as Alan Simpson recalled: 'It gave us a chance to get complete variation of situation and circumstance – he could be a window-cleaner one week and a Shakespearean actor the next – it didn't seem to bother anybody.'

Lack of continuity certainly didn't worry the listening public. They loved the show. 'So did the cast,' recounted Ray Galton. 'Bill Kerr would often break off into laughter, beginning with a giggle that opened out into a huge guffaw!' 'Sid James once took thirteen attempts at one line before he could stop laughing and get it right,' added Alan. 'And I well remember the time we had to literally pick Tony Hancock up off the floor, where he had been rolling about with tears streaming down his cheeks!'

'The Pet Dog', the first show of this third series, concerned a puppy that wouldn't stop growing, originating as a birthday present for Andrée and ending up occupying the whole house.

Also in this series was 'The Bequest', in which Hancock's uncle ('Ah poor old Uncle Ebadiah – gone – and never called me "nephew"'), left him a fortune with the proviso that he had to get married.

Hancock's attempts to find himself a wife take him to the dance-hall, where he insists on wearing his 'correct dancing clobber', complete with his number pinned to his back. The fact that the Palais now reverberates to a dance-band playing jive does not deter him from asking:

'Excuse me, young lady, if your dance card is not full, perhaps you would care to have the next fox-trot?'

And back comes the reply: 'Get lost, fatty!'

Galton and Simpson really showed their comic genius in this cameo, taking a slice

of reality in the form of the new youth scene, and presenting us with Bill Kerr splendidly playing (as well as his usual character) the Marlon Brando street-wise tough guy who begins to threaten Hancock.

'Don't let him hit me, Sid . . .'

Sid's intervention only succeeds in separating the whole dance floor as a fight seems inevitable. 'I've never seen the Hokey-Cokey break up so fast,' says Hancock.

Then from the danger of the dance-hall, the writers take us to the safety of romance, with Hancock playing the great lover hoping to woo young Andrée with soft music (from the piped bands of the Royal Grenadiers?) and cheap champagne. Even this isn't safe because there is a knock at the door and in walks . . . 'Good Evening, does Mr Hancock live here?' . . . 'Snide'.

Hancock tells him that Mr Hancock has gone up Everest with Hillary, Snide tells him that he's got another will, a later one, for Mr Hancock.

Tony then admits, 'I'm Mr Hancock.'

'Snide': 'Oooooh hallo, how's Mr Hiliary?'

The sixth show of the series was 'The Blackboard Jungle', a gentle send-up of the film of the same name. This sort of comedy was extremely popular at the time (much in the same way that most non-situation comedy in 1987 lampoons contemporary television programmes); and of course, as Alan Simpson pointed out, it was much easier to write because you didn't have to think up the plot.

Incidentally, just deviating slightly, in 1986 one of our THAS members came across this marvellous headline in his local newspaper: 'HOW THE LAD FROM EAST CHEAM USHERED IN THE TEENAGE REVOLUTION'.

Aghast, I read on!

The sub-headline followed: 'John Ogden sets the record straight at last about 'Ancock, unsung father of be-bop-a-lula'.

Interested? I certainly was. John goes on to say that 'In just one programme on November 23rd 1955, the lad from East Cheam brought the sound of rock and roll into millions of homes in his parody of the film, *The Blackboard Jungle*.'

The theory followed that the only exposure for 'pop' music on BBC radio networks in 1955 was *Family Favourites* which tended to concentrate on ballads, and that when Bill Haley's recording of 'Rock Around the Clock' (from the film *Blackboard Jungle*) was broadcast in this episode of *Hancock's Half-Hour*, it was heard by an audience worth three of that gained by today's *Top of the Pops* appearances. John attributed the greater part of Bill Haley's record success in this country to this one 'H.H.H.' show, and after discussing the 'rock and roll revival', added 'How I wish there could be a Hancock revival!'

Other notable episodes from this third series were 'Hancock's Hair', opening with a true scene from life – Hancock counting the number of hairs found on his hair brush each morning; 'The Student Prince', a clever variation on a theme; 'The Greyhound Track', another fine mess Sid got him into; and that lovely dream sequence in 'The Test Match', wherein Hancock is destined to be the cricketing hero, with assistance from John Arlott, Colin Cowdrey, Godfrey Evans and Frank Tyson.

Tony Hancock, the person, had a great passion for cricket, both as a spectator and a player, so this dream sequence had a special significance for him and he was, by all accounts, thrilled at the opportunity of meeting his own cricketing heroes. Freddie Hancock (Tony and Freddie were married in 1965) received a letter from the

headmaster at Tony's public school not long after Tony's death, saying that 'He will always be remembered as a very good cricketer', and one of our THAS members recalled meeting Tony at Lord's cricket ground and spending some time with him talking about not comedy but cricket.

'The Test Match' was the last programme in the third series and it was noticeable that Andrée's lines had been cut quite dramatically to the point where she had almost less to say than Alan Simpson's 'stranger' in the previous series.

Andrée was not surprised when she was not invited back for another series. 'Galton and Simpson were finding it increasingly difficult to write for my character. Tony really needed someone a bit more domineering, less passive.' That certain someone didn't turn up until show five of the fourth series, but before that series began, Tony and 'the boys', as Galton and Simpson were affectionately called, had been busy on their first television series for BBC television.

Between the end of the third and beginning of the fourth series there had been an all-out musicians' union strike at the BBC in protest at the use of recorded music. One of the side effects of this dispute, once settled, was that Wally Stott was commissioned to rewrite the musical 'link' pieces and arrange them for a much smaller orchestra, which, as it turned out, was more in keeping with the new, settled style that was to follow.

Hancock's radio voice, possibly as a result of the much slower pace of his television work, had now developed the style of delivery which we normally associate with him. Sid James' character, though still erring in the criminal underworld, was to deepen and become softer, more friendly towards Hancock as this series progressed, and the Bill Kerr character was relaxing and graduating towards the naive innocence of the boy from the bush.

The first show, transmitted on 14 October 1956, 'Back from Holiday', saw Hancock (Tubs) and Bill coming home from a holiday abroad a little earlier than expected, to find that Sid had rented out their house to Kenneth Williams, who had filled it with cats. As a result, the homeless couple had to retire to a doss-house where they slept 'over the rope'.

Sid was again up to his usual tricks in 'The Bolshoi Ballet', with Hancock seeking an injection of popular culture and Sid James selling him down the river.

The fourth show of this fourth series, 'The Income Tax Demand', is a very good example of the way in which Galton and Simpson were finalising their character of the radio Hancock, and after these finishing touches had been added to the overall picture of Anthony Aloysius St John Hancock, their canvas was to remain substantially unchanged from this point forward. Hancock is immediately appalled at, what seems to us to be, a thoroughly reasonable tax demand, and rebels against the red tape of the establishment that engineered it. He is preparing for a fight, withdraws, hesitates, re-enters the fray with Sid James, hesitates again, apologises for ever having started in the first place and ends up where, in reality, he imagined he would be from the onset, in failure. The reason why Galton and Simpson are so exceptional in creating these miniature playlets about life, is that they are able to send Hancock down in a way that he takes the establishment down with him.

When the chips are down, you either laugh or cry, and it was the Galton and Simpson philosophy to laugh, and in doing so to make others laugh with them.

The very location of 23 Railway Cuttings, a purely fictional address, was all part of

the character-building that the writers did so well. 'We wanted Cheam, as it seemed to us a pretty posh sort of area,' said Alan, 'but thought that he was the sort of bloke who would never actually quite make it to Cheam, so we got as close as we could and put him in *East* Cheam. We also wanted to make it in a slightly less desirable part of Cheam, so we made it Railway Cuttings. It could as easily have been Oil Drum Lane.'

The fictional pub, the Hand and Racquet, was based upon the pub of the same name (still serving beer on the corners of Orange and Whitcombe Streets, just off the Haymarket) where the writers and members of the cast would meet for a drink between rehearsals, and, incidentally, the place where I met Alan Simpson for the first time. He pointed out a location where once sat a café which provided them with lunch – usually steak-and-kidney pudding and two veg, which the owner referred to as 'Baby's head and two.'

Meanwhile, back at 23 Railway Cuttings, Bill and Tony had decided that they needed some secretarial assistance and, with thoughts aspiring to someone of the same dimensions as Shirley Eaton, they advertised for 'The New Secretary', (programme five, fourth series). Dreams disturbed and silence shattered, Griselda Pugh, played by Hattie Jacques, stormed in and the whole fabric of *Hancock's Half-Hour* was to change.

Although, at first, the character of Griselda 'Grizzly' Pugh was a trifle harsh and over-aggressive, it mellowed very quickly through the next few shows and soon developed into the affectionate, occasionally sentimental, dominating mother-figure of a she-devil that is so much part of our nostalgic reminiscences of the radio shows.

TONY   Miss Pugh! Come here, I need you!

HATTIE   I can't – I'm busy! I'm doing some filing!

TONY   Well, finish it later . . .

HATTIE   I can't – I've only done four fingers . . .

(Just part of the interchange between secretary and employer in the show (episode six), 'Michelangelo Hancock', or 'Hancock the Sculptor', in which Hancock plans to win the town council statue competition.)

HATTIE   Ha . . . what do you know about statues?

TONY   Quite a lot, from the speed you work at . . . (*aside*) hallo, there's another one gone home!

Miss Pugh agrees to be the model, bringing the comment from Kenneth Williams, as one of the judges, 'Barrage balloon on a stick!'; Sid James acquires the blocks of stone, from Westminster Bridge and various other London locations, and Hancock gets the bird from an 'extra' in the crowd scene, played by Ray Galton, 'What about the drains in River Road.'

Episode seven, by direct contrast, is a straight lampooning of the popular contemporary film *The King and I*, renamed *Anna and the King of Siam*, with Hancock having his head shaved for the Yul Brynner role, and the ninth episode, 'The Stolen Petrol', was a topical skit on the return of petrol rationing, as a result of the Suez Crisis.

The episode (eight) that was sandwiched between those two, and in which Hancock himself is sandwiched between Griselda and Sid, was called 'Cyrano de Hancock', and was a sort of eternal triangle with a big difference. In demonstrating to Sid the technicalities of a romantic proposal, Hancock inadvertently asks for Miss Pugh's hand in marriage.

SIDNEY Go back in there and tell her it was a mistake.

TONY It's too late, Sid, she'll have written the invitations by now.

His attempts to call off the wedding are as hilarious as they are futile, but all is not lost, as the registrar turns out to be none other than Kenneth Williams' 'Snide' character, the upshot being that Snide and Hancock emerge married while Griselda is escorted away in tears by Sid.

It could have ended there quite easily, but Galton and Simpson took it further to show the resilience in the Hancock character. Okay, the situation had turned full circle and he was in a right predicament but he'd paid for the photographer and he wasn't going to waste it: 'No, not that side, this side . . . get the old sweep of the nose in there . . .'

And in another masterful stroke of the ridiculous, Hancock, Galton and Simpson ask us to visualise the seductive picture of 'Grizzly' in split skirt and fishnet stockings, standing in a gondola dishing out cups of coffee to the customers, the gondola being stationed on the open sewer which runs through the 'Expresso Bar' (episode ten).

'Hancock's Happy Christmas' or 'Christmas – East Cheam Style' (episode eleven), a festive special, brought all the joyous wonder and excitement of the yuletide season to the merry inmates of 23 Railway Cuttings, well everyone except Hancock, that is. 'We're having no decorations in this house, thank you . . . dirty great pinholes all over the place . . .'

After 'The Diary', one of the scripts included herein, we come to 'The Thirteenth of the Series' and a return to the more involved 'plot' situation, but which does contain some pre-Python surrealism: for instance the policeman, played by Kenneth Williams, has to guard the stones of Stonehenge by taking them home with him each night, on his bike.

Episode fourteen, 'Almost a Gentleman', is, according to my good friend, Alwyn W. Turner, a perfect example of how the Hancock character felt alienated from the reality of society. The fact is that this show, along with 'Wild Man of the Woods' and 'Hancock in the Police' (episodes sixteen and eighteen), are, with 'The Old School Reunion' (included here), such excellent shows that, if you buy enough copies of this book to satisfy the BBC powers that be, maybe we can persuade them to do another one, and we'll include those in it.

These, and 'Agricultural 'Ancock', in which Sid sells him a farm which looks suspiciously like Lord's Cricket Ground (episode seventeen), were reviewed in *Punch* magazine in 1957, by Bernard Hollowood: '. . . his scriptwriters have a brilliant line in literary cliché and the humour of the goonbeam lunacy, and by a strong cast . . .' This show was one of Richard Briers' favourites: 'I just love the bit where the "milkmaids" are coming out with their padded gloves on. . . .'

After episode nineteen, 'The Emigrant', which was transferred to television a few years later, the last show of the fourth series was 'The Last of the McHancocks', with James Robertson Justice spitting blood and hellfire on the clan of the McHancocks and calling Griselda, 'a wee lassie', much to the amusement of cast and studio audience alike.

Seamus McNasty (James Robertson Justice) is the Scottish Bluto-type character whose clan, the McNastys, have sworn vengeance upon the Sassenach McHancocks, but is confused by the arrival of Bonny Prince Sidney. The Highland Games are disrupted when the rocket-powered hammer thrown by Bonny Prince Sidney lands on a spectator, 'Snide'.

So the fourth series ended an unqualified success: Tony Hancock was a star. During that series run, he also appeared in his own TV show series for Associated Rediffusion, starred in the radio play, *The Man Who Could Work Miracles* by H. G. Wells, and first played the now famous 'budgerigar sketch' for a Royal Variety Performance.

It so happened that the period of time which elapsed between series on this occasion was the longest yet, going to a full eleven months between the end of the fourth and the beginning of the fifth, during which time Tony Hancock starred in his second television series for the BBC, did a short variety tour, made the third BBC TV series, and also appeared, choosing his eight favourite records, on *Desert Island Discs*.

During this time, Dennis Main Wilson had decided to concentrate his energies on the expanding medium of television, and a new producer was found in Tom Ronald; although the first show, 'The New Radio Series', was produced by Pat Dixon. This episode centred around Hancock being over-inflated with the success of his TV series and deciding to retire. He fires Miss Pugh, tells Sid and Bill that 'I've carried you two for far too long', and altogether is presented in rather a harsh light.

Next up, 'The Scandal Magazine', is a beauty, however, in which Sid James runs a scandal magazine exposing the sordid exploits of Hancock: 'What was Tony Hancock doing, under the table with the cigarette girl, at the "Bag of Nuts"?', and 'Mabel the cigarette girl tells all!'

Not only is it a brilliant script by Galton and Simpson, but the whole team joined in the fun and produced a classic piece of radio comedy, with Tony Hancock coming in with a few uncharacteristic ad-libs with the studio audience.

Sometimes, as in this recording, the studio audience was liable to be over-enthusiastic, which tended to slow things down, but this could be excused, or at least explained, by the pre-show 'warm ups'. Robin Boyle, continuity announcer, recalled, in an interview for the THAS magazine conducted by fellow member, Graeme Stevenson: 'For the warm up, Tony liked to do his impression of a light-house, for which he would revolve slowly, silently opening and closing his mouth each time he faced the front of the house, never changing that famous lugubrious expression.'

For this fifth series, Bill Kerr's character had now slowed right down and was assuming that wide-eyed childlike innocence that was to become the butt of so many Hancockian jests. This trait was displayed particularly well in 'The Insurance Policy' or 'Sid James Insurance' (episode four), where Bill had divided his morning's attention equally between investigating the new pin-ball machine at the café, and watching the buses come and go at the bus depot. Hancock, meanwhile, seems at last to have become wise to the schemings of Sidney Balmoral James, though not strong enough to stand the second onslaught of the James brand of salesmanship.

'The Publicity Photograph' (fifth) features Kenneth Williams as the photographer, Hilary Sinclair, engaged by Sid to take a few 'snaps' of Hancock ('I don't take "snaps" – I paint with light!'), and sees the virtual demise of the 'snide' character, with Ken, throughout this series, assuming other major roles such as the Commander of the Bomb Disposal Squad ('I'm with the Catering Corps, really . . .') in 'The Unexploded Bomb' (sixth). Peter Black, TV and Radio critic, once commented on the quality of the *Hancock's Half-Hour* writers: '. . . the building of visual images

that, like animated cartoons, soared free of plausibility – pure fun'; and how true that is in this show, where the main plot is excellently served by numerous sub-plots, with a sense of the utterly ridiculous that asks us to imagine Hancock plugging his electric razor into the street lighting and only getting one half of his face shaved before the street lights go out.

'Hancock's School' (seventh), shows Bill's character at its lowest intellectual level, as Hancock takes up the gown that he had cast off from *Educating Archie* and teaches Bill the rudiments of the three 'r's. As ever, Sid James is the catalyst that promotes the explosion and there are definite memories of the Will Hay influence, with Ken Williams playing the all-too-bright schoolboy (Charles Hawtrey) and Hancock resorting to fiction for the areas of fact of which he is unsure.

'Around the World in Eighty Days' (eighth) is an excellent skit on the movie, whilst 'US Air Force Comes to Cheam' deserves more than just a few words in this potted history. This show, along with 'Hancock's Car' (eleven) and 'The Foreign Legion' (thirteenth), are perfect examples of the need for a second volume of radio scripts!

Programme twelve, 'The East Cheam Drama Festival', was another departure from situation comedy to witness Hancock masterminding, from the Scout Hall, Cheam, 'a trilogy of three plays'. The first is an unusual spoof on Victorian melodrama in *Jack's Return Home*, with hilarious results, the second is a semi-satirical parody of *Look Back in Anger*, and the third is an odd-ball pastiche of the life and times of Beethoven – and the music that made him famous!

After 'Sunday Afternoon at Home', probably the most famous comedy in the world, we come to 'The Wrestling Match', a.k.a. 'The Grappling Game', where we are given a ringside seat as 'Grizzly' finds a new vocation in life.

The great thing, in looking back over these tremendously varied and fun-filled scripts, is that somewhere along the trail you come up with one particularly favourite sequence that, like classical music, you can hear again and again without ever tiring. I am now about to give you my favourite piece. It is taken from 'The Junk Man', episode sixteen, where Bill has been given some string to wind up into a ball. Bill has managed to wrap it round his hand, making his fingers go blue. He tries various unsuccessful ways of removing the string from his throbbing fingers before approaching Hancock again, who is at the front door talking to Sid.

BILL   Er . . . Tubs?
TONY   Oh, what?
BILL   Hallo, Sid!
TONY   Well?
BILL   Well what?
TONY   You called me!
BILL   Did I?
TONY   Yes – you said 'Tubs?', and I said 'Oh, what?', and you said 'Hallo, Sid', and I said 'Well?', and you said 'Well what?' and I said 'You called me!', now – I want to know why you called me in the first place.
BILL   Er . . . um . . .
TONY   Think, man, what was it?
BILL   Er . . . um . . .
TONY   Are your shoes hurting you?

BILL No.

TONY Are you hungry?

BILL No.

TONY Think hard. It'll come – don't get flustered. Now, keep calm now, what was it?

BILL Er . . . um . . . Hallo, Sid!

TONY You've said that! Stop wasting my time – what do you want? It must have been something!

BILL Oh, yeah, I remember what it was – I've got the string off my fingers!

TONY Oh, good lad – how did you do it?

BILL Well, I unwound it off me fingers like you told me to do . . .

TONY See – a little bit of thought – what have you done with the string?

BILL It's wound round me other fingers now, and it's tighter and it's hurting twice as much this time!

TONY (exasperated) Sid – you can buy him if you like. . . .

The very thought of poor Bill stood there with throbbing fingers, trying to remember what he had to say . . . magic! A combination of the imagination of the writers and the sheer class of the performers!

And on the subject of performances, we couldn't let this fifth series pass by without recalling the superb portrayal of the man, alone and threatened with imminent disaster, drawing on every facet of his imagination: Tony Hancock in 'The Threatening Letters'.

There is a 'crank' writing threatening letters to famous people and Hancock's name is top of the list – and there are many Hancock fans who name this show among their favourite five. One such member – he's one of our honorary members, actually – is Richard Briers, who told me: 'I love it when he's totally alone and there's footsteps coming up the path – he goes through all the voices of the imaginary people in the house – "Are the machine guns ready, Sergeant?" – "Yes, sir" – "Ah, sir" – "And the paratroopers hidden in the garden?" – sheer brilliance!'

Richard Briers, as an honorary member of the Tony Hancock Appreciation Society, is in the good company of Freddie Hancock, Andrée Melly, Bill Kerr, George Fairweather, Alec Bregonzi, Jim McManus, Bill Wyman, Alan Simpson and Ray Galton. Alan, Ray and I were recently discussing which shows we would best like to hear repeated on the radio, and both Alan and Ray plumped for 'The Threatening Letters' as being a particular favourite.

The series ended with 'The Sleepless Night' in June 1958, but the cast reassembled in December for a Christmas special, 'Bill and Father Christmas'. That was to be the last appearance in a *Hancock's Half-Hour* by Hattie Jacques and was also the end of a 'way of life', regarding the recording procedures.

Freddie Hancock, who at the time was Hancock's publicity agent but who was later to become his second wife, recalled 'the system would involve Tony doing a read-through with the cast, and that was probably the first time he'd seen the script – then it would be timed, so as to give the sound effects people some idea of what they had to do, and then a rehearsal. The audience would then be brought in, and after a few warm ups from, usually, Alan Simpson, they would go straight into the main recording.'

The show which was recorded on a Sunday, for instance, would be broadcast on

the next Tuesday or Wednesday, and the scripts could be written between shows. Alan recalled that as soon as one recording was complete, they would be back at the typewriter the next day working on the next script.

The sixth radio series, however, was scheduled for transmission in September 1959, to run concurrently with the BBC TV series, so it was decided that the radio series should be recorded in advance. The scripts were written in a very short time and the whole series was recorded in a few weeks during the summer.

In that sixth and final radio series Hattie Jacques, who had left to have a baby, was sadly missed. Nobody can dispute the tremendous talent and warmth that Hattie had brought to the programmes, for although she only appeared in thirty-six shows, those are the ones that are best remembered with nostalgic affection.

Kenneth Williams, too, was a much valued and well-loved member of the team, and made a vital contribution to the show's success and popularity, initially through 'Snide', and progressively through the wide range of marvellous characterisations that he produced from his repertoire. Kenneth left the show after episode two of this series, and the characters that he would normally have made his own were taken by established 'straight' actors, such as Warren Mitchell, Hugh Morton and Wilfred Babbage. This move away from the comic voice and the supplementary comic characters was in keeping with the casting in the television shows and was the direction in which Hancock, Galton and Simpson had been moving: towards a situation comedy that was to be as true to life as possible.

This is particularly evident in the first show, 'The Smugglers', transmitted on 29 September 1959, in which the character of Sidney Balmoral James, now settled as a firm friend of 'the family' rather than a mere casual acquaintance, displays the need to continue his fringe criminal activities with a 'bit of business on the side'. This forms the main plot, with Sid trying to smuggle a few watches through the customs with the aid, unwittingly given, of Hancock, whilst there is also a strong and hilarious sub-plot whereby Tony and Bill plan to take the scooter to Clacton, posing as foreign students to 'impress the birds'.

Bill, of course, had great difficulty in understanding even the very basic subterfuge involved in 'bird deception', confusing himself, and everyone else, in the comprehension of fantasy and reality, and exposing Tony to the customs officer's close examination in the culmination of an intricate, plausible and very clever script.

This was followed by 'The Childhood Sweetheart', where Tony drifts into sentimental nostalgia for a girl he once 'courted' in his youth: 'I'm going to see my little Olive again, after all this time – I'm glad I remained pure all these years – saved meself for her – it was a bit of a strain, fighting off all those other women, but somehow today it all seems worthwhile!'

The Hancock character, when threatened, was quite resilient and always ready to fight back, that is until actual physical violence became an inevitable feature of the fight, when he would retreat with honour. The imagined spectacle of Tony and Sid coming very close to exchanging blows is a highlight of 'The Last Bus Home', when the two characters, tired and weary after missing the last bus, begin to argue and actually square up to each other.

'The Picnic', featured herein, was followed by 'The Gourmet', in which Tony's long and considered perusal of a menu leads him, through various manipulations, to an eating contest, and 'The Elopement', another script which deserves full appreciation.

'Fred's Pie Stall' and 'The Waxwork', both excellent scripts, were succeeded by the classic 'Mystery Tours', with Tony being conned into running a coach firm, by Sid, taking unsuspecting American tourists on a trip around the sights of East Cheam. 'Sid's Mystery Tours' has a quality of a fully-fledged play in which the characters are given time to indulge themselves in some of life's most ordinary pleasures, like reading the morning newspaper, before tackling the plot. Alan Simpson remembers the show for the sight of Tony Hancock and Sid James having hysterics over the classic 'tortoise' routine. This has great similarities to the much later, and equally famous, 'dead parrot sketch' from Monty Python, and concerns a tortoise which Hancock bought from Sid: 'It didn't move for three weeks.' Hancock has poked it with a stick, looked down all the holes and still hasn't been able to find a tortoise. And this is just a small sub-routine, one of many, in a show that is packed with incidents, fun and fantasy.

'The Fête' opens at a council meeting, with Hancock's ideas for the proposed fête being totally ignored until, in desperation, he suggests that he can get Laurence Olivier to perform the opening ceremony. Suddenly, and before Hancock can withdraw his motion, it is accepted and the rest of the plot follows his attempts to get Lord Olivier to the fête!

'The Poetry Society' and 'Hancock in Hospital', both featured here, were followed by the penultimate show, 'The Christmas Club', recorded out of sequence some six months later and thereby being the last *Hancock's Half-Hour* show recorded for radio. Again the plot is easy-going and plausible and features a lovely scene where Sid and Tony are sitting comfortably by the fire while someone is knocking at the door, and neither is prepared to leave their chairs to answer it.

The very last radio show of all was 'The Impersonator', and revolved around Hancock venturing into 'straight' acting. Richard Briers, as an actor himself, finds this show particularly funny, especially the 'bit where he comes home and finds Sid and Bill with their feet on the mantelpiece, waiting to watch the television.' Whilst they are watching television, there appears an advertisement seeming to be in Hancock's own voice, pronouncing the virtues of Harper's Cornflakes.

'It was my job,' Peter Goodwright told me, 'to reproduce an exact copy of Tony's voice. This I could do, but was a little dismayed during the rehearsals because I sounded more like Tony Hancock than Tony himself did. What surprised me was that no one else seemed to be very worried about this. The producer was most complimentary about my part in the show, and the writers were pleased to find that their idea worked so well. After the rehearsal I mentioned my thoughts to Alan Simpson and Ray Galton and they said: "Don't worry – that was only a read-through – it will be different at the performance." And sure enough it was. Hancock was superb, garnering every available laugh, timing his lines perfectly and sounding (much to my relief) exactly like Hancock! "Stone me," he exclaimed, after one of our sections in the script, "It's like talking to a mirror!"'

The plot takes Tony into court to sue the impersonator (Peter Goodwright) for damages resulting from loss of earnings, and ends with the impersonator being offered the leading role in *Hancock's Half-Hour*.

Peter remembered enjoying the show immensely: 'Everyone was happy and friendly and I appreciated the warm welcome I had received from Tony and the rest of the cast. At this time in his career, Tony was immensely popular and I was

delighted to have had the opportunity of working with him.'

And so ended one of the most popular and best remembered radio comedy series of all time, and so, too, ends my brief history of the radio series.

Why was it so popular?

Peter Dickinson summed it up in a radio review written for *Punch* magazine, in 1958: 'Hancock manages to avoid the well-worn pitfalls of the genre [situation comedy]; he is a reasonable man, expecting reason in his relations with the rest of the world and not getting it; he does not keep dropping the pretence that he is an ordinary man in order to make jokes about his being a famous comedian . . .'

And here, in talking about Hancock, Peter Dickinson is, of course, making reference to the Hancock radio character, which was a totally unique blend of input from Hancock himself and his writers.

Why are the shows so very popular today?

Basically for all the various reasons that they were so successful in the first place. When comedy is written and performed so very well it doesn't stop being funny a week or a month later – it remains alive and vibrant for ever. Some of the terminology, perhaps, may get lost through the years, which is why I have included a glossary (at no extra expense), to explain some of the forgotten phraseology; and as there are occasional references to contemporary events, which today would need some knowledge of history, I have included a brief introduction to each script, merely to place the time period and to give a few pointers – after all, you don't get Beethoven's '1812' symphony on Radio Three without a brief introduction, and these scripts are as much classics as anything she composed.

In the Tony Hancock Appreciation Society in 1987, we have probably got more members who were too young to have heard the original broadcasts than members who, like me, can just about remember hearing them the first time around; and what appeals to the young of today is still that marvellous sense of fun that was enjoyed by the previous generation.

There have been at least five radio programmes over the last ten years which were devoted to examining the success of *Hancock's Half-Hour* on the 'wireless', a brief analysis in the *Omnibus* television programme of 1986, numerous books devoting whole chapters to the radio shows and a stage play in which the scripts have been performed. Now, for the very first time, a selection of those golden scripts is being published in this very book.

It is important to note, too, that these scripts are presented in their original and unedited state. The text in square brackets is that which was removed by Galton and Simpson after the first read-through, on finding that the whole product was over-running the allotted time. Further discrepancies between the written script and the broadcast show exist because of final editing by the producer. Dennis Main Wilson told me that he might sometimes spend as much as eight hours in the editing process.

'More often than not,' he recalled, 'I would have to remove the "visual" laughter, wherein Tony may have noticed a giggler in the audience and given him or her one of his famous stares, and this in turn would provoke even more laughter. There was so much fun being enjoyed by both cast and audience that the shows very rarely kept to time and inevitably something had to be edited out.'

No other radio show produced such 'fun' or had such an effect; no other radio comedy show has been so accurately and well documented, talked about and

honoured. The Queen Mother, for instance, selected an extract from *Hancock's Half-Hour* for inclusion in a special birthday compilation. Robbie Coltrane, in an interview for the *New Musical Express,* summed it up when he said: 'If you want to know what ordinary people were thinking in the fifties . . . listen to Hancock!'

There is a wealth of history, occasion, warmth, talent and innocent humour locked away in these superb scripts by Alan Simpson and Ray Galton – all you have to do is to . . . read on . . . it's 'Radio Fun'.

THE STORY SO FAR. . .

Four fictional biographies of 'characters'

by Chris Bumstead

A short series of fictional narratives, devised by Chris Bumstead, to take the discerning student of the *Hancock's Half-Hour* radio shows back in time to the events that happened prior to that period.

In essence, then, to present a mythical, 'mirthical' meditation on each 'character' prior to his or her arrival at 23 Railway Cuttings, East Cheam.

ANTHONY ALOYSIUS ST JOHN HANCOCK
(nee Hemlock)

An undefinable character

Born Thomas Algernon Hemlock, *circa* 1926, in a linen basket backstage at the Glasgow Empire, where his parents, Elsie Dolores and Boris Fitzgibbon Hemlock, alias 'The Flying Hemlocks', were doing a week's variety in the *George Fanshaw Myriad Miracles and Minstrel Show*.

Boris Hemlock, though the eldest son in the Hemlock family and pre-ordained to inherit the Hemlock castle, estates and fortune, was completely disowned by the Hemlock dynasty when he announced to the press that he was entering show business, doing impersonations of Napoleon III.

While his three brothers went off to join the forces, young Tommy, who was stagestruck, followed in his father's footsteps. He decided to become an impressionist – Tommy Hemlock, man of a few faces – but, although he had appeared on stage many times as a child performer, he had yet to appear in the theatre programme.

His performance as the hump, in *Hunchback of Notre Dame*, went unnoticed by his profession . . . and his parents, who had moved to Bolton and wondered where he was.

As a teenager, he took whatever work the theatres could provide, and appeared as the forest in *Babes in the Wood*, as a nest of tables in *Anything You Can Do*, and did a successful three-month tour of Penzance as a penguin in Maria Fortsbridge's Performing Penguins.

He began work on his impressions when he took Agatha Purbright, assistant catering attendant at the Fred Flackersleigh Pie and Whelk stall, to the pictures one Saturday evening. The projectionist, slightly inebriated after a lunchtime session of heavy drinking at the Cinematographers Arms, had lost the last reel of the film and the manager called to the audience for anyone prepared to show their talents. Tommy Hemlock strode eagerly on to the stage and stunned the auditorium with his impressions of King James I, Alfred Stubbs the tobacconist, and Rudolph Valentino.

On the strength of this performance, he wrote to his parents, 'Dear Mater and Pater, Have been a big success in the Grand Metropolitan Cinema, Oil Drum Lane, and am assured of my future.' Two days later he received a reply, asking him for money.

However, the talents of the young aspiring Tommy Hemlock could not be overlooked for ever, and, at the age of twenty-six, he auditioned for a lead in the Arnold Grumby's Group of Boy Troopers, to tour the south of England. 'You couldn't forget Tommy Whatsisname,' said Arnold Grumby, now a successful deckchair salesman in Manchester, 'He were vibrant . . . yes, vibrant, he were . . . bloody vibrant!' And did he pass the audition? 'Not blooming likely,' recalled Mr Grumby. 'Too bloody vibrant!'

But, as it turned out, this was a lucky break because the very next day Tommy Hemlock was stood on a corner near Oxford Street, counting the buses go by, when he espied the premises of Kosher Fashbaum, theatrical impresario.

It was there that Hemlock acquired the big break that he had been waiting for, but before we go further we must backtrack a little to 1947 when his father, Boris Fitzgibbon Hemlock, retired from the stage and took up the position of assistant tram-driver on the number 83 route. Returning to London, the Hemlocks moved into rooms let by Victoria Smethers, a blood donor of considerable proportions.

As luck would have it Boris's route took him through Sutton and East Cheam – the tram-drivers' union had funded an extra stretch of tramline to go up the back of Firebox Terrace, along Railway Cuttings to the shunters yard, where a daily poker school was held for off-duty drivers. It was there that Boris noticed a house for sale, at a very reasonable rate due to subsidence and coal deposits (it was customary at that time for passing train-drivers to heave any unwanted bits of nutty slack at the most run-down house in the district). It was then that the Hemlocks moved in to 23 Railway Cuttings, and soon afterwards Thomas, the prodigal son, came home.

Tommy had not been there but three weeks when he returned from a hard day's train spotting on Cheam bridge to find that his parents had emigrated to Canada.

We now come back to the moment of the big break in Tommy Hemlock's career, when Kosher Fashbaum offered him a twelve-week run at the Dog and Duck, East Cheam, as one half of *The Whistling Hillbillies*; the other half was a wandering Australian.

Keeping up the payments on the house was very difficult, however, and Tommy was forced to take up the post of Resident Master of Music at the Hand and Racquet Snug Bar, East Cheam, under his new professional name (to befit the circumstances of such a position): Anthony Aloysius St John Hancock. It was there that he first made the acquaintance of a certain Sidney Balmoral James.

SIDNEY BALMORAL JAMES

An undesirable character

Born in the basement of a pawn shop in the Mile End Road, to Agnes and Harold 'Fency' James, he was named Sidney, after his uncle Edward who had been deported there, Balmoral, because of his father's great interest in royalty (with particular attention to their jewellery), and James, because that was his father's name and it seemed like a good idea at the time.

As soon as young Sidney could walk, his father, President of the Mile End Road Round Table and Trader's Association, would take him on late-night shopping excursions, after the shops had shut. The young lad felt a strong bond between himself and his father, despite the fact that he had been sold to gypsies on numerous occasions by his paternal parent, who knew full well that Sidney would come running back home, if only to get his commission.

Sidney Balmoral was educated at Eton, between the years of 1936 and 1937, and his parents were very proud of the fact that their son had been taught all he knew at the Eton and Harrow Approved Reform School.

Graduating in 'Tote Formulations', and excelling on the sports field, where he ran off with every trophy that was available, he returned home to take up a career as a bookie's runner, during which time he also, according to local ministers, took a great interest in religious architecture, with a particular leaning towards lead roofing.

He made his début at Court in 1946, at the Old Bailey, where he was successful in denying the charge of stealing a gold ring from a jeweller's shop window. In his evidence he claimed that he had thrown the brick into the window accidentally and that the ring slipped onto his finger as he reached in to remove the brick. It was noticed, shortly afterwards, that the foreman of the jury had an unexpected win on the greyhounds.

Despite his many criminal affiliations, Sidney Balmoral 'Effervescent' James was much respected in the neighbourhood for his many charitable acts and works for the community. He was singularly responsible for the St Nicholas Church Roof Restoration, was treasurer of the Escaped Convicts Rehabilitation Trust fund and was particularly successful in his attempts to save fallen women.

When, in 1954, the celebrated theatrical impresario, Kosher Fashbaum, was mysteriously lost in a boating accident on the Serpentine, it was a great shock to his family to learn that Sidney Balmoral James had been named sole beneficiary of the theatrical agency. The family, quite naturally, contested the will, which was written on the back of a betting slip for the two o'clock at Newmarket, but the judge, who soon afterwards went on a three-week holiday to the Bahamas, ruled that the will was perfectly legal, despite the fact that it was written in crayon and had the words 'This is perfectly true and legal, signed Kosher' added as an afterthought.

Changing the name of the business to the Sid James Theatrical Agency and Scrap Metal Dealers, he scoured the surrounding areas for likely up-and-coming talent. Whilst sitting in the Snug Bar of the Hand and Racquet, East Cheam, he noticed the amazing talents of one Tommy Hemlock, who could play 'Knees Up Mother Brown' on the piano whilst drinking a pint of brown ale and not spilling a drop.

Impressed by the man's obvious talents and his equally obvious gullibility, Sidney Balmoral James signed up the erstwhile music-hall entertainer with a contract, pencilled on the back of a beer mat, which generously allowed Mr Hemlock to keep ten per cent of everything he earned.

GRISELDA GERMAINE PUGH

A vast character

Born in Sandwich, Kent, in August 1925, Griselda was the only daughter of Esmeralda Pugh (nee Willsdent) and Colonel Ashburton Nelson Pugh, of the Army Catering Corps.

When the child was two years old, Esmeralda wrote, in a letter to her mother, 'Our hopes for a large family initially envisaged as containing three, or possibly four children, are now all condensed, if condensed be the word, into Griselda, who already eats more than her dear father. If it were not for the Red Cross parcels, and the little bits and pieces that Ashburton brings home from work, I positively swear that we could not manage.'

Griselda was educated at St Petra's College for the Undernourished and was not the easiest of pupils to teach, according to Emily Banks, her form teacher: 'We couldn't get her into a desk, for a start, and if we put her by the window, nobody could see anything . . . it was ridiculous!' But despite all the drawbacks, little Miss Pugh went on to Finishing School, where she took cooking and weight-lifting.

At the age of fifteen, Griselda found herself caught up in the war effort at home, when her vest was inflated with helium and she was used as a barrage balloon to defend the vital railway link between Cheam and Sutton.

Shortly after the war, much against her parents' wishes, Griselda Germaine Pugh spent three years as an advertising hoarding in Piccadilly, where she slowly rotated on the spot whilst hundreds of fairy lights, attached to her duffle coat, flashed on and off to display the merits of Simpkin's Slimline Tonic.

Distraught by the public humiliation of their daughter's activities, Mr and Mrs Pugh arranged to have Griselda dismantled and sent to America, where she spent six months on a box, holding a candle, in New York harbour, while the Statue of Liberty was taken away for cleaning. It was there that she was spotted by a Hollywood talent scout and was offered the part of Moby Dick in the film of the same name.

On her return to England in 1953 Griselda attended the Cynthia Smallpiece School of Catering, but failed to gain a diploma when the *Creation De La Pugh, et Pudding Cabinet* exploded, injuring five people and severely damaging a passing omnibus, three lorries and a government building.

Undaunted by this mishap, Miss Pugh set up her bell tent outside the American Air Force Base at Cheam, where she was most gratified at being awarded a contract to supply the Base with ten gallons of rice pudding a day, which they used to fill sandbags for their firing ranges.

It was there that she first turned her thoughts towards domestic service, for when the Base had filled all their sandbags, she was again looking for a permanent position. Advertising her services in several quality Ladies' magazines, as an 'established cook – excellent recipe for cabinet pudding boiled in an enamel bath over six gas rings – some typing and light duties', she was on the point of giving up when she noticed an advertisement in the tobacconist's window in East Cheam High Street.

WILLIAM 'BILLABONG' MONTBEAURENCY KERR
A wandering character

There is a very famous, almost classic, poem in Australia, revered by literary critics and sheep farmers alike, and it begins thus: 'There was a young man from Wagga Wagga, who put . . .', but I guess you know the rest. The identity of the young man has, up till now, been a mystery; many learned scholars have tried in vain to fathom out the secret, and many have even suggested that this 'young man from Wagga Wagga' is a distant relation of Mathilda, the 'sheila what's always dancing!'

The legend follows the story of the Hopalong Kerrs, forced by circumstance and huge debts, to live wild in the outback, feeding on koala bears and wombats. (The fair dinkum, referred to in the poem incidentally, is a small blond animal resembling a turnip.) Their child, a boy, was, according to legend, stolen by a herd of rogue kangaroos and cared for by one of the elders until rescued by a party of 'swagmen' returning, somewhat drunkenly, from the annual sheep-shearers convention at Whourouly.

The boy, then aged twenty-four, was placed in a crate marked fragile, and despatched to England, and it was here that Professor Hackman first became acquainted with 'Billabong' Kerr. It was Hackman who, in 1948, wrote the now famous thesis on *Kerr – The Missing Link*, in which he claimed he could trace a direct line of descendancy to 'Billabong' Kerr (whom he rechristened William Montbeaurency after the famous pedantologist) from Neanderthal man. Mocked by his fellow scientists and debunked as a fraud, Hackman sold Kerr to a travelling showman, Barnum O'Toole, who set William on the road to success in his *All-moving, All-wiggling, Unusual Show*.

For three years, Kerr toured the provinces with such companions as the bearded lady, the cyclops of Cirencester, and Charles, the lizard eater, and for a time he was particularly friendly with the alligator woman, a highly-strung individual who could get a little snappy at times.

[You can tell that Galton and Simpson didn't write this, can't you, eh?]

Professor Hackman, meanwhile, determined to rebuild his reputation and to rescue as much as he could from his defamed thesis, caught up with the circus at Wapping and released 'Billabong' Kerr from his contract, taking him to the East Cheam Institute Research Facilities run by a gentleman called Victorian Fred.

Subjecting the little man to several tests and experiments, they at last decided to have Kerr carbon-dated, to prove once and for all whether or not there was any genuine connection between the boy from the crate and the famous poem.

Alas, when the results came back from the Quick-Flick Clear-Print Processing Company, all was disappointingly negative. William 'Billabong' Montbeaurency Kerr was turned out onto the street and Professor Hackman went into hibernation in a cave just off Studland Bay. His thesis is still talked about in scientific circles and is often referred to in after-dinner speeches, where it is guaranteed to bring welcome light relief.

Thus, while his past remained a mystery, his future was certain. 'Billabong' became a busker, establishing himself a 'stake' outside the Clean-Easy Dry Cleaning establishment in East Cheam High Street, where he would whistle 'The Wild Colonial Boy' to the passing housewives.

It was there that he was spotted by Arnold Dukes, landlord of the Dog and Duck: 'I said to him – would you like a job in my saloon bar? 'Cos the piano's broke. He said, "Yeah, right on cobber, true blue, and how's yer billabong".'

Dukes left him there. It was some time before Dukes saw him again. 'He walked

into the pub and said he'd come for a job and that he was one half of a team called *The Whistling Hillbillies* – so I said, where's the other half? And he said "I don't know, I haven't got one".'

Dukes threw him out. Kosher Fashbaum, the theatrical agent, doing a pre-Christmas rummage through the slums, happened upon 'Billabong' and was so impressed by the wide-eyed innocent that he signed him up on the spot, teamed him with a certain Thomas Hemlock and they became the *Whistling Hillbillies*.

Abridged by Terry Gompertz
Read by Grizelda Hervey
The second of fifteen instalments

3.0 Greenwich Time Signal
CRICKET
England v. South Africa
Further commentary

3.45 MUSIC WHILE YOU WORK
Band of the Corps of
Royal Engineers (Chatham)
Conducted by Major A. Young
Director of Music

4.15 MRS. DALE'S DIARY
(BBC recording)
To be repeated tomorrow at 11.0 a.m.

4.30 ERIC SPRUCE
at the BBC theatre organ

5.0 GERALDO
and his Orchestra
with Roy Edwards and Anne Haven

5.30 CRICKET
England v. South Africa
Further commentaries
and summaries
If play continues until 6.30 the commentary will be extended

6.15 CALLING
ALL SPORTSMEN
An up-to-the-minute round-up of
events and personalities—at home
and abroad—ranging from:
Angling to Athletics
Bowls to Boxing
Bat and Trap to Billiards
Rowing to Racing
with latest news of sport of the day
Introduced by Cliff Michelmore

6.45 'THE ARCHERS'
A story of country folk
Written by Geoffrey Webb
and Edward J. Mason
Edited by Godfrey Baseley
Produced by Tony Shryane
(BBC recording)

7.0 Greenwich Time Signal
News and
RADIO NEWSREEL

7.25 app.   Sport

7.30 FAMILY FAVOURITES
Tunes you have asked us to play,
including some records chosen by
Service men and women overseas

8.0 NIGHTS
OF GLADNESS
Archibald Joyce
and his Edwardian contemporaries
Introduced by Ivan Samson
Singers:
Grace Nevern
Raymond Newell
with the
London Theatre Orchestra
(Leader, Sidney Sax)

'DEAD CIRCUIT'
A serial by Elleston Trevor
Adapted from the novel
by Simon Rattray
3—'Mantrap'

Hugo Bishop............Robert Eddison
Major Craddock..........Austin Trevor
Georgina Hutton.........Mary Wimbush
Starling.................George Merritt
Doctor Veiss.............Olaf Pooley
Gorry....................Noel Hood
Detective Inspector Frisnay
Raf de la Torre
Police Sergeant..........Jeffrey Segal
Sergeant Flack.........James Thomason
Vic Levinson..........Virginia Winter
Boy.....................James Doran
Other parts played by Annabel Maule
Production by Audrey Cameron
(BBC recording)

9.30 Tony Hancock
with Bill Kerr, Sidney James
and Andrée Melly in
HANCOCK'S HALF-HOUR
also featuring Kenneth Williams
The 'Hancock Theme'
and other incidental music
composed by Wally Stott
The Augmented BBC Revue Orchestra
Conductor, Harry Rabinowitz
Written by
Alan Simpson and Ray Galton
Produced by Dennis Main Wilson
(BBC recording)
(Sidney James is in 'Wonderful Town' at the Prince's Theatre, London)
Repeated on Sunday at 3.0 p.m.

10.0 Greenwich Time Signal
NEWS

10.15 TOPIC FOR TONIGHT

10.20 CRICKET
England v. South Africa
First Test Match: Fifth Day
A summary of the day's play
by Rex Alston

10.25 BBC SWING SESSION
with
Ted Heath and his Music
Kathy Lloyd
Bobbie Britton, Peter Lowe
On the Beat
with
The Kirchin Band
Introduced by Ted Heath
Produced by John Hooper

11.5 A BOOK AT BEDTIME
'A Man in the Zoo'
by David Garnett
(to be read in ten instalments)
Read by David Garth
Abridged by Alastair Dunnett
7—'Mr. Cromartie's Neighbour'

11.20 BBC SWING SESSION
with
Ted Heath and his Music
Kathy Lloyd
Bobbie Britton, Peter Lowe
and
The Kirchin Band
Introduced by Alan Dell
Produced by John Hooper

11.50 Weather Forecast
Highlights
of tomorrow's programmes

The Tim
PROGRAMME
464 m. (647 kc/s)
194 m. (1,546 kc/s) 91.3 Mc/s

6.0 p.m. PIANO RECITAL
by Kendall Taylor
Prelude, Elegy, and Toccata...
Sonata in A flat, Op. 110.....Beet
(BBC recording)

6.35 'HISTORICAL
INEVITABILITY'
Pieter Geyl, Professor of Modern
tory in the University of Utrech
views the book by Isaiah Berlin.
(The recorded broadcast of Mar

6.55 HANDEL
Music for the Royal Fire
played by the Berlin Philhar
Orchestra, conducted by
Lehman: on gramophone re

7.25 FOREIGN REVIEW
A monthly report
on the arts, science, and politics a
Compiled by Alan Pryce-Jon
Including a report by Christopher
on the German mood in the art
politics, and an illustrated talk by
Heyworth on recent performances
Hamburg State Opera of Dallap
Voli di Notte and Schoenberg's *Erwa*
(BBC recording)
To be repeated on Wednesday a

7.55 EARLY SCOTTISH M
The second of four programme
devised and edited by
Thurston Dart and Kenneth El
Sixteenth-century Scottish S
sung by the Saltire Singe
O lusty May; Depart, depart;
that same sweet face; Richt
opprest; O mortal man; Now
sing; Evin dead behold I bre
In through the windows of
eyes; That mighty motion?; A
desie of delight
Texts of songs edited by Helena
(BBC recording)
Instrumental music: June 2

8.30 EMMY DESTINN
Alec Robertson talks about the (
born soprano who sang leading
at the Berlin Royal Opera, at (
Garden, and at the Metropolitan (
New York, between 1898 and 1
Illustrations include arias from 'The
Dutchman,' 'Aida,' 'Robert the
'Madam Butterfly,' and 'Der Freis
followed by an interlude at 9

9.5 Arthur Hill in
'THE GOOD SOLDIE
A novel by Ford Madox Fo
Adapted and produced for broadc
by Wilfrid Grantham
For details see Saturday at 6
(BBC recording)
*(Arthur Hill is appearing in 'The
maker' at the Haymarket Theatre, L*

10.50 REGER
Quartet No. 1 in G minor, Op.
played by the Allegri Quarte
(Recorded broadcast of Nov. 3,
First of five programmes in wh
Reger's string quartets will be p
Quartet No. 2: June 20

11.20 Close Down

THE TELEVISION SET

There comes a time in the affairs of man . . .
or
To buy, or not to buy . . .

The latest in a long line of status symbols, an H-shaped aerial strapped to the chimney and a 9in. viewing screen surrounded by a mahogany wardrobe; the television set.

'Ooooh, you go' a telly . . .'

First comes the decision to buy – the excitement – the anticipation – the television licence!

At the time that this script was written, radio was still by far the more popular medium; there was only one television channel (commercial television did not get fully under way until September 1955) and the television licence cost all of £3.00, but it did cover you for the use of the radio as well, so that you could watch *What's My Line?* or *The Brains Trust* and listen to *England Calling the Commonwealth* on the radio at the same time.

For, despite the fact that many homes had specially installed a television set for the purpose of watching the Coronation in 1953, there were only 4,500,000 television licences issued in 1955. This situation is firmly established in this script when Hancock says 'we'll pop down to the radio shop' – to buy a television! Radio Rentals Ltd (large television rental company in 1987) did not even mention televisions in their advertisements in 1955, which concentrated solely on the renting of radio sets. By 1957 the company acknowledged the growing popularity of TV with a small paragraph in the advertisement, stating that television sets could also be rented, but by 1959 the advertisements were predominantly for the hire of televisions.

However, the cynical among you, and those of a younger disposition, will no doubt query the validity of the Do-It-Yourself television kit, as assembled in this show, but, yes – they did actually exist. I embarked on some extensive research, but was unable to produce an advertisement for such equipment. I was slightly disappointed about this, because the reproduction of such indisputable evidence in this book would have silenced the sceptical, so imagine my surprise and delight when, in conversation with Ray Galton, he recalled having watched the Coronation on just such a set, built by his future brother-in-law. The screen, being green in colour, resembled that of a radar scanner. I wonder if they had to have a television licence or a permit from the Royal Navy?

All this is to prove that television was still very much a luxury novelty. It was also a pawn in the gamesmanship of life. One can imagine the queue for the morning bus. 'Did you see that programme last night? . . . Oh, you haven't got a set. . . . Oh, what a shame!'

But what was there to entice the public away from radio? An average of six hours television a day: three-minute interludes between the programmes, constant breaks in transmission, a few light-hearted but heavy-handed panel games, the occasional play, an old film or two, and *Muffin the Mule*.

Radio still had the pick of the crop in the light entertainment world because television could not provide the same sort of money that could then be earned on radio, and, quite naturally, there was the same fear of that medium that had occurred when radio first began.

For all that, the anticipation of owning a television set must have been a tremendously exciting experience, although now, with four channels, eighteen or more hours of transmission daily, videos and satellite television, it is difficult to capture the excitement that abounded in 23 Railway Cuttings as the television set whirred into life.

Let me try to place this script in the time period (because of all the scripts in this book, this one is the most dated by way of circumstance): 1955 was only a year on from the last of the food rationing, and while 'Cherry Pink and Apple Blossom

White' was the number one 'hit' record, on 78 rpm, later that same year the music scene would change radically with the arrival of Bill Haley and his Comets and their 'platter' entitled 'Rock Around the Clock'. A few years later there was to be a huge consumer boom flooding the eager public with washing machines, electric cookers, record players, televisions and cars, all on the hire-purchase credit system. But in 1955 the washing was often still done in the kitchen sink, scrubbed on a washboard long before Lonnie Donegan found another use for it, a bike was the ordinary family's means of transport . . .

. . . And the 'Television Set' was on the Light Programme on 14 June in a series called 'H-H-*Hancock's Half-Hour*'.

THE TELEVISION SET

Script by
ALAN SIMPSON AND RAY GALTON

Recorded: 13 June 1955
Broadcast: 14 June 1955
Starring:
TONY HANCOCK
SIDNEY JAMES
BILL KERR
ANDREE MELLY
KENNETH WILLIAMS
ALAN SIMPSON

Produced by
DENNIS MAIN WILSON

KENNETH   There comes a time in the affairs of man, when he must throw off the petty tyrannies that beset him, and once and for all make the final decision that eventually we all – each and every one of us – one day will have to make.

TONY   . . . So that's all there is to it, I'm going to buy a television set.

BILL   Yeah but Tub . . .

TONY   Don't try to talk me out of it, I've made up my mind. I'm going to buy a television set.

ANDREE   (*tearful*) You monster. You've lost interest in me. (*grizzles*).

TONY   What's the matter with you?

ANDREE   What do you want a television set for?

TONY   To entertain me in the evening.

ANDREE   That's what I mean. You didn't need a television set when you first met me.

TONY   Ah well, that was different I . . .

ANDREE   You used to clear the tea things away, send Bill to the pictures and you'd still be chasing me round the table when he got back. You're tired of me.

TONY   No I'm not. I'll still be able to spare you a few minutes while the interval's on.

BILL   But I still don't see the point in spending all that money. We've managed perfectly well without a television set up till now.

TONY   That's just it. We're the only house down our street that hasn't got one. Oooh, the disgrace. How can I hold my head up. When I walk down the street they point at me and snigger.

BILL   You're imagining things. Nobody round here knows we haven't got a television. That wooden aerial we put up on the roof would fool anybody.

TONY   I tell you they've found out. It was that window cleaner – he passed it around. I told you to draw the curtains when he calls. He's told 'em about the hole in the carpet too. It's just what they needed. That crowd of old women that go down to the butcher's shop. They've been trying to get some dirt on me ever since I moved out here.

BILL   So what?

TONY   Well it's embarrassing. Now they've found out me secret – they plot. They try and trick me. They ask me what I thought of Barbara Kelly's ear-rings last night, I say very nice . . . and they say 'that's funny, she wasn't on'. It's getting so I have to read all the newspaper critics before I can indulge in normal conversation. It's that Mrs Higgins. She's the ringleader. She don't like me. Ever since I played in the cricket team with her husband.

ANDREE   What has that got to do with it?

TONY   My whites were cleaner than his. And I was a bit sarky when she asked me how I did it.

BILL   What did you tell her?

TONY   I told her I knew that girl in the cinema.

ANDREE   What girl?

TONY   The one with the pigtails who walks into that soap flake packet.

ANDREE   Oh Tony, you shouldn't have been so rude.

TONY   Well I can't stand that Mrs Higgins. She's a sight too snooty by far. Do you

know . . . this is straight up . . . I know it's true, I heard it in the fish queue last Monday. Do you know . . . she bought a television set last year – now she votes Conservative.

BILL   I still don't like the idea of spending all this money. There are much more important things we could buy.

TONY   Such as.

BILL   Things for my bedroom.

TONY   What things?

BILL   Weeeel . . . bedclothes, bedspread . . . a bed.

TONY   No. When you start paying your rent I'll furnish your room out. Until then you'll have to make do with the top of the wardrobe.

BILL   Yeah but . . .

TONY   Enough. We're getting a television set. It's more important than you think.

BILL   How do you mean?

TONY   Mrs Higgins and the Women's Institute have complained to the Town Hall. They say I'm lowering the dignity of the neighbourhood. They're getting a petition up. Either I get a television set or I move to a poorer district. Come on, we'll pop down to the radio shop in the High Street and choose one.

TONY   Well, they've got quite a nice selection haven't they?

ANDREE   Yes. We should be able to find a set we like out of all these.

BILL   Yeah . . . but it's a bit expensive this place Tub. Look at that little table model – eight inch screen – they want two hundred and forty for it.

TONY   Two hundred and . . . that's volts.

BILL   I don't care what currency it is, it's a lot of money.

TONY   Look, just keep quiet and let me deal with it. They look after me here. I'm one of their best customers.

ANDREE   You are?

TONY   Certainly. I get all me fuse wire here. We'll have a word with the salesman.

KENNETH   Good afternoon sirs . . . modom. Can I be of any assistance?

TONY   Yes, I'd like to have a look at your television sets.

KENNETH   Yes, they all do on Test Match days.

TONY   No, we want to buy one.

KENNETH   (*interested*) Oh, I see. Well we have several models here that might interest you. This of course is a very popular model. A combined television, radio, record player, cocktail cabinet and bookcase.

BILL   Has it got a bed in it?

KENNETH   No I'm afraid not.

BILL   We're not interested.

KENNETH   Then how about this one? Our latest de luxe model. All the latest refinements. A giant thirty-six inch screen, a pair of curtains and a miniature organ that comes up and down during the intervals. Very tasteful.

TONY   No, I don't think so.

KENNETH   (*coaxing*) You wouldn't require an outdoor aerial for this model.

TONY   Oh yes I would. A great big one . . . lit up by a searchlight. If I'm paying that much money for one, I want people to know I've got it.

ANDREE   [What else have you got?

KENNETH Well . . . I do recommend this one. In my opinion it's the best model we have in the shop. Wonderful reception. It picks up all the programmes . . . *The Goon Show, Take It From Here, The Frankie Howerd Show* . . .

BILL But they're radio shows.

KENNETH Oh! I thought they were too good for television.]

TONY Look, quite frankly I haven't seen anything I really like yet.

KENNETH I see . . . well . . . what sort of price did you have in mind?

TONY Well I want something good.

KENNETH Naturally.

TONY I mean if you're buying a television set, there's no point in getting a cheap one.

KENNETH Of course not.

TONY They're more trouble than they're worth.

KENNETH Quite.

TONY Always buy quality. It's cheaper in the long run.

KENNETH I agree.

TONY So taking everything into consideration, I'm quite willing to go up to . . . oooh . . . anything up to about fifteen quid.

KENNETH Fifteen pounds?

TONY It's the only way. If you want class you've got to pay for it.

KENNETH Yes . . . but fifteen pounds . . .

TONY Sssssshhhh – not so loud. Cor dear, I don't want everybody to know I've got that much money on me. I might be attacked.

KENNETH My dear sir, stop wasting my time . . . fifteen pounds. The cheapest set we have in this shop is sixty guineas.

TONY Sixty guineas? I'd want Sabrina sitting on me lap while Philip Harben cooks the dinner for that.

KENNETH I'm afraid I can't help you. Would you mind, I have other more solvent customers awaiting my attention.

TONY Very well, I shall bid you good-day.

KENNETH If you would.

TONY Oh I see. Very well, if that's the way it is, in future I shall buy my fuse wire elsewhere. Good-day.

(*Door shuts. Street noises & footsteps*)

TONY Sixty guineas! I'll never be able to afford that.

ANDREE Never mind Tony, you can still chase me round the table if you like.

TONY Thank you Andrée, it's very kind of you to offer . . . but I've set me mind on a television set.

ANDREE I won't run so fast.

TONY Oh. Well in that case I . . . no. Be strong Hancock. Get thee behind me Satan. You can't tempt me with your apples. I want a television set. Sixty guineas.

BILL Yeah. It's a lot of money Tub.

TONY Yes.

BILL Yeah. (*pause*) You could get a great bed for fifteen pounds.

TONY (*quickly*) You're not getting a bed. We're getting a television set, so shut up. I'm going to get one by hook or by crook.

SIDNEY Somebody mention me?

BILL   Sid.

TONY   Good afternoon Sidney.

ANDREE   Hallo Mr James.

SIDNEY   Somebody said they wanted a television set.

TONY   That's right, me. But they're so dear.

SIDNEY   You mean you've been into a shop?

TONY   Yes.

SIDNEY   To buy one?

TONY   Yes.

SIDNEY   That's an expensive way of doing business ain't it? You should have come to me.

BILL   You. Televisions?

SIDNEY   Certainly, I can get hold of anything like that. Just give me the nod. What sort of television set are you looking for?

TONY   Can you get me one like Jimmy Edwards has got?

SIDNEY   Certainly. Where does he live?

TONY   I don't want any stolen stuff.

SIDNEY   Ooh you've got a suspicious mind you have. I've never yet sold you anything that's been stolen.

TONY   What about that car you sold me?

SIDNEY   I didn't steal it. I found it parked outside a cemetery, so I figured the owner wouldn't be needing it any more. Now do you want a television set or not?

TONY   Well yes but . . .

SIDNEY   Say no more. Come down and have a look round my warehouse. [I've got loads of stuff down there.] I'm sure I can dig you up a television set to suit your pocket.

TONY   I want one bigger than that.

SIDNEY   Come on, let's see what we've got.

TONY   Right. Come on Andrée, Bill. Bill, stop looking in that furniture window.

BILL   They've got some nice beds in here.

TONY   You're not having one.

BILL   Oh Tub, please. It's all right for you, you've got one. What's it like sleeping in a bed Tub? I sat on yours once, oh it was great. Please buy me a bed Tub . . . eh Tub . . . Tub?

(Hollow atmosphere as if in warehouse. Hollow footsteps)

BILL   . . . and I don't care if some of the springs are broken Tub, I just want a little bed so I can curl up and . . . I fall off the top of the wardrobe some nights and . . .

TONY   For the last time, no. N - O - E, no!

SIDNEY   Well here we are. This is me furniture department. Stocked right up at the moment.

BILL   Say, you've got some great stuff here Sid. Must be worth thousands. Where did you get it from?

SIDNEY   Me and my boys pick most of it up at sales. The auctioneers let us have it dirt cheap.

TONY   Why?

SIDNEY   We've got bigger hammers than they have. Have a look round. [There's a lot of stuff you might like.] What about this lovely gramophone? Thirty-five quid

and it's yours.

TONY   Thirty-five pounds? Bit ancient isn't it?

SIDNEY   All right then. Twenty quid and I'll give you a dog to look down it.

TONY   No, I don't think so.

ANDREE   Where are these television sets?

SIDNEY   Oh yes. Now let's see. I've only got one . . . it's here somewhere. Ah here it is. I forget how much I've priced this one at. Er . . . how much did you say you've got?

TONY   Fifteen pounds.

SIDNEY   That's it. Lovely set this. Ultra Modern 1955 de Luxe Exhibition Model. Just rolled off the assembly line.

BILL   Who pushed it?

SIDNEY   There's nothing wrong with this set. Wait till you see it work. Just give the handle a few turns.

TONY   What's the handle for?

SIDNEY   You want the pictures to move, don't you?

TONY   Well, it helps I suppose. But you shouldn't have to turn handles to make the pictures move. We pay our licence money. Let the BBC turn the handle at their end.

ANDREE   And another thing. There isn't a screen.

SIDNEY   Of course there is. You put your eyes up against that window and look down it.

ANDREE   I can't see anything.

SIDNEY   Well you haven't put the penny in the slot yet [have you?]

TONY   This is a funny television set.

BILL   Let's have a look.

SIDNEY   Ready?

BILL   Yeah.

SIDNEY   Right. Start turning.

(*whirr of What the Butler Saw machine handle*)

BILL   Oh yeah, yeah, I can see it.

ANDREE   What programme is on Bill?

BILL   Er . . . just a minute . . . oh yeah . . . it's called *What the Butler Saw*.

SIDNEY   Yeah . . . it's a . . . it's a new panel game.

TONY   Show us. Oooh . . . whoo, whoo. Hallo. My word. Which one's Lady Barnet? Har har. Oooh dear . . . that was a good mime. Whoo, whoo. This is much better than the *Flowerpot Men*. Skobollob. Wait a minute, wait a minute, slow the handle down. Back a bit. That's it. Har har. My word. Cor dear. I can guess her story. Ooooh. Dear oh dear. Tch, tch, tch. Ah. Cor. Whoo whoo. Har har.

(*Click of machine. Whirr stops*)

SIDNEY   Well?

TONY   Well I can't see the ITA topping that.

ANDREE   Tony, that isn't a television set.

TONY   It doesn't matter, let's buy it whatever it is.

BILL   Hear, hear.

ANDREE   I thought you wanted a bed.

BILL Who wants to sleep with that in the house?

ANDREE You're not buying it. [He's trying to cheat you. You came here to buy a television set, not one of those things.

TONY I know what I'm doing. With Kerr in the house, at the end of a fortnight there'll be enough pennies in there to buy a ten-channel, giant screen consul model with a golden aerial.

ANDREE No there won't. He'll use the same thing he uses for the gas meter. A handful of flattened out beer bottle tops. No,] if Mr James hasn't got a real television set, we'll go somewhere else.

SIDNEY Look wait a minute. I admit I haven't got a television set . . . well not a made up one . . . but I tell you what I have got – a complete home construction kit. Make it up yourself. It's got all the parts.

TONY Well I don't know . . .

SIDNEY Ten quid the lot. Easy to make up. All the parts are numbered. Can't go wrong. A child of three could put it together in ten minutes.

TONY Really?

SIDNEY Yeah. So if you allow yourself a couple of hours, you shouldn't have any trouble.

TONY All right then, I'll have a go. Won't get a set anywhere cheaper than that. I'll take it.

SIDNEY You won't regret it. Ten nicker please.

TONY Here you are. (*quickly*) One, two, three, four, five, six, seven, eight, nine, ten. Check 'em up.

SIDNEY One, two, three, four, five.

TONY Oh well, if you're going to unfold 'em.

SIDNEY Come on, and the rest.

TONY [All right, here's a five pound note.

SIDNEY Here wait a minute, isn't this the one I paid you back last week?

TONY Yes.

SIDNEY Well you get rid of your duds on someone else, I don't want it. Oncers, if you please.]

TONY Oh here you are. Come on Andrée, let's go home and make the television set. Hurry up, look at the time. I'll miss Sooty if I'm not careful. Come on Bill. Bill. Bill!

BILL (*snores*)

TONY Get off that bed. Come on, get off, you're not getting one. Come on, untie yourself, we're going home. Come on . . .

(*clinks & clunks, taps etc, of putting the set together*)

ANDREE Haven't you two finished putting that television set together yet?

TONY Won't be long Andrée.

ANDREE Well hurry up, I'm afraid to walk with all these parts strewn all over the house.

TONY They're not strewn. There are five thousand parts all laid out in order. Now please stand back and don't interfere Andrée – this is a job for the men. (*calls*) Bill!

BILL (*way off mike*) Yeah?

TONY Part seven hundred and eight. I think it's in the bedroom.

44

BILL [(*off mike*) Seven hundred and eight? No, not in here. What is it?

TONY   A valve I think.

BILL   (*off mike*) I've got it. Halfway down the stairs. Coming down. Catch.

(*smash of glass valve*)

TONY   (*calls*) Bill.

BILL   (*off*) Yeah?

TONY   (*calls*) Part seven hundred and eight . . .

BILL   (*off mike*) Wait a minute, where did I see that? Um . . .

TONY   (*calls*) It's laying] on my bed.

BILL   (*off*) Oh, I'll get it.

TONY   (*very long pause*) If he's gone to sleep I'll bash the daylights out of him.

BILL   (*coming on*)   Here it is Tub. Seven O Eight.

TONY   Give us it [here] I think it plugs in just over here. There.

ANDREE   Are you sure you're doing this properly?

TONY   Of course we are.

ANDREE   But it's getting so big. It should be more compact. You've still got half the parts to put on . . . and I've already had to move the table and three armchairs into the other room.

BILL   She's right Tub. I feel sure it's not supposed to dominate the house like this. I'm sure we're supposed to get it all in that little wooden cabinet.

TONY   Oh that stupid little thing. I used that up before I got to part number six. I can't understand it. It's got out of hand somehow.

BILL   What a mess. Wires, valves, knobs, switches, plugs, all soldered into one glorious impenetrable mass. Professor Lumière could send Garth to another world on half this lot.

ANDREE   Why don't you pull it all down and start again?

TONY   No. We'll just have to carry on and see what we can do with it when it's finished. Now come on, get the ladder out and knock that wall down, part seven o nine's got to go on.

TONY   There we are. Just solder on part five thousand . . . there. Finished.

BILL   Oh great. Trapped in our own bathroom.

TONY   [We're not trapped.] We can get out. Simple. There's a window behind you. Just open it and shin down the drainpipe.

BILL   [That's OK – but how do we get back in?

TONY   Easy. Just break the basement window and hack our way through parts eight, nine, ten and eleven.

ANDREE   A child of three could do it. Four days I've watched it grow . . . pushing me back . . . back, stifling me until . . .

TONY   Steady woman, steady. It's all over now. It's dead, dead . . . sorry – I was thinking of the *Quatermass Experiment*.]

ANDREE   Well, anyway, it's finished. We now have a television set . . . all over the house. All we've got to do now is find a way of looking at it.

TONY   Easy. Sit on the front doorstep and look through the letter box.

ANDREE   Well go on, switch it on.

TONY   Right . . . there. Can you see the screen Bill?

BILL   Yeah, if I look down the stairs I can just see the reflection of it in the hall mirror.

TONY   Well?

BILL   It's blank.

TONY   Strange, we followed the instructions.

BILL   Did you put the earth in?

TONY   Yes. Two bucketfuls.

BILL   Well no wonder it won't . . . just a minute. It's lighting up. Yes. It's getting brighter . . . brighter . . .

ANDREE   Now what's it doing?

BILL   Smoking. Switch it off!

(*loud explosion*)

TONY   I think a valve blew. Oh well . . . Andrée . . . that kid next door.

ANDREE   Yes. . . ?

TONY   How old is he?

ANDREE   Three.

TONY   Ask him to pop in for ten minutes.

ANDREE   There you are, I told you it could be done. Ten minutes and that little boy has got it all into the cabinet . . . all ready to work. He certainly showed you two up.

BILL   He wasn't so clever. He didn't even know how to open that bottle of beer I offered him.

ANDREE   He's only three.

BILL   That's no excuse for ignorance.

TONY   Of course not. Do you know he can't even tell the time. He had to ask me.

ANDREE   Well your answer wasn't very brilliant, was it? (*disgusted*) The big long hand's on five and the little short hand's on seven.

BILL   Well anyway, it's all finished. Now we can all settle down for our first evening's viewing.

TONY   Oooh I am excited. There's a good play on tonight. I've been looking forward to this all week.

ANDREE   We'd better draw the curtains and switch the light off.

TONY   Ah no. Leave the curtains open . . . so the neighbours can see the glare.

ANDREE   Move the chairs round in front of the set.

(*scrape of chairs*)

ANDREE   That's it. Now all sit down.

TONY   (*howls*) I'll murder that perishing kid. What a daft place to leave a hot soldering iron.

ANDREE   Sit down and keep quiet. Have you switched on Bill?

BILL   Yeah. The picture should be on any minute.

TONY   Hallo look . . . there's a twopenny stamp stuck on the front.

BILL   That's the screen.

TONY   Oh yes, one of those female announcers.

ANDREE   [Isn't the screen just a little bit small?

BILL   No, no, that'll be all right. You'll get used to it.

TONY   Hallo, the picture's gone. It's broken. It's gone black.

ANDREE   Shoo. Get away. Shoo. Shoo. It's all right now.

TONY What was it?

ANDREE A fly.

TONY This is ridiculous. How can you watch a tiny screen like that.

BILL Don't worry, we can easily put a magnifier over it.

TONY Good idea, hold this jeweller's glass in front of it. Ah that's better.] Ooh, look, the programme's starting.

(*BBC television identification music*)

TONY Nation shall speak peace unto nation. Quite right too. Here, here. I was telling Charlie down the pub . . . ooooh look, there they are.

BILL What?

TONY Them five Eiffel Towers with the rings coming out the top. Hallo, here's the weather man. Ooh, I don't like him. I don't like him at all. I don't like his face.

ANDREE He's quite good-looking.

TONY Who asked you. Smarmy he is. Look at him. All teeth and trousers. Aaaaaaah . . . (*mimics*) Cold depression over Ireland. Rain front covering all of eastern England by midday tomorrow. Aaah, what does he know. Look what he's doing to those maps. Ruining 'em. Perfectly good maps and he's chalking all over 'em. I bet they're not his. He doesn't care. The BBC . . . we pay for them. Look at the way he laughed when he said 'rain'. Go on . . . get off, go on, go home. And goodnight to you too. Bighead.

[(*BBC television newsreel signature*)

TONY Ah the newsreel.

ALAN State Opening of Parliament.

TONY Ah. State Opening of Parliament.

ALAN Scimpshoms, scrampshoms, rhubarb, Parliament, Westminster, etc.

TONY There they go. Look at 'em. All the layabouts. Trooping in. State Opening of Parliament. Half of 'em are missing already. Here! Look . . . look! There goes our bloke. Just going through the door. Oh well, that's the last we'll see of him for the next five years.]

BILL It's not a bad little set, eh Tub?

TONY Just the job. Sit back and relax . . . all set for the evening. Marvellous. I'm looking forward to this play. What's it say in the *Radio Times*? Here it is. Hallo, it's a bit thin this week. Still want the same money for it I notice. They're a saucy lot . . . Ah, this is the life. Cosy way to spend an evening, just the three of us, in our own little home. Hmmmmm! Lovely.

(*doorbell*)

TONY Hallo. Visitors. Go and see who it is, Bill.

BILL Right.

(*door opens*)

SIDNEY Hallo boys.

BILL Sid! Come in.

TONY Hallo Sidney.

SIDNEY Blimey! You've got it working.

TONY Naturally. It didn't take me five minutes.

ANDREE Tony!

TONY Weeelllll. I held the spanners for him, didn't I?

ANDREE Are you stopping, Mr James?

SIDNEY Yes, if you don't mind. There's some telefilms of today's dog meeting at White City. I want to make sure no one saw me throwing the cat on the track.

ANDREE Do sit down, Mr James. Tony, give Mr James your chair.

TONY But I want to see the play . . .

ANDREE You can have the chair behind.

TONY Bill's got the chair behind. Come on William, get out. Move.

BILL No. You sit on the stool.

TONY Oh all right. (*yells!*) Who put the soldering iron on it?

BILL You did. Sit down.

TONY (*groans*) Me whipcord gabs. Ruined!

SIDNEY D'you mind? I'm trying to watch the television.

BILL Yeah. Shuttup, Tub.

ANDREE Oooh. What's this on now?'

TONY Aaaaah. It's that cooking bloke, Philip Harben. Hallo it's about time he got his hair cut, isn't it?

SIDNEY The picture's upside-down.

TONY Don't touch it, I'll do it! Don't panic. Soon put it right. Leave it to the lad. He knows. Framehold to the right . . . Contrast down a bit . . . Horizontal . . . bit this way. Brightness up a bit . . . There.

SIDNEY Hasn't made any difference.

TONY Ah well, I haven't kicked it yet.

(*sickening wooden kerlunk*)

TONY There.

BILL What?

TONY Big hole in the side.

ANDREE Never mind, the picture's come back. What's on now?

TONY Ah, the play's just starting. Just what I've been waiting for. Isn't half good. Tragic love story. About two people thrown together, and their impossible love that never can be.

ANDREE Who's in it?

TONY Diana Dors and Gilbert Harding. Quiet now. No interruptions. I don't want to miss any of it.

(*lush film music*)

TONY Aaah. Oooh look. They're in a restaurant. Sitting at different tables. Aaah. You can tell he's in love with her. Look – he's trying to attract her attention. He's flicking bits of celery at her. Oooh, isn't it sad.

SIDNEY When's the racing come on?

TONY Shuttup.

SIDNEY Well this is mushy.

TONY Be quiet. She's seen him. Look – she's thrown a roll at him. Ooh I'm going to enjoy this.

(*door bell*)

TONY (*annoyed*) Oh who's this.

ANDREE Go and see, you're nearest the door.

TONY But me play. I don't want to miss any of it. He's weighing up the rice pudding there.

(*door bell*)

BILL   Go and answer it.

TONY   Oh all right. Perishing people. Right in the middle of a play . . .

(*door opens*)

TONY   Yes.

KENNETH   (*as Snide*) Good evening.

TONY   Oh cor blimey, it's him.

KENNETH   I'm your next door neighbour.

TONY   Well make the most of it, I'm moving tomorrow.

KENNETH   I've just come round to borrow a pint of milk. My Tibby hasn't had anything to drink all day.

TONY   Well I'm very sorry to hear it I . . .

KENNETH   Course he only gets fed when I come home from work you see . . . and he does like the top of the milk . . .

TONY   Yes well look, here's a quart. Must go.

KENNETH   You haven't got any fish as well have you? Any old little bits'll do, he's not fussy, cod fillet, bit of plaice, anything like that. Nice cat he is.

TONY   Yes I've seen him, digging up me rhubarb. Now look I must go, its been very nice . . .

KENNETH   Ooooooohhh, you've got a telly.

TONY   Yes, we're watching the play, so if you don't mind . . .

KENNETH   You don't mind if I step inside for a minute and watch it do you?

TONY   Well I . . .

KENNETH   Thanks. Good evening all.

(*good evenings*)

KENNETH   I'll sit down here, shall I?

TONY   No, well that's my seat you see and . . .

KENNETH   You can sit behind me can't you?

TONY   Yes . . . but I can't see the screen . . . and the play . . .

KENNETH   Oh dear!

TONY   What?

KENNETH   You haven't bought one of those sets have you?

TONY   Well yes . . . and we're trying to watch the play you see . . .

KENNETH   You've bought trouble there you have.

TONY   Yes well . . .

KENNETH   I'll give it three weeks and you'll need a new tube. [It's happened to everybody who's got one of those. They're notorious, I thought you would have known better.

TONY   Yes well it's going all right at the moment, so if you'll keep quiet we can all watch the play, eh?]

KENNETH   Have you had any trouble with the valves yet?

TONY   No.

KENNETH   You will. They go in bunches. Cost you a fortune. (*laughs*)

TONY   Yes well let's see if they last to the end of the play shall we . . . I've been waiting all week to see this and . . .

KENNETH   You've got it too bright you know.

TONY   Oh cor . . .

KENNETH   Of course it's nothing to do with me, but quite frankly, I think you've

bought a lot of rubbish there.

SIDNEY Oi . . . pimples.

KENNETH Are you talking to me?

SIDNEY Yes, and if you keep on, I'll probably be the last person to do so.

KENNETH Oh.

SIDNEY Shut your cakehole and watch the play.

TONY Ah good, I haven't missed much of it. This is where it starts to get interesting . . .

ANDREE It's no good Henry. It . . . it just won't work.

BILL But Helen . . .

ANDREE No Henry, my mind is made up.

BILL But Helen . . . dearest Helen . . . not even . . . for the children?

ANDREE Never. Unless . . .

BILL Yes?

ANDREE Unless you tell me.

BILL (*crafty*) But dearest heart, there is nothing to tell.

ANDREE (*tears*) Then . . . we're through Henry . . . do you hear me, through.

BILL (*building down*) But you can't just say 'we're through'. Does all . . . this mean . . . nothing to you.

ANDREE (*sadly T. S. Eliot*) Yes. Everything . . . yet nothing.

BILL All right then . . .

ANDREE (*alarm*) Henry – No. (*sickly laugh*) No – you wouldn't . . . Henry, you'd never escape the police. (*hysteria*) Henry! Don't be a fool!

(*Revolver shot. Body slumps to floor*)

BILL (*Tragic pause. Horror in voice*) Helen – Helen . . . (*sobs*) What have I done . . . (*choking tears & sobs*) Helen . . . Helen . . . (*sobs*)

KENNETH (*very long pause*) Where's the sandwiches?

TONY Where's the what?

KENNETH Where's the sandwiches? Every time I go into people's houses to watch television they always offer me sandwiches.

TONY We haven't got any sandwiches.

KENNETH But I'm hungry. It won't take you long to cut some bread up, open a tin of meat, make some cocoa and a few cakes . . . I only want a mouthful of something.

SIDNEY How about teeth?

KENNETH Oh I'm sorry – you're watching the play, aren't you.

TONY It's nearly finished now. Still, they tell me the end's very exciting. Best bit in the play. Surprise ending. As long as you see this bit you haven't missed anything.

KENNETH (*builds up to tremendous climax*) Here.

TONY What?

KENNETH The screen's gone funny.

TONY Me play. Me twist ending. Them perishing cars. (*calls*) Put a suppressor on! Just because there's a railway strike, you think you're everybody. Oooh me play.

KENNETH You know what's wrong with it, don't you? It's the distributor.

TONY Is it?

KENNETH Oh yes. I can tell, cos I know all about tellys you know.

TONY I thought you would.

KENNETH I'll soon put it right for you. It's this knob here.

TONY Don't touch it. I'll do it.

KENNETH No, no, no, I'll do it. You've got to know what you're doing with the telly sets. They're very delicate. Have you got a hammer and chisel?

TONY Now wait a minute, go easy . . .

KENNETH Just wrench the back off.

(*splintering of wood*)

KENNETH That's better. Now we can really have a go can't we?

TONY Please be careful.

KENNETH Of course. Now what shall I start on? There's so much here to choose from. Oooh I am going to enjoy this, I am. It's a challenge.

TONY Come out, come out. I know you're in there, I can see your face on the screen.

KENNETH I think the best idea is to go round tapping everything with the hammer. Never know what you'll find that way.

TONY No look . . . please . . . (*carries on protesting*)

(*Several light taps with hammer, then terrific metallic crash as TV set falls to bits. Odd bits drop off*)

KENNETH I thought so.

TONY What?

KENNETH There was something loose. (*laughs*)

TONY (*sour laugh*) Me television set. Ruined.

KENNETH Don't worry, we can soon . . . here, can you smell something burning?

TONY Yes I can. (*sniffs*) Can't be the soldering iron, I haven't sat down for half an hour.

KENNETH Here, it's the telly. It's on fire. There must have been a short circuit.

TONY Mind the curtains. They've caught alight. Water. Quick. Stamp it out. Call the fire brigade.

(*fire engines drawing up*)

KENNETH Well I don't think I can be of any further assistance gentlemen, so I'll say goodnight. I did enjoy the play. Goodnight.

TONY Goodnight he says. Me furniture's ruined. All me clothes are gone. Me house has been burnt down . . . and it wasn't insured. (*slight pause*) He only came in for some milk for his cat. Television. I'm finished with it. Look what it's done to me. I'm ruined. Poverty stricken. I've got nothing left.

BILL Yes you have Tub. I managed to save one thing from the fire.

TONY What?

BILL The bed. Goodnight Tub. (*snores*)

(from New Zealand)
Mike McKenzie
(from the West Indies)
The Bob Brown Singers
with the Frank Baron Trio
BBC Revue Orchestra
Conductor, Harry Rabinowitz
(from South Africa)
Produced by Glyn Jones
(United Kingdom)
(BBC recording)

0.30   THE
MONTMARTRE PLAYERS
Directed by Henry Krein
with Edward Rubach
and Robert Docker (two pianos)
(BBC recording)

11.0   SONGS
FROM MANY LANDS
Entertainments Choir of the
Danish State Radio
Conductor, Svend Saaby
Accompanist, Charles Spinks
(BBC recording)

11.30 PEOPLE'S SERVICE
These things I remember
(Psalm 42, v. 4)

Thanks at the End of the Year
Service from Nicolson Square
Methodist Church, Edinburgh,
conducted by the Rev. Professor
John Foster, D.D., assisted by the
Minister, the Rev. Kenneth G.
Bloxham

11.55   1,500 m.
Shipping Forecast

247 m. and VHF
'Good Listening'
Some news of current programmes

12.0 Greenwich Time Signal
TWO-WAY
FAMILY FAVOURITES
For Service men and women
stationed abroad and their
families at home
Presented from London and Cologne
by Jean Metcalfe and Dennis Scuse

---

gramme
6 kc/s)   91.3 Mc/s VHF

mpton, and Ursula Howells in

..........................Stephen Murray
..........................Fay Compton
..........................Ursula Howells
..........................Simon Lack
..........................June Tobin
..........................Arthur Young
..........................Allan Jeayes
..........................Alban Blakelock
..........................Frank Partington
..........................Bunny May
AN..........................Molly Rankin
..........................Haydn Jones
..........................Robert Sansom

yed by
, Emerton Court, Humphrey Morton,
y, Arthur Keane, John Graham,
atrice Kane, Ronald Sidney
TION BY VAL GIELGUD

NTERVAL (4.10-4.20 app):
rud
Op. 20, played by the

A WINTER PROGRAMME
LOOKING BACK
TO LAST SUMMER
AND FORWARD TO NEXT

Memories of sunlit days and leisure hours to come

THIS WEEK YOU ARE INVITED TO HEAR ABOUT:

A holiday in Barmouth   *A riding holiday in Switzerland*
with Stephen Grenfell   *with Georgie Henschel*

Ted Appleton, our travel expert, will be on hand
with up-to-the-minute items of holiday interest

INTRODUCED BY FRANKLIN ENGELMANN

Produced by Arthur Phillips and Harold Rogers

at 3.15

1.15 THE BILLY COTTON
BAND SHOW
The Boys with the Laughs
Alan Breeze, Doreen Stephens
The Bandits
Mr. Wakey Wakey (himself)
Script by
Eddie Gurney and Arthur Pastor
Produced by Glyn Jones

1.45   Peter Brough
and Archie Andrews in
EDUCATING ARCHIE
(Last Wednesday's recorded broadcast)

2.15   Bebe Daniels
and Ben Lyon
LIFE WITH THE LYONS
8—'A Star is Born'
with Barbara Lyon, Richard Lyon
Doris Rogers, Molly Weir
Richard Bellaers, Horace Percival
BBC Variety Orchestra
Conductor, Paul Fenoulhet
Written by Bob Block
Ronnie Hanbury and Bebe Daniels
Production by Tom Ronald
(BBC recording)
To be repeated on Thursday at 8.0

2.45 MOVIE-GO-ROUND
A sound approach to the cinema
introduced by Peter Haigh
Music from a New Release
Pearl Bailey sings
'Zing went the Strings of my Heart'
from 'That Certain Feeling'
Elvis Presley sings
'Poor Boy' from 'Love Me Tender'
Picturegoers' Quiz
Test your ear and your memory for
familiar and once-familiar voices
Stargazing
Anna Neagle talks about her career
and illustrates it with
extracts from films she has made
Presented by Desmond Carrington
and Spencer Hale
Pocket Preview
'Giant'
starring
Elizabeth Taylor, Rock Hudson
and James Dean
Adapted by Roy Bradford
Produced by Ruth Dennis
Sound-track Memories
including the voices of
Bob Hope and Dorothy Lamour
The programme edited and

3.15 HOLIDAY HOUR
See above and page 5
(BBC recording)

4.0   Tony Hancock in
HANCOCK'S HALF-HOUR
with Sidney James
Bill Kerr, Hattie Jacques
and Kenneth Williams
Written by
Alan Simpson and Ray Galton
Theme and incidental music com
and conducted by Wally Stott
Produced by Dennis Main Wilson
(BBC recording)
To be repeated on Tuesday at 8.0

4.30 QUESTION TIME
Young people in the F
Macdonald Y.M.C.A. Cen
Inverness, put questions with
Hogmanay flavour to Is
Peterkin, John Bannerman,
Sorley Maclean
Chairman, Jack House
(BBC recording)

From the Continent

Every Day. 'The French Have a
for It': 7.45 a.m. (41.44 m.; 7240
7.45 p.m. (25.06 m.; 11970 kc/s). *Mo*
to Friday: 10.0 p.m. (218 m.; 1370
Saturdays and Sundays: 2.0 p.m. (
m.; 7240 kc/s).
Sunday. 9.0 a.m. High Mass (F
National Programme 348, 249, 235 m
12.20 p.m. *Pelléas et Mélisande*, dram
Maeterlinck, with music by Fauré (F
National Programme 348, 249, 235 m
12.45 p.m. 'Jazz in the Champs-Elys
(Paris 1829 m.)
1.20 p.m. *Job*, oratorio by Ton de L
(Hilversum 298 m.)
2.30 p.m. *La Vie Parisienne*, operett
Offenbach (French National Progra
348, 249, 235 m.)
2.35 p.m. Hans Henkemans (piano):
by Debussy (Hilversum 298 m.)
4.45 p.m. Pasdeloup Concert: choral r
by Mozart (French National Progra
348, 249, 235 m.)
7.0 p.m. 'La Vie Parisienne': ca
programme (Paris 1829 m.)
8.0 p.m. Symphony Concert, conducte
Ernest Ansermet, with Pierre Fou
(cello): Beethoven, Lalo, Boccherini,
Bartok (Paris 1829 m.)
8.20 p.m. *Love for Three Oranges*, o
by Prokofiev (Italian Third Progra
75.09 m.)
9.30 p.m. 'By the Blue Danube' (
1829 m.)
11.5 p.m. Symphony Concert, condu

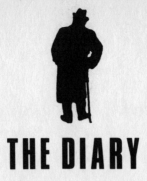

THE DIARY

'This morning I had an egg for breakfast . . .'

Of all the scripts in this book, indeed of all the scripts that Alan and Ray composed, this is the least dated, or indeed datable, simply because ninety-five per cent is pure fantasy and the rest is of such an everyday, ordinary run-of-the-mill reality that it could be set in 1987, 1997 or even 1956.

The reason for choosing this particular show is to provide an example, of which this script is certainly the best, of the flights of fancy that the writers would occasionally indulge in, without departing in any way from the main characteristics of the Hancock radio persona.

Whilst Hancock may dream of greater things, as is the human wont, reality is never very far away and the return to it is usually accompanied with a bang. Whereas the previous script was nearly all plot and very little character analysis, this show presents a great advancement in the work and talents of both writers and performer, for although the script could be given to any comedy actor worth their salt, nobody could have given it the depth of conviction that came from Tony Hancock.

As I have mentioned before, it was through this show, indirectly, that I first heard of Tony Hancock, though even then I was not aware of his name but just thought of him as a very funny man. I was, by all accounts, a very serious child, and one of my few concessions to the lighter side of life involved listening to *Children's Favourites* on BBC radio, compèred by 'Uncle Mac', originally from *Children's Hour*. It was a simple request programme for younger listeners, in which children from places I'd never heard of would write and ask to hear 'The Runaway Train' or 'The Laughing Policeman' and, nearly every week, one could almost guarantee hearing an extract from 'The Test Pilot'.

'The Test Pilot', also known as 'The Secret Life of Anthony Hancock', was taken from an album called 'Pieces of Hancock', and is, in effect, the last of the three fantasy sequences in 'The Diary'.

This excerpt, along with several other extracts from the radio shows, was introduced by, and interspersed with a specially written commentary by Galton and Simpson, and was produced for PYE records by the late Alan A. Freeman. There were some copyright problems concerning the use of the 'Dambusters' March' which was featured in the original radio programme, and Alan A. Freeman had to very carefully edit out the music. This was hampered by the fact that some of the dialogue over-ran, so he got over this problem by recording over it with the sound of jet aircraft taking off. He told me that if you listen very closely to the record you can still hear the faint soundtrack of the 'Dambusters' March'.

So with Sid James' acting experience showing through his accents, and the whole cast having a whale of a time, I can say no more about this script other than 'I want eggs for tea when I get back, James . . .'

THE DIARY

Script by
ALAN SIMPSON AND RAY GALTON

Recorded: 23 December 1956
Broadcast: 30 December 1956
Starring:
TONY HANCOCK
SIDNEY JAMES
BILL KERR
KENNETH WILLIAMS
HATTIE JACQUES

Produced by
DENNIS MAIN WILSON

TONY   Oh well, December the thirty-first. Another year over.

BILL   Yeah. It's been a good year for me personally. The first year I've ever really felt relaxed and at ease.

TONY   Yes of course, you've been out of work all year haven't you?

BILL   Yeah. I reckon another couple of years like that, and I'll be completely recovered.

TONY   From what?

BILL   From the two days I worked the year before last.

TONY   Yes, it's been very hard for you hasn't it. I don't know how you've kept your reason. I'm not even sure that you have. There must be some marbles missing somewhere, it's not natural to be as idle as you. You could write a book on *How To Be Lazy*, if you weren't so lazy.

BILL   Don't keep getting at me, it's not my fault I'm weak. My war wound keeps playing me up.

TONY   Oh please, don't give me that stuff about your war wound. You're talking to a man who's seen it . . . and knows how you got it. A little scratch on the arm from the officer's nails as he pulled your stripe off. Let's get one thing straight, we're not having a repetition of bone idleness in 1957. You are going out to work.

BILL   Don't exaggerate, I wasn't bone idle last year, I must have done some work somewhere, even if it was just helping around the house.

TONY   You did not. Nothing. Not a dickey bird. I've got it all down in my diary. Everything that goes on in this house goes down in my giant chemist shop diary.

BILL   (*interested*) Say, I didn't know you kept a diary Tub.

TONY   Of course I keep a diary. All great men keep diaries. Pepys, Boswell, Shaw, all we literary herberts. Every little thing that happens in my life goes down in this book. Well you never know, they might want to publish it in years to come . . . or dramatise it on the radio. With a harp accompaniment in front of it, it'd be a sensation.

BILL   Show us it.

TONY   Careful, careful. That's for posterity. Future historians don't want a load of jammy finger-prints to cover up me revelations.

BILL   Who's going to be interested in your diary? What's happened in your life that could be of any value to anyone else?

TONY   They'll probably marvel at me perspicuity.

BILL   What's that?

TONY   It doesn't matter what it is, as long as people marvel at it, that's good enough for me. You've always underestimated me haven't you, right from the first moment I carried you into the house. You've never reckoned me. Never suspected the spark of greatness that pulsates within me eager breast. There's nothing I couldn't have achieved if I'd set me mind to it.

BILL   Daah, I'm going to bed.

TONY   Yes it's about time. It's nearly dinner time, and you've had a hard morning sitting there cracking nuts. And seeing me cristed Madeira home by the bottleful. Go on, be off with you . . . leave me here with me diary . . . to reminisce.

BILL   You're just a nobody. The diary of a nobody.

TONY   Go on . . . up to bed, you ratbag.

(*door shuts*)

56

TONY A nobody indeed. That's what they all think. None of them realise. I could have been somebody. I didn't feel like it that's all. I've got it in me. It's all in me diary. There's not an entry in here that doesn't serve to remind me of what I could have been had I chosen a different path. The Personal Diary of Anthony Hancock Gent, 1956. Where's the key, let me unlock it.

(*diary being unlocked*)

TONY January the first, 1956. Dear Diary, the beginning of another year. I sense a year of great importance in my life. A year of momentous last personal triumph. I feel fate will take a hand and if I am equal to its challenge I know this will be a year of great achievement. This morning I had an egg for breakfast. January the second. Pussy ran away with my dinner. January the third. It is raining. But what is rain to a man of greatness? I shall go out. January the fourth. I have a cold. January the fifth. I fed the goldfish. January the sixth. I cleaned my bike. January the seventh. Pussy brought my dinner back. January the eighth. I fed the goldfish. January the ninth. Nothing of any interest happened today. January the tenth. At last, drama. Bill cut his finger. I bandaged it. Should I devote my life to medicine?

KENNETH Calling Doctor Hancock . . . calling Doctor Hancock . . . you're wanted in casualty ward. This is an emergency.

TONY Curse, isn't there any other competent doctor in this hospital? I can't do every operation that comes in. Seventy-four before lunch, isn't that enough for them?

HATTIE But Doctor, you're the world's foremost authority on everything. The other doctors don't dare to operate while you're in the hospital. You'd better go doctor.

TONY Good grief woman, I can't. Don't you realise I'm just about to start on a delicate brain operation.

HATTIE Whose?

TONY My own. Scalpel.

HATTIE Scalpel.

TONY Forceps.

HATTIE Forceps.

TONY Mirror. There it is, good heavens what a size! No wonder I'm a genius.

KENNETH Calling Doctor Hancock, will you please come to casualty immediately . . . this is an emergency.

TONY Oh heavens what's wrong?

KENNETH I'm not feeling very well.

TONY Very well, I'll come. Bandage me up nurse, I'll finish it when I get back.

BILL Ah, there you are Hancock. Thank heavens you're here.

TONY Good afternoon Professor Kerr.

BILL This is Professor Sigmund James.

SIDNEY How are you?

TONY A slight arteriosis of the cardiacal tube. How are you?

SIDNEY Chronic dilation of the anterior notochord thanks.

TONY Glad to hear it.

BILL You know of course Professor James is *the* Professor James, the world famous specialist on aberrations and abnormalities.

57

TONY Oh yes indeed, I read your book while I was operating once . . . it's the only time I get you know.

SIDNEY Ah yes, that book was the result of twenty years research. What did you think Hancock?

TONY I enjoyed it. Most amusing. Bit naive in parts, and I can't agree with your chapter on neuro pathology, but I've made a few notes that should put you right.

SIDNEY Oh thank you Hancock, that's most kind, I'm very grateful.

TONY Not at all, the least I can do . . . till I get a day or two to spare, I'll write a book on the lot then, might help some of you. What seems to be the trouble gentlemen?

BILL Doctor Hancock, we are faced with the most baffling case in medical history. Only you can solve it.

TONY Naturally. I shall operate.

SIDNEY But you don't know what it is yet.

TONY Do you know a better way of finding out?

SIDNEY We could ask the patient.

BILL We've tried that, he won't tell us.

TONY What time is it?

SIDNEY Eleven o'clock.

TONY Then that settles it doesn't it. There's only one thing to do.

BILL What?

TONY Golf. I always think better on the golf course.

SIDNEY But what about the patient?

TONY Bring him with us. He can carry the clubs.

BILL But he's desperately ill.

TONY Well, bring him anyway. If we solve the problem we can operate in a bunker. Stand him in my golf bag, there's plenty of room, I only use one iron to go round with.

SIDNEY I refuse to operate on a golf course. I insist we do it in the hospital.

TONY Oh how tiresome, very well. Lay my instruments out nurse.

HATTIE Which ones Doctor?

TONY Violin and snare drums. They sooth me while I'm thinking.

BILL Well if you're ready Doctor, I would class it as an honour to assist you during the operation.

TONY There's nothing you can do really.

BILL There must be, perhaps I could turn your music for you.

TONY Excellent idea, shall we begin?

HATTIE The patient is ready Doctor, shall I wheel him in?

TONY Please do. So much more convenient when they're here.

SIDNEY Shall I get your rubber gloves Doctor?

TONY No thank you. I think I'll have the fur-lined driving gauntlets today, it's rather chilly in here.

BILL (*in awe*) The most delicate operation known to medical science and he wears gauntlets. How does he do it?

SIDNEY The man must be the greatest surgeon in the world.

TONY I am.

BILL Doctor, before you begin I must warn you . . . the most eminent surgeons

from Europe have flown over to watch you perform this operation. They're up there in the gallery. I trust you have no objection to them watching?

TONY Not at all, but do tell them, when I get to the exciting bits not to rustle their popcorn bags. Right gentlemen . . . I am ready.

TONY (*low and tense*) Scalpel.

HATTIE Scalpel.

TONY Suture.

HATTIE Suture.

TONY Scissors . . . scissors, scissors quickly, scissors. Good. Forceps.

HATTIE Forceps.

TONY There we are. That's got his pyjamas off. They (*gently remonstrative*) should have been off before he got here you know nurse.

HATTIE (*tearfully*) I'm sorry Doctor, I'm so nervous at working with such a brilliant man.

TONY Of course, of course, don't worry little goose. Well gentlemen, this is it. Watch carefully, you might miss something the speed I go at . . . and I can't do it again, it wouldn't be fair on the patient. Right.

TONY & HATTIE (*as fast as they can do it without getting tonguetied*) Scalpel.
Scalpel.
Sutures.
Sutures.
Scissors.
Scissors.
Clamp.
Clamp.
Forceps.
Forceps.
Swabs.
Swabs.
Needle.
Needle.
Thread.
Thread.
Scissors.
Scissors.

TONY There we are gentlemen, finished.

BILL That's amazing. Fantastic. This operation normally cannot be done in less than seven hours. You have done it in . . . one minute, twenty-three point four seconds!

TONY Yes, I'm sorry I took so long. But while I was at it, I removed his appendix, his tonsils, cleared up his catarrh and straightened out his hammer toe. Well, if there are no other operations for me to attend to before lunch, how about a quick game of rugger?

SIDNEY Impossible. We haven't time.

TONY I'm talking to the patient. When I cure somebody, I don't mess about old man.

(*Hancock fanfare*)

KENNETH And for his services to the advancement of medical science, for his work on behalf of all mankind surpassing even the achievements of Lister, Pasteur, and Curie, I have great pride in awarding to Doctor Anthony Hancock the Nobel Prize for Medicine.

(*tremendous massed crowd cheering*)

TONY January the eleventh. Bandage fell off Bill's finger, finger turned blue, took him round to doctor's. Don't think I'll take up medicine after all. I don't know enough, I reckon I could have made a go of it if I'd had the training. Seen *Doctor in the House* through a couple of times, I would have been all right. Still, there are plenty of other fields one can achieve greatness in. I'm glad I kept this diary. Just flicking through it, one can see more and more the chronicles of a great mind. February the sixth. Mended gramophone. February the seventh. Looked at telly, went to bed early. February the eighth. Went to the pictures. Rotten film, but smashing flavour of the month. Winked at girl coming out. February the ninth. Chased mouse across kitchen with broom and poker. (*thoughtful*) Chased mouse across kitchen with broom and poker.

(*Hancock chords*)

(*Cageful of lions roaring. Whip cracking now and again*)

TONY Back. Back Rajah. Back I say. (*whip*) Ha ha you may be King of the Jungle, but you've met your master now haven't you? Yes go on sulk. Lick my face go on. That's it, now hup. Up on the stool. On the stool I say.

(*single lion growl*)

TONY On the stool. (*whip*) That's it, stay there.

SIDNEY What a great lion tamer that boy is. The biggest sensation I've ever had in my circus. Captain Mad Jack Hancock.

HATTIE He's so brave, father. He tackles those beasts bare handed with no fear at all. He must have nerves of steel.

SIDNEY Yeah, that Rajah's killed three trainers already. But you'd think he was a mouse the way that boy deals with him. I don't know how he does it. He makes them lions do tricks I've never seen before. Sticking your head in your mouth, yes . . . but not in as far as your knee caps. That's asking for it.

HATTIE He doesn't care. He's wonderful.

SIDNEY Are you in love with him Gladys?

HATTIE Can I be blamed if I am. Every time he looks at me I feel I could jump through a hoop for him.

SIDNEY Listen Gladys, you know there's nothing I want more than for you to marry in the circus. I had great hopes of you and the sword swallower. What happened to him?

HATTIE You remember, he swallowed a seven foot sword and we had to leave him stuck in that field outside Wolverhampton.

SIDNEY Oh yes, well you and Hancock have my blessing, but stay away from him until after the season. I can't afford to have him distracted. He's the only draw we've got left. I've had nothing but trouble these last few weeks. All those accidents.

HATTIE They couldn't be helped.

SIDNEY They could have been avoided. I told the Bearded Lady to stop smoking.

Nobody's going to come and see her now . . . the Lady with the Five o'clock Shadow. And then the India Rubber Man had to go and fall in love with the Tattooed Lady. What a tragedy. Rubbed all her tattoos off.

HATTIE Nothing like that's going to happen to us father.

SIDNEY I don't want Hancock worrying about you. One slip of concentration in the cage and he's had it. I can't afford to lose him, I'll be ruined.

HATTIE Sssh, here he comes.

TONY Well there we are Mr James, that's the act I shall be doing when we open tomorrow night. What do you think?

SIDNEY Sensational son, sensational.

TONY I thought you'd like it. I can do anything with those cats. I was going to have them riding round on motor bikes, but Rajah chewed his ration book up, so that coalboxed that.

SIDNEY Doesn't matter, it's a great act boy, a great act.

TONY Well it's the best I can do with those lions. What a rough old lot they are. Weak-kneed spineless things. They're not wild enough, been in captivity too long. Two days behind bars is enough to soften any animal. I want some fresh stuff, straight off the boat. Then I'll teach 'em tricks that'll make their manes stand on end.

SIDNEY That's great son. I'm relying on you to pull the customers in. Come over to my caravan, I want to discuss the lay out of the cage with you.

TONY Right. By the way, the lions haven't been fed today, you'd better sling another clown in.

HATTIE What a man. Oh I hope he tames me like he does those other wild beasts.

BILL Hallo Miss Gladys.

HATTIE Why it's Billo the Sad Faced Clown. Billo, why don't you take your make-up off when you're not working?

BILL I've taken it off Miss Gladys . . . this is me.

HATTIE (*tinkly laugh*) What a funny face you have Billo. So sad and ugly. (*laughs*)

BILL I'm glad you like it Miss Gladys. Miss Gladys.

HATTIE Yes Billo.

BILL Miss Gladys, I've been standing outside in the pouring rain for hours just looking at you and waiting for you.

HATTIE How sweet. Goodbye Billo.

BILL I'm soaking wet.

HATTIE Well, of course you are . . . it's been raining. Good night Billo.

BILL I'm your slave. I'd do anything for you, I worship the ground you walk on. I know I'm only a clown, but I love you, my heart aches for you, I throw myself down on the ground at your feet, so you can trample on me.

HATTIE How nice, goodnight Billo.

BILL Don't go Miss Gladys . . . Miss Gladys.

HATTIE Hurry up Billo, I'm in a hurry.

BILL Miss Gladys, I've got two tickets for the village dance, would you like to come?

HATTIE Go to a dance with you . . . you're just a clown. (*laughs*)

BILL You only think of me as a clown, but I'm a man as well. Underneath this grease paint, there's something else.

HATTIE   What?

BILL   Dirt. But there's a heart as well, brimming over with love and devotion for you.

HATTIE   Oh don't be ridiculous. I couldn't be seen out with a clown.

BILL   But Miss Gladys . . .

TONY   On your way, clown.

BILL   Mad Jack Hancock.

TONY   Yes, Mad Jack Hancock the greatest lion tamer in the world. Miss Gladys is not for you clown, a village dance indeed . . . she's coming up to London with me in my high powered sports car. (*mocking laugh*)

BILL   You don't care who you hurt, do you Mad Jack? You think you're rather grand standing there in your white jodhpurs, shiny boots, black wavy hair and sideboards.

TONY   Racy eh?

BILL   You're not for Miss Gladys, you and your dashing devil-may-care manner blind a woman to your true nature. Some of those simple village girls know that to their cost.

HATTIE   Is this true, Jack?

TONY   Heed him not Gladys. He's just a poor jealous clown, don't be bothered with him. Come . . . to my caravan, I will change into my Oxford bags, we will jump into my car and leap forward into the night.

HATTIE & TONY   (*go off laughing gaily*)

(*hearts & flowers music*)

BILL   Alone I stand. She's gone with him. I must do something to protect her honour, the poor innocent girl is blinded by his too obvious good looks. I must save her, but how? She will not listen to me, Billo, the lonely sad faced clown. An accident, that's it . . . an accident in the lion cage tomorrow night. Then I'll be rid of him and claim Miss Gladys for myself.

(*circus music*)

(*murmur of crowds*)

SIDNEY   Well this is it Jack. The biggest test of your career. The biggest town we've played . . . and a cageful of fresh lions, straight from the jungle.

HATTIE   Do be careful, Jack. These lions are so savage, they've never seen a man before.

TONY   How many are in there?

SIDNEY   Six.

TONY   Not enough. Three dozen I want. And throw some crocodiles in, just to make it more interesting.

SIDNEY   What tricks are you going to do with thirty-six savage lions?

TONY   I curl myself up, lay in the middle of the cage and they have a game of rugby.

HATTIE   This is madness, you won't be able to control them.

TONY   Don't worry, the lion hasn't been born that can get the better of Mad Jack. But . . . if it makes your mind any easier, I have my Derringer in the top of my boot, with live cartridges.

HATTIE   Before you go into the cage Jack . . . tell me . . . while you were drinking champagne out of my slipper last night, did you . . . did you mean what you said?

TONY   You mean . . . about marriage?

HATTIE   Yes.

TONY   (*sly laugh*) My dear girl, Mad Jack never gives the elephant a bun after it's done its dance. Announce me Ringmaster.

(*fanfare*)

KENNETH   My Lords, ladies and gentlemen, introducing the world's greatest lion tamer, Captain Mad Jack Hancock, who will enter the cage, completely unarmed, to face thirty-six savage man-eating lions.

(*music*)

BILL   Miss Gladys.

HATTIE   Not now Billo, Mad Jack is on.

BILL   I thought you might like these.

HATTIE   (*catches her breath*) Billo, what are they?

BILL   The cartridges from Mad Jack's Derringer.

HATTIE   He won't have a chance if they turn on him . . . we must stop him.

BILL   It's too late . . . he's in the cage.

(*cageful of lions roaring*)

TONY   Now listen lads. I curl myself up and lay down in the middle. When I blow the whistle you kick off. No scratching or you'll be sent off. Twickenham rules, and let's have a good clean game. Right.

(*Referee's whistle. Lions roar. Crowd roars*)

HATTIE   Look, just as we feared . . . they're not doing what he says.

SIDNEY   I knew they weren't trained enough. They've got him cornered. He's in trouble.

(*lions roaring*)

TONY   Get back. Back I say. I've got a gun here. Get back. All right you brutes, I'll just have to shoot you. There.

(*click of empty revolver*)

TONY   What's this, no bullets. This is Billo's work. Very well, bare hands it is.

(*Lions roaring. Crowd roaring*)

HATTIE   I can't watch it, they'll tear him to bits.

KENNETH   My Lords, ladies and gentlemen, and now we will send *another* thirty-six lions in for Mad Jack to tear to pieces. Is there no limit to this man's courage. Yes, the greatest lion tamer of all time, Captain Mad Jack Hancock.

(*crowd cheering their heads off*)

TONY   February the tenth. In hospital suffering from shock. The mouse turned on me, I jumped on a chair and fainted. No, well, fair's fair, he was a big mouse and they can turn nasty when they're cornered. It's just as well we bought the kitten. Though *he* gets a bit umpty at times. Still, I'm clever, I don't budge out of me room till Bill's locked him up. Not that I couldn't have been a great lion tamer. It's just that I think it's such a worthless profession for a great thinker. Erudite philosophers like me shouldn't waste themselves like that. Let's have a flip through . . . ah these pages . . . living history this. What drama happened in July? July second. Went to a dance. Didn't click. Walked home and went to bed. July third. My birthday. Threw party. No one came. Went to bed. July fourth. Ah . . . Went to fair on common. Had threepenny go on roundabout. Little bus was full up, had to sit in aeroplane instead.

(*Hancock chords*)

(*door opens*)

TONY   Wing Commander Hancock reporting sir.

BILL   Come in Hancock. You know why I've sent for you?

TONY   I can guess sir. P64?

BILL   P64 it is. According to specifications it should top well over 2000 miles an hour.

TONY   That's not bad for a take-off, what does it do when it leaves the ground?

BILL   That is its air speed, Hancock. As you are the best test pilot we have on the drome, you have been picked to take it on its test flight.

TONY   (*casually*) Jolly good show.

BILL   Quite frankly, no one knows exactly what will happen when you get up there. All we know is at that speed metal does peculiar things. Once you've gone through the heat barrier, metal can melt into a jelly.

TONY   What flavour sir?

BILL   (*short laugh*) Same old Hancock. Does nothing frighten you?

TONY   Nothing in the air, sir.

BILL   Here is a scale model of the aircraft. As you can see, the design is quite revolutionary. No wings. Vertical take-off. You lie flat on your stomach in the cockpit. And you will notice it is approximately half the size of anything else we have.

TONY   I'm a bit worried about that sir.

BILL   Ah, so you are human after all. What's worrying you?

TONY   Will there be enough room for my moustache?

BILL   We thought of that Hancock, the best thing to do is tie it around the back of your neck. It'll also cut down wind resistance. Any questions?

TONY   I don't think so sir, it's just another job.

BILL   When you're up there the atmospheric pressure is enormous, no human body could stand it, so we have a special pressurised rubber suit and helmet for you.

TONY   Oh I don't think so sir. It's such a lovely day the usual blazer and flannels I think. Besides I'm going to a dance when I get back, can't waste time changing.

BILL   You're a cool customer. No different now as you were when you destroyed the German Air Force in '43.

TONY   A little older sir.

BILL   Good luck Hancock, England is proud of you. It's in the hangar waiting for you. Everything depends on you.

TONY   If . . . if anything should go wrong sir, promise me . . .

BILL   Anything Hancock.

TONY   Don't abandon the project sir. Keep 'em flying. Melt all my medals down and build another one. There are plenty of chaps willing to have a crack. Goodbye sir.

BILL   Goodbye Hancock. Sergeant James.

SIDNEY   Sir.

BILL   Show Wing Commander Hancock to the plane.

('*Dambusters' march*')

SIDNEY   There she is sir. All ready for you. We've been up all night polishing it. We put your favourite white-wall tyres on for you.

TONY Thank you James, you're a good egg. Have you tied my teddy-bear on the control panel?

SIDNEY Of course sir, we all know you never go up without that.

TONY It's silly really, but . . . it was hers you see.

SIDNEY Miss Linda's sir.

TONY Yes, she gave it to me during the war . . . in London. We were so happy. We pledged our undying devotion and then not an hour later . . . it happened.

SIDNEY She went off with that American Private?

TONY Yes. Damn him. He dazzled her with his after-shave lotion. The cad, he knew we couldn't get any. Oh well, time to put her through her paces. I want eggs for tea when I get back, James.

SIDNEY Oh that I had his moral fibre.

TONY *(slightly off)* Ready to start engines.

(engines start)

SIDNEY Don't forget it's a vertical take-off sir.

TONY I know, don't bother to open the hangar door, I'll go out through the fanlight.

(rocket taking off)

('Dambusters' march')

(Jet plane travelling. Radio static)

TONY H for Hancock calling Control Tower. Levelling out at 1800 miles per hour. Everything going to plan. Fine plane, tell the designer chappie.

HATTIE Control Tower. Control Tower, to Hancock. We're worried about possible sabotage. The mechanic who was working on your aircraft is missing. Think you should come down. Land immediately, repeat, land immediately.

TONY Nonsense, she's going beautifully. I don't know a thing about any mechanic. Taking her up to 2400 miles an hour.

(banging on windscreen)

TONY Hancock to Control Tower. Something strange is happening. There is a peculiar knocking sound on the windscreen. It seems to be coming from outside the plane. Am slowing down to 1800 miles an hour. Will slide cockpit open to see what's wrong.

(cockpit cover being slid back)

KENNETH *(as Snide)* Good evening. It ain't half cold out here, can I come in?

TONY There's no room, get off.

KENNETH Oh don't be like that. Move over, I'll sit on your lap.

TONY Get your boot off me joystick, do you mind! Who are you?

KENNETH I'm the mechanic. I was still working on the tail when you took off. Frightened the life out of me, I mean I wasn't expecting it. I was sitting there quite happily singing to myself, and the next minute, whoosh . . . I was up here.

TONY Well you can get off again, you're upsetting the balance.

KENNETH If me spanner hadn't been round a tight nut, I would have been off ages ago.

TONY Sit still, I can't control the plane with you jumping about.

KENNETH I'm only trying to get comfortable. All these knobs and levers here, sticking in me. What's this one?

TONY Don't touch it.

(*ejector seat going off*)

KENNETH   Oooh, it's the ejector seat. Come back, where are you?

TONY   I'm out here sitting on the tail.

KENNETH   Oh stop messing about. Come back in. It's no use sitting out there sulking. I can't drive the thing.

TONY   Well go into a dive, so I can slide down.

KENNETH   All right, I'll try this lever.

(*ejector seat again*)

KENNETH   Hallo.

TONY   Hallo.

KENNETH   You might have told me there was another ejector seat.

TONY   All right, so we're both out here. Now what do we do?

KENNETH   Oooh look we're going up.

TONY   Well what do you expect when we're both sitting on the tail?

KENNETH   Isn't life funny? In the papers this morning, the stars said this was my lucky day.

TONY   If we keep going up at this rate, you'll be able to tell them they're wrong.

KENNETH   Well come on, we've had a little skylark, and a little giggle, let's go down now.

TONY   How can we go down. Look, we're finished, the engine's falling off.

KENNETH   That's all right, they've got plenty more down there.

TONY   We want one up here. We're going into a dive. We're out of control.

KENNETH   Oooh that's dangerous isn't it?

TONY   If we don't do something immediately, we'll be dead in thirty seconds.

KENNETH   Oh, just my luck, it's pay-day. What are you going to do?

TONY   I've got to try and pull the plane out of the dive. We can't get back to the cabin. Give me a piece of string.

KENNETH   Oooh, I'm scared. Oooh.

TONY   Don't panic man. This is the RAF. Where's that stiff upper lip?

KENNETH   Just above this loose flabby chin.

TONY   Give me that string. I'll get you down safely.

('*Dambusters' march*')

BILL   Well Hancock, you've done it again. Saved the plane. Any other man would have baled out.

TONY   You should know me sir, as long as there's a seat and a pair of wheels, I'll bring it down.

BILL   How did you manage it? Sitting on the tail like that?

TONY   Quite simple. I took a piece of string, lassoed the controls, and steered it home. Lucky I was a cox at Oxford eh sir?

BILL   Brilliant work Hancock. You've won another medal. What's it to be this time?

TONY   I can't make up my mind sir. I've already got two of everything. Have you got anything in red and green, to match my blazer sir?

BILL   Certainly Hancock, here you are.

TONY   There's no room on my jacket sir, you'd better throw it in the wheelbarrow with the others.

BILL   No, as it's New Year, I'll hang it on your moustache. You're a brave man,

Hancock. You will go down in history as the most courageous and decorated pilot in the RAF.
(*Hancock chords*)

TONY July the fifth. Last time I go on the roundabouts. Been in bed all day with dizzy spells. No, well it wasn't my fault, that bloke cranking the handle got a bit worked up. I remember me mother walking round holding me hand, had a job keeping up with me. Oh well, so much for me diary. Just one more entry to be made. December the thirty-first. Did radio show today. Sued by man who wrote *The Secret Life of Walter Mitty*. Oh well you can't please everybody. I'm going to bed.

1.30 PEOPLE'S SERVICE

Not as I will, but as thou wilt . . .
(St. Matthew 26, v. 39)

Crossing Your Bridges

3—' The Bridge of Fear '

'rom Yardley Parish Church,
Birmingham; conducted by the
'icar, the Rev. Charles Crowson

1.55 1,500 m.: **Shipping Forecast**
'47 m. and VHF: ' Good Listening '
Some news of current programmes

2.0 Greenwich Time Signal

**TWO-WAY
FAMILY FAVOURITES**

'resented from London and Cologne
y Jean Metcalfe and Dennis Scuse

.15 Sid Phillips in

CLARINET CAPERS

with Ray Burns
Reg Wale, Norman Cave
and Sid Phillips and his Band

Introduced by Michael Brooke
Produced by John Kingdon

.45 Peter Brough
and Archie Andrews in

EDUCATING ARCHIE

with Ken Platt

Last Wednesday's recorded broad-
ast)

.15 Bebe Daniels, Ben Lyon in

LIFE WITH THE LYONS

11—' You Are My Lucky Star '

vith Barbara Lyon, Richard Lyon
Doris Rogers, Molly Weir
tichard Bellaers, Horace Percival

BBC Variety Orchestra
Conductor, Paul Fenoulhet
Written by Bob Block
Ronnie Hanbury and Bebe Daniels
Production by Tom Ronald
(BBC recording)
Repeated on Thursday at 8.0 p.m.

2.45 MOVIE-GO-ROUND

Introduced by Peter Haigh

Music from a Recent Release
' Natasha's Waltz '
from Nino Rota's score
for ' War and Peace '

Picturegoers' Quiz
Test your ear and your memory

Stargazing: Frank Sinatra
talks about his career and
illustrates it with excerpts
from films he has made

Presented by Desmond Carrington
and Spencer Hale

Popular Musical: ' The King and I '
Deborah Kerr sings
' Hello, Young Lovers '

Pocket Edition: ' Lisbon ' starring
Ray Milland, Maureen O'Hara
and Claude Rains
Adapted by Roy Bradford
Produced by Ruth Dennis

Sound-track Memories
including the voices of
Marlene Dietrich and Marilyn Monroe
The programme edited and
produced by Trafford Whitelock
(Recording)

3.15 HOLIDAY HOUR

A winter programme
looking back to last summer
and forward to next

This week you are invited to hear about

A touring holiday in Southern Sweden
from C. Gordon Glover

A day trip down the Clyde with
Jameson Clark

Ted Appleton and Bill Cormack, travel
experts, give items of holiday interest
and answer your queries

Introduced by Franklin Engelmann

Produced by Arthur Phillips
and Harold Rogers
(BBC recording)

.0 Tony Hancock in

HANCOCK'S HALF-HOUR

with Sidney James, Bill Ke
Hattie Jacques, Kenneth Will

Written by
Alan Simpson and Ray Galton

Theme and incidental music com
and conducted by Wally Stot
Produced by Dennis Main Wil
(BBC recording)
To be repeated on Tuesday at 8.9

4.30 QUESTION TIME

A group of young people in
Community Centre t Cra
New Town put questions a
he houses and towns we live

Elizabeth Chesterton
Robert Furneaux-Jordan
Colin MacInnes

Tony Gibson is in the cha
(BBC recording)

From the Continer

1.20 p.m. Radio Orchestra: Sm
Weber, and Dohnanyi (Hilversum 402
1.30 p.m. Willem Andriessen (p
Sonatas by Beethoven (Hilversum 298
4.45 p.m. Symphony Concert (F
National Programme 348, 249, 235 m
5.30 p.m. Sascha Elmo and his
Orchestra: Light music (Hilversum 40
7.0 p.m. Concertgebouw Orchestra (F
sum 16, 25, 31, and 49 metre bands)
7.0 p.m. ' La Vie Parisienne ': cabare
gramme (Paris 1829 m.)
8.0 p.m. Band of the Garde Républ
Weber, Falla, Liszt (Paris 1829 m.)

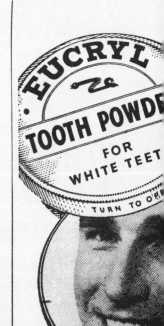
Third Programme

464 m. (647 kc/s)   194 m. (1,546 kc/s)   91.3 Mc/s VHF

.0 **THE FIRST STAGE**

A chronicle
of the
development of
English drama
from its
beginnings
to the 1580s

Arranged for broadcasting and
introduced by John Barton
Edited and produced
by Raymond Raikes

4—**Mystery Plays: The Betrayal,
Trial, and Crucifixion**

ilate.....................James McKechnie
aiaphas.................Howieson Culff

Music composed by Elizabeth Poston
played by the Goldsbrough Orchestra
conducted by Douglas Robinson
(BBC recording)

*(Douglas Robinson broadcasts by permis-
sion of the General Administrator, Royal
Opera House Covent Garden, Ltd.)*

To be repeated on Tuesday at 9.20
Basil Ashmore writes on page 4

Mysteries, Miracles, and Moralities:
February 17 and 22

Full details of the thirteen programmes in
the series are contained in *The First Stage,*
a handbook by John Barton, which may be
obtained through newsagents and book-
sellers or post free by crossed postal order
for 2s. 6d. from BBC Publications, 35
Marylebone High Street, London, W.1.

4.5-4.55 ' IL SEGRETO

THE OLD SCHOOL REUNION

'One and one are two, two and two are four, four and four are . . .
. . . one and one are two . . .'

Greystones, that cultural training ground, that edifice of intellectual instruction, that purveyor of philosophical dreams, revisited now by a 'red-nosed music-hall comic', who romanticised as if to say, 'I remember the first time I saw Mandalay' – following that with 'and I parked me bike against the gates!'

In those halcyon days of 1957 a public-school education was reserved exclusively for the established, the ruling classes, the privileged few, for those discerning parents who were rich enough to keep their infants away from the riff-raff and the Teddy boys.

For in 1957 the 'Teds', the English phenomena from the rock 'n' roll explosion, were well established; it was the year of Marty Wilde, Terry Dene and Wee Willie Harris, of skiffle and of hula-hoops; it was the year that Harold Macmillan made his now famous speech: 'Some of our people have never had it so good'; and it was also the year that the Schools Broadcasting service began on television.

'William . . . a school is a collection of children, and a pile of books, surrounded by bricks to keep the rain off.'

Comparing this with the previous example, 'The Diary', you may be forgiven for thinking that this script, too, is just another excursion into flights of fancy, with Hancock dreaming of higher ideals; but it goes much further than that in character analysis and provides all sorts of clues as to the gradual build up of the Hancock radio character.

Tony Hancock, himself, had a good education and was, quite rightly, proud of it, though it appeared at times that he might have felt a twinge or two of guilt – as though his education kept him at some distance from being what he most wanted to be, ordinary. As a pupil he was quite ordinary and undistinguished academically. One of his prep school teachers at Durlston Court recently recalled that whereas most of the boys wanted to be politicians or test pilots, the young Tony Hancock wanted to be a comedian.

At Bradfield College, however, he did distinguish himself, if not in the classroom. According to his former tutor there, besides his being a very capable footballer, he excelled on the cricket pitch where he was a first-rate all-rounder. So the Ian Botham of Bradfield College, who went on to be the most popular and best-loved comedian in Britain, was well thought of at school and perhaps it was this that gave Galton and Simpson the inspiration to write this marvellous story of what-might-have-been.

The Bradfield College Register, incidentally, contains this extract:

4799 GRANT Lieutenant . . . Bank of England . . . [etc.]
4800 HANCOCK Anthony John, born May 1924, arrived September 1938, left December '39. In G house.
4801 HENDERSON Captain . . . Director Ulster TV, MP 1952–58 . . . [etc]

Which I like to think is something that Tony would find amusing, in the vein of the much later television series, 'He came, He went and in between . . . nothing!'

However, although most of the action takes place in the fantasy world of *Tom Brown's Schooldays* and Billy 'Yarooh' Bunter's school, Greyfriars, I did come across one 1957-dated item in the script that may need some elucidation: 'Supplementary' – as in: 'Ah, good . . . me supplementary's come through . . .', which referred to the issue of supplementary petrol coupons, a continuing effect of the Suez Crisis.

THE OLD SCHOOL REUNION

Script by
ALAN SIMPSON AND RAY GALTON

Recorded: 13 January 1957
Broadcast: 20 January 1957
Starring:
TONY HANCOCK
SIDNEY JAMES
BILL KERR
KENNETH WILLIAMS
HATTIE JACQUES

Produced by
DENNIS MAIN WILSON

(*Knock on door. Door opens*)

TONY Ah good morning, postman.

KENNETH Morning. Merry Christmas.

TONY Merry what?

KENNETH Christmas.

TONY Bit late aren't you?

KENNETH Better late than never. Merry Christmas.

TONY You've said that. What are you holding your hand out for?

KENNETH What do you think?

TONY You want me to shake it.

KENNETH No I don't. I want a tip.

TONY How dare you! How dare you come knocking on doors so long after Christmas asking for gratuities?

KENNETH Not my fault. It's the first time you've opened the door since November the twenty-ninth.

TONY Well you're too late. I've given out all me Christmas boxes. And you can tell the dustman, the baker, and the milkman if you see them. Now kindly give me my post and remove your great plates off me foot scraper.

KENNETH All right, here you are.

TONY Thank you. Good day.

KENNETH What about my Christmas box?

TONY Oh, here you are. Have the stamp off this envelope – it hasn't been cancelled.

KENNETH Thank you I'm sure.

TONY Better than nothing. Cut the perforation off, you'll make a fortune. Good day.

KENNETH Skinflint. I'd make the most of those letters. They're the last ones you'll get off me that are readable.

(*door shuts*)

TONY I'll have to see about him. I'll have a stiff spring put on me letter box next week, that'll have his fingers. Now, what have we got here?

(*letter being opened*)

TONY (*reads*) 'Dear sir, or madam, you are required to appear at Bow Street Police Court on a charge of parking your car and causing an obstruction.' Well that can't be me, it's been up on blocks for three weeks.

BILL Yeah . . . in the middle of Regent Street.

TONY Oh you're up are you? I didn't expect you until the warm weather.

BILL Are you going to answer the summons?

TONY Course I'm not. I've got a valid excuse. They were digging the road up, and I wanted to take some tar blocks home, when I ran out of petrol. I couldn't carry the tar blocks, I couldn't move the car, so I put the blocks under the car, took the wheels off, sold the tyres and cut me losses.

BILL Forty bob fine at least.

TONY Disgusting. I only got five and six on the tyres. Ah, good.

BILL What?

TONY Me supplementary's come through. Be able to run me road haulage business now.

BILL You didn't tell them you've got a road haulage business.

TONY Certainly. Six ten-tonners, four articulates, half a dozen eight-wheelers, twenty-four vans, and a couple of lorries.

BILL How much have they given you?

TONY Four gallons. Hallo, what's this? A letter postmarked Greystones, Wiltshire. Greystones . . . Greystones. Who do I know in Greystones?

BILL Open it, perhaps there's something in the envelope.

(*rustling of paper*)

TONY Of course. Greystones. My old school.

BILL Greystones?

TONY Yes, the finest public school in the country. I was there for seven years.

BILL I had no idea you were a public schoolboy, Tub.

TONY What? Oh my gosh, haroo, leggo, yes. Haven't you seen me striped blazer hanging up in the wardrobe?

BILL Is that a blazer? I thought it was a deckchair.

TONY They were the school colours, I'll have you know. Red, green, mauve and heliotrope. I hope the moths haven't got at it.

BILL They wouldn't go near that without dark glasses.

TONY You are mocking the most cherished of our institutions, the British Public School. I'll not have it sir, I've a good mind to take me tie to you.

BILL I'm sorry Tub, I didn't realise you English felt so strongly about your old school. You see, back home things are a bit different. We didn't have schools. The teacher used to come round once a month on a kangaroo.

TONY A qualified professor was he? What was his name? Perhaps I've heard of him.

BILL Jumping Bluey Smith. Does it ring a bell?

TONY No, no I can't say it does. Probably an Eton man, certainly not Greystones. Ah dear old Greystones, seven of the happiest years of my life. I started off as a fag, and worked me way up to Head Cigar. That's what we called the Captain. Do you know, William, I haven't been back to the old school in fifteen years. Ho hum, tempus fugit.

BILL What does that mean?

TONY I don't know, ask Jumping Bluey Smith next time he comes leaping round.

BILL Well, what does this letter say?

TONY Let's see. Here, it's from old Ding-Dong.

BILL Who?

TONY Doctor Clanger, our Headmaster. A gentleman and a scholar William. A classical education of course. It was him who translated my stage act from the original Greek.

BILL And now he's written for the money.

TONY No he hasn't. He says it's Speech Day next week, and they've decided to have an old boys' reunion, and would I like to go. Ah it'll be wonderful to renew old acquaintances after all these years. I wonder how old Stinks is getting on.

BILL The chemistry master?

TONY No, his wife. Ooh, that horrible perfume she used to wear. Afternoon in Gallipoli I think it was. Well, I must get my togs cleaned and pressed. Haven't worn the old blazer in years. Not since that week I did with the Kentucky

Minstrels. Now then . . . let's try it on.

BILL   It won't fit you after all these years.

TONY   Course it will. I haven't put an inch on since I was fifteen. (*struggling*) See . . . it . . . fits . . . like . . . a glove . . . just do . . . the buttons . . . up . . . and . . . (*hoarse with suffocation*) There. Perfect fit.

(*three pings as buttons pop off*)

TONY   That's better, where did the buttons go?

BILL   I don't know where the other two are, but this isn't a monocle in my eye. Take that blazer off, you look stupid in it.

TONY   Stupid? The girls didn't think so in the old days. With me white flannels and me straw hat, punting down the River Cam on a summer's afternoon. A beautiful girl in her crinolines, a big picture hat and a little fluffy white parasol, smiling softly at me, poling her way down the river for all she was worth. Yes, this blazer's seen some action in its time.

SIDNEY   Aye, aye, anybody home?

TONY   Hallo Sid, come in.

SIDNEY   How much do you want for your four gallons supplementary, cos I've got a . . . cor blimey.

TONY   What's the matter?

SIDNEY   What have you got that roll of lino wrapped round you for?

TONY   This is my school blazer.

SIDNEY   Looks like a colour chart from a paint firm.

TONY   I'll have you know I'm proud of this. When people see me out in this they know immediately I'm an Old Greystonian.

SIDNEY   Well what are you wearing it for anyway? You left school a couple of years ago.

TONY   If you must know it's for the old boys' reunion next week. I've been invited down.

SIDNEY   Don't tell me you're going.

TONY   Of course I'm going.

SIDNEY   You must be off your chump. A famous public school like Greystones. You're going to meet all the boys you went to school with and grew up with?

TONY   Of course, I'm looking forward to meeting them again.

SIDNEY   But they're probably all bankers, and stock-brokers, business men and cabinet ministers now.

TONY   Well?

SIDNEY   You'll be the only failure there.

TONY   I suppose I will real . . . what do you mean failure? I've made me mark in my chosen profession.

SIDNEY   You've got your name up on the board outside the Windmill, what weight's that going to carry?

TONY   They won't worry about that, what do you think they've invited me for?

SIDNEY   Probably to show off to the pupils . . . as an example of what happens to little boys who are lazy.

BILL   Sid's right Tub. You'd feel out of place amongst the sort of people who'll be there. You'll be right out of your class.

TONY   But they were friends of mine. We were in the Upper Fifth together. We

used to do prep together, and play rugger together and sleep in the same dorm. Chaps don't forget those sort of things. We were chums . . . me and Spotty Cholmondley, and Hairy Wilkins, and Scruffy Thompson . . .

SIDNEY These boys . . . what are they doing now?

TONY Well . . . Spotty Cholmondley, he's in the House of Lords . . . Hairy Wilkins, he's an Archbishop somewhere, and Scruffy Thompson, he was a British Ambassador in Cairo.

SIDNEY Well there you are. They're all respectable gentlemen these days. They won't want to know Fat Legs Hancock.

TONY Who told you my nickname?

SIDNEY Well what else could they call you? They won't talk to you, a red-nosed music-hall comic, it'll be very embarrassing for you.

BILL Yeah, I wouldn't go Tub, they might think you're trying to touch them for a few bob. It'd be very humiliating.

TONY Well I was going to put the pressure on a bit, the old hard luck story and the limp . . . but now you come to mention, I suppose things have changed over the years.

SIDNEY (kindly) Of course they have. You stick with people in your own class. Layabouts like us.

TONY Yes, you're right. What a pity, they would probably have asked me to hand out the prizes.

SIDNEY (pause) What prizes?

TONY Prizes for the best pupils. The usual stuff . . . silver cups, gold watches . . .

SIDNEY Well, you'd better sew the buttons on your blazer, you want to look smart for the prize-giving.

(train going along)

SIDNEY Well . . . another few minutes, we pull into Greystones.

TONY I still don't see why you insisted on coming along Sid. It's my old school.

SIDNEY I wouldn't want you to feel alone down there. You might be glad of a bit of moral support. And someone to give you a hand with the prizes.

TONY That's very kind of you. I don't think you needed to bring six suitcases with you though. We won't be staying down here all that long.

SIDNEY No, I reckon about ten minutes should see it through.

BILL Boy, I'm looking forward to this trip. I've never seen a school before. What are they like Tub?

TONY Well William . . . Plato summed it up best when he said . . . a school is a collection of children, and a pile of books, surrounded by bricks to keep the rain off.

BILL Plato said that?

TONY Yeah, old Arthur Plato, the barman at the Dog and Duck.

SIDNEY Hallo, the train's slowing down.

TONY We're arriving, this is it.

BILL (excited) Where's the school, where's the school?

TONY Out the other window. There it is look, behind the trees.

('Eton Boating Song')

TONY See its noble spires rising majestically above the oak trees there across the meadows. Oh, this is a wonderful moment. Twenty years since this same train steamed into Greystones station, a child's face pressed eagerly against the window gazing in wonder at those dreamy spires, just as we are now. A young lad, his first day at a new school, what lay in store for him as he clasped his mother's hand, in school cap, blazer and short trousers?

BILL What was your mother doing in short trousers?

TONY I was in short trousers, oaf. Me mother had long trousers on.

(*'Eton Boating Song'*)

TONY As the train slowly drew to a halt, my young little eyes couldn't tear themselves away from the sight of those ivy covered walls, that great clock tower with that bell that summoned us all to assembly.

(*sonorous bell in distance*)

TONY This then was Greystones, the finest public school in England, my home for the next seven years. Twenty years ago.

(*Bell still ringing. Train letting off steam*)

(*calls*) Greystones. Greystones.

HATTIE Come along Anthony, lift your cases down.

TONY Righty-ho, mater, I'm ready.

HATTIE Anthony, this is the first time you've ever been away from home . . . you must be a brave little soldier.

TONY Oh I will mater, I will.

HATTIE I want you to promise to write to me every week. Study hard, and don't get into bad company.

TONY Yes mater. I'll try jolly hard to make myself a credit to you and pater.

HATTIE Your father would have been proud to see you now. He worked so hard so that he could send you to a school like this.

TONY Yes. What a pity he got caught.

HATTIE Why . . . oh why did the Inspector have to jump on his tram and check the tickets just at that moment? Go now Anthony . . . I . . . I . . .

TONY Mother . . . mother, you're crying.

HATTIE Am I?

TONY Yes. Mother, mother don't cry, I'll be all right.

HATTIE It's . . . it's not that Anthony.

TONY Then why mother? Why are you crying?

HATTIE The pubs are open and I've left my handbag at home.

KENNETH Excuse me young sir. Are you for Greystones?

HATTIE Yes, that's right.

KENNETH Oim Perkins, I drive the horse and trap up to the school. Give me your cases and we'll set off.

TONY Goodbye . . . mother.

HATTIE (*tearful*) Goodbye . . . my darling. (*cries*)

TONY Oh please don't mother . . . mother . . . look, here's half a crown, pop in the off-licence and buy yourself a miniature.

KENNETH Ready young sir?

TONY Coming. Goodbye mater.

76

(horse and trap setting off)

HATTIE   Goodbye, Anthony . . . *(further off)* Goodbye.

KENNETH   Cheer up young sir. You'll soon settle down when you meet the other young gentlemen.

TONY   What is Greystones like Perkins?

KENNETH   It's a fine place sir. Battles are won and lost on the playing fields of Greystones . . . so say the village girls.

TONY   And the chaps, Perkins, what are they like?

KENNETH   Oh as fine a bunch of young gentlemen as you'll find anywhere . . . except Rogers of the Upper Sixth. You keep clear of him. He's a bully and a coward. Picks on you young 'uns. Pulls them around by their ears.

TONY   Oooh the rotter.

KENNETH   You can always pick out the boys who have fagged for Rogers. One good ear and a flapper. Well here's the gates, I'll drive you up to the quadrangle and you report to the Headmaster.

(knock on door)

KENNETH   *(as headmaster)* Come in.

(door opens)

TONY   Doctor Clanger, sir?

KENNETH   Yes boy, what is it?

TONY   I'm the new boy, sir, Hancock.

KENNETH   Come in boy, come in, welcome to Greystones. You are going to like it here eh, eh, what, eh?

TONY   Oh yes sir.

KENNETH   How do you know, you idiot? You've only just got here. Come out and get the cane.

(swish and whack)

TONY   Oooh!

KENNETH   You're a lucky and privileged boy to be coming here to Greystones. What are you?

TONY   A lucky and privileged boy, sir.

KENNETH   That's it, speak up. Greystones is the oldest public school in the country. What is it?

TONY   The oldest public school in the country, sir.

KENNETH   That's it, speak up. Greystones has great traditions you must live up to. What must you do?

TONY   Live up to, sir.

KENNETH   That's it, speak up. And if you don't live up to them you want the cane. What do you want?

TONY   The cane sir.

KENNETH   A pleasure, bend over.

(whack)

TONY   Oooh!

KENNETH   That's better, I've got my eye in now, I'm landing them just where I want them. I think I'll pay a surprise visit to the gym, I always catch a few bending round there. That will be all boy, you're in the Upper Second, and you will fag for Rogers.

TONY Not Rogers sir.

KENNETH Yes Rogers sir.

TONY Good grief sir, it's me for a flapper.

TONY Dear mother, I am enclosing five shillings, as requested. Why don't you give it up and start sending me money like all the other chaps' mothers? I have been here three weeks now, and they have given me a cap four sizes too big for me. But it doesn't matter, as my ear keeps it up . . .

KENNETH (*as Rogers*) Fag . . . fag . . . where's Hancock? Hancock.

TONY Coming Rogers.

KENNETH Where have you been, you young puppy?

TONY Sorry Rogers, I've been checking your football pools.

KENNETH Did I win?

TONY No. Ow my ear, leggo you beastly rotter, it wasn't my fault . . . I wasn't playing.

KENNETH (*evil*) Let's see if I can twist it right off.

TONY Oooh. Ow, leggo. Yaroo. Ow.

KENNETH Curse, it won't go any more.

TONY It's upside down, what more do you want?

KENNETH Here's fourpence, run down to the village and get me five cigarettes. I've got a woman coming here tonight.

TONY You are a bounder, Rogers, you know Dr Clanger said we must keep away from women till after Sports Day.

KENNETH I'm having my own private Sports Day, starting as soon as Gladys arrives.

TONY Not Gladys, the charlady? I shall tell.

KENNETH You sneaking little prig. I'll teach you some manners.

TONY I'm not frightened of you any more, Rogers. Twist my ear, do what you like, you're not going to bully me any more. The worm has turned.

('*Happy Hancock*' music)

BILL Gee that was great Tub, what happened?

TONY He threw me out of the window. Look Bill, Sid . . . over here, in the quadrangle. You can still see the crack in the cement, twenty years later. Ah, this brings back memories.

SIDNEY Hey look, over there, some of the old boys have started to arrive.

TONY Oh yes, I wonder if I can recognise any of them.

SIDNEY That must be Rogers over there, with that woman.

TONY How do you know?

SIDNEY Well look at the size of her ear.

BILL Yeah, what about your ear Tub? I don't notice anything wrong with it.

TONY Ah well no, I played it clever. Rogers always used to pull me left ear, see. So when he left I fagged for Jessop. He used to pull right ears, so between us we balanced it up.

SIDNEY Where's the cups and gold watches?

TONY Later Sid, later, there's plenty of time. Let's have a look round, let me drink in the memories it all conjures of those spacious halcyon days of yore.

SIDNEY   Oh blimey he's off again.

BILL   What about the bird you used to go punting with on the river?

TONY   Oh Gladys.

BILL   Gladys?

TONY   Well she was the only woman in the school, we had to pass her around. They were the days when I was in the Upper Fourth. Fifteen years old and in love for the first time. I carved our initials on the oak tree here. Where are we . . . yes, look here it is. A.H. loves G.B. Gladys Biggs. I remember the day I carved that . . . 16 years ago . . . A.H. loves G.B.

(*chipping on oak tree*)

TONY   There you are Gladys, proof of our eternal love. Till Clanger doth us part.

HATTIE   Oh Fat Legs, you're so romantic.

TONY   Gladys, if you wish to carry on keeping company with me, don't call me Fat Legs.

HATTIE   But all the boys call you Fat Legs.

TONY   It's an unfortunate nickname I have acquired on account of my legs tend to swell up when my garters are too tight. But I don't want the name to stick through life, so please call me by my correct name.

HATTIE   All right then. Big Feet.

TONY   What?

HATTIE   How old are you?

TONY   Fifteen.

HATTIE   What do you hope to be?

TONY   Sixteen.

HATTIE   What are you going to do when you leave school?

TONY   Oooh I don't know. Might be Prime Minister. A great lawyer. Famous surgeon. Banker, international financier, Archbishop, tram driver.

HATTIE   Tram driver.

TONY   Well it's the family trade. It's been handed down. We Hancocks have been spinning the old handles round up front there for years. Break me father's heart if I took up any other trade.

HATTIE   But what are you spending seven years at a public school for?

TONY   Well I can be an educated tram driver can't I? Very impressive to be able to call out the place names in Latin. The Elephantus and Castleus. The Ballus Pondus Roadus. Gladys, when are we going to get married?

HATTIE   Oh don't be daft. You're fifteen and I'm seventeen.

TONY   That's old enough Gladys. Why, out in the East they get married when they're eight and nine.

HATTIE   I don't care what they do in Aldgate, this is Greystones. There's plenty of time.

TONY   No, let's get married now. We can manage. I've got four and six . . . plenty of chaps have started on less than that.

HATTIE   No, no you must give me time to think. Four and six?

TONY   Yes. Unless of course mother gets thirsty again, then we'll have to wait another six months. Will you wait for me Gladys?

HATTIE   Why, where are you going?

TONY Oh Gladys, you're a provocative little minx. Do you know what I think I'm going to do?

HATTIE What?

TONY I think I'm going to kiss you.

HATTIE (*giggles*) You mustn't.

TONY Yes I must. I think I shall kiss you like John Boles kissed Mary Astor at the flicks last night.

HATTIE No, no Anthony, this is madness, you'll be sent down if we're caught.

TONY I don't care, my blood is up.

HATTIE No Anthony please, you mustn't. I can see the reflection of Dr Clanger's telescope from his study window.

KENNETH Boy! Who are you?

TONY Hancock sir, Upper Fourth.

KENNETH Disgusting behaviour. Come to my study immediately.

TONY Yes sir.

KENNETH Not you . . . the girl.

('*Happy Hancock*' music)

BILL Gee that's sad Tub. Did you see her again?

TONY No. I haven't seen her since that day. That tree trunk is the only thing left to remind me of her. It looks just like her.

SIDNEY Very sad. Where's the prizes? Come on, I think we ought to go round and have a look at them before they're given out.

TONY There's plenty of time Sid. People are still arriving. Let's have a look round, there are so many memories here. Look, that's my old classroom when I was in the Upper Sixth, a husky young athlete of eighteen. Six foot two inches tall, broad shoulders, slim waist . . .

BILL Wait a minute, wait a minute . . . you're five foot six and flabby.

TONY If I told you I was mending a lift once and the cable broke and it fell on top of me, you wouldn't believe me would you?

BILL No.

TONY Well it'll have to do for now. Look, there's my study up there. I had a special room being school captain, me own fag. I used to relax there with me friends after leading the school cricket team to victory.

('*Eton Boating Song*')

TONY Sit down Farnsworth, my fag will be here in a minute with some muffins.

BILL Great innings you played today Hankers.

TONY Sorry I let you all down getting out like that.

BILL But great scott man, you scored two hundred and seventy-three.

TONY Ah yes, but it was only against Yorkshire.

BILL You must be the greatest school captain Greystones ever had, Hankers. Rugger, there's no one to touch you. I mean look how you routed Wales last week. Rowing, you practically finish the course before they get their boat in the water.

TONY I'm lucky to have my health.

BILL But you're not just brawn, it's brain as well. Distinctions in everything you touch . . . this study is a mecca of literary discussion . . . professors gathering here

every evening just to listen to you.

TONY (*modest*) Ah it's just my sherry they like. Where's that boy with the muffins? (*knock on door*)

TONY Here he is. Come in.

(*door opens*)

KENNETH (*as Snide*) Good evening.

TONY Good heavens, who are you boy?

KENNETH I'm your fag.

TONY Well lay down on the floor, I'll tread on you.

KENNETH On no don't be like that. Dr Clanger said I was to be your fag.

TONY What form are you in?

KENNETH The First Form.

TONY How old are you?

KENNETH Twenty-seven.

TONY Well, how long have you been in the First Form?

KENNETH Sixteen years. Between you and me I'm not very bright. Go on, you try me out, go on, ask me something.

TONY All right . . . um . . . what's three sixes?

KENNETH Er . . . six hundred and sixty-six.

TONY Well, what's wrong with that? You didn't even have to think about it. When did Julius Caesar conquer Britain?

KENNETH I don't know, I wasn't there.

TONY Well that's reasonable, of course you weren't. I can't understand it, why haven't they moved you up higher these last fifteen years?

KENNETH I was stuck in me desk. Cos you do when you grow. I've only just got out. It's awkward you know, being in the First Form. Cos they're all ten year olds, they all talk about things like cowboys and indians, cigarette cards, trains . . . I feel right out of it.

TONY I can quite believe it.

KENNETH So I just sit there with me bricks and ignore them.

TONY I don't blame you.

KENNETH Still I'm not worried, when I'm sixty-five I'll retire, whatever form I'm in. Now, what do you want me to do sir?

TONY If you're going to be my fag, you must be punctual, you must press my gown, clean my shoes, cook my tea, warm my slippers, light my fire, run my errands, and clean my study.

KENNETH Oh no, stop messing about, I've only got one pair of hands. Here's your muffins, I've cooked them for you.

TONY They're black, you've burnt them.

KENNETH My hands aren't much better.

TONY Where's the toasting fork?

KENNETH Oh, nobody tells you do they? I just poked me finger through one of the little holes and held it there.

TONY You idiot.

KENNETH Yes I am aren't I? Still it wouldn't do for us all to be alike would it? Here you are, I've cleaned your shoes. All lovely and black and shining.

TONY Oh yes . . . there's just one thing wrong.

KENNETH   What?

TONY   When I gave them to you they were brown and shiny.

KENNETH   Oooh yes, I believe you're right. Never mind, give us your black ones, I'll make them all brown or something. I'll see what colours I've got. If you want anything, just open the window and attract me attention.

TONY   Yes all right, I'll sling a brick at you.

KENNETH   Yes that'll do. (*goes off singing*) One and one are two, two and two are four, four and four are four and four are . . . one and one are two, two and two are . . .

(*door slams*)

('*Eton Boating Song*')

BILL   Gee Tub, your own fag, you must have been a pretty important person.

TONY   Just about the most distinguished pupil they've ever had at Greystones. Rugger hero, cricket champion, athletics, distinctions in every subject. I've got me own honours board up in the Grand Hall, I'm a legend here, that's why they asked me down. Hallo, who's that being chased across the playing field?

BILL   It's . . . it's Sid. Now what's he done?

SIDNEY   (*puffing up to mike*) Come on you two, the prize-giving's been cancelled, we can just get the last train if we're lucky.

TONY   We can't go now, I want to meet all me old school chums.

SIDNEY   They're right behind me. Here you are, cop hold of the suitcase, I'm off.

KENNETH   (*as headmaster*) (*coming on*) Stop that man, stop that man, he's a thief! What is he?

TONY   A thief . . . Dr Clanger . . . after all these years.

KENNETH   Ah an accomplice, you've got the suitcase . . . you thief!

TONY   I'm not a thief. Dr Clanger, you remember me . . .

KENNETH   No, no, I've never seen you before. Police . . .

TONY   Yes you have. I was here twenty years ago . . . Here I'll roll up me trouser legs. There.

KENNETH   Fat Legs Hancock, of course. Now I place you. You crook, I knew you'd come to no good. Sneaking back after all these years just to steal the school trophies.

BILL   Hey, you can't talk to the greatest scholar and athlete you've ever had like that.

KENNETH   Scholar? Athlete? Him? Rubbish.

BILL   He was at Greystones for seven years.

KENNETH   I know, and the worst school porter we've ever had. Bend over.

BILL   Allow me Dr Clanger.

(*swishes and whacks as Bill canes Tony*)

TONY   (*interspersed with yells as Bill hits him*) No Bill, I can explain . . . I remember now, I wasn't a pupil here . . . I got the school mixed up. It wasn't Greystones . . . Gray's Inn Road LCC Classes I meant, it's a mistake anyone could make. No Bill . . .

ORAL AND
TRAL CONCERT

from the
..iths' Hall, London
..INA MILKINA
(piano)
..IS   BARRY TUCKWELL
(horn)
..OW   TREVOR ANTHONY
(bass-baritone)
..URNE FESTIVAL CHORUS
..aster, Peter Gellhorn)
..HARLES SPINKS
..sichord continuo)
..CHAMBER ORCHESTRA
..d by Eli Goren)
..CTOR, COLIN DAVIS
Part 1
142: Uns ist ein Kind
..................................Bach
..to No. 5, in E flat (K.271)
Mozart

ER OF METHOD

..erenson (1865-1959)
..llis Waterhouse
..rofessor of Fine Art
..versity of Birmingham
..terhouse discusses Beren-
..on the history of art.
..BC recording)

HORAL AND
..STRAL CONCERT
Part 2
.. 31, for tenor, horn, and
..................................Britten
..eligieuse..............Berlioz
..neuse....................Berlioz
..broadcasts by permission of
..Opera Company)

..nthony Jacobs in
E LETTER'
..hilip O'Connor
..a by Douglas Cleverdon
..n..............Anthony Jacobs
..harles.......Frank Duncan
..embers..Cécile Chevreau,
..rey Segal, and Joe Sterne
..............Hilda Schroder,
..arold Reese, Basil Jones,
..and Philip O'Connor
..............David Spenser,
..imett, and Martin Starkie
.., Michal Hambourg

.. a letter requesting his
.. a worthy cause, Henry
..ogressive ' but middle-aged
.. the so many progressive
..at he has supported during
..y-five years.

..ding: second broadcast)

RAL AND
..HESTRAL
ONCERT

..by the Third Programme
..ration with the City
..ciety before an invited
..udience in the
..IITHS' HALL, LONDON

**TUESDAY
TUNETIME**
★
The ladies of the
**Showboat
Singers**
★
Olga Gwynne
(left) and
Cherry Lind
AT 9.30

5.0 AT YOUR REQUEST
(Continued)
The music you have asked for
introduced and played by
Sandy Macpherson
at the BBC theatre organ

5.15 GEOFFREY WALLIS
at the piano

5.30   News Summary
ROUNDABOUT
News, views and music
Tuesday edition
Introduced by
McDonald Hobley
with
Bill McGuffie
Records from the Theatre:
' South Pacific '
Topic for Motorists: Phil Drackett
A Sporting Memory: John Arlott
Woman's Page: Josephine Douglas

6.29 Weather and News Headlines
followed by Tonight's Topic
BBC West of England Light Orchestra
(Leader, Frederick Lunnon)
Conductor, Frank Cantell
Produced by Denys Jones

Shipping Forecast at 5.58 on 1,500 m.

6.45   ' THE ARCHERS '
A story of country folk
Written by
Edward J. Mason and Geoffrey Webb
Edited by Godfrey Baseley
Produced by Tony Shryane
(BBC recording)

7.0   Greenwich Time Signal
RADIO NEWSREEL

7.25   SPORT

7.30   News Summary
Wilfred Pickles in
HAVE A GO!
visits
The Gornals, Staffordshire

8.0   Tony Hancock in
HANCOCK'S HALF-HOUR
with Sidney James, Bill Kerr
Patricia Hayes, Joan Frank
Written by
Alan Simpson and Ray Galton
Produced by Tom Ronald
(BBC recording)
To be repeated on Sunday at 6.30 p.m.

8.30   News Summary
' THE DREAMING SUBURB '
A serial in twelve parts
adapted from his novel
by R. F. Delderfield
EPISODE 10
Miss Baker......Dorothy Holmes-Gore
The Carvers
  Jim.........................Malcolm Hayes
  Judy...........................Sheila Grant
  Archie.........................David March
  Anthony...................Glyn Dearman
The Frasers
  Esme...............................Simon Lack
  Elaine..............................June Tobin
The Hartnells
  Ted...........................Trevor Martin
  Margy....................Betty Baskcomb
Louise Strawbridge........Beryl Calder
Edith Clegg..........Catherine Salkeld
Esther Frith....................Ella Milne
Harold Godbeer...........John Bryning
Tim Ascham.................Rolf Lefebvre
Edited by Cynthia Pughe
Produced by Norman Wright
(BBC recording)

9.0   Alan Dell's
DATE WITH A DISC

9.30   News Summary
TUESDAY TUNETIME
presents
THE SHOWBOAT
Music and songs
from the world of entertainment
Sidney Torch conducts the
BBC Concert Orchestra
(Leader, William Armon)
and the Showboat Singers
Olga Gwynne, Cherry Lind
Bill Newman
with contrasts from
The Dennis Wilson Trio

THE ELECTION CANDIDATE

'She's never seventeen . . .'

One of the difficulties of introducing these script selections is not to give away too much of the essence of the script itself. 'So why bother?' one may ask oneself. Because, as I stated earlier, these scripts are akin to classical music whereby some aspects of the whole composition are better understood or more noticeable when some background is provided. It's like visiting Winchester Cathedral without the use of a guidebook: you can still see all there is to wonder at, but it would have helped to know why you are wondering at it; and the guide book might have pointed out interesting items that you have missed. So, without making this a kind of history lesson, let me take you back to around 1957 when the shadow of war had passed, the Cuban crisis was a long way off and people, in general, were looking imaginatively towards a brighter, more prosperous future.

The European Economic Community had been formed in March 1957, and there was a growing political awareness in Britain. Coincidentally, in that month the Liberal Party had lost another seat in the House of Commons, reducing their number of seats to only five, and contemporary political commentators were concerned about the possible demise of this once great party.

Towards the end of 1957 and throughout 1958 there was an amazing upturn in the fortunes of the Liberal Party that coincided with the growing popularity of television, for a number of Liberal supporters were appearing from this new medium. These people, such as Robin Day, Jaqueline Mackenzie and Ludovic Kennedy, were already well-known, almost household names to families across Britain, and the new vigour of their contribution to the political scene was becoming increasingly recognised at the polling booth in by-elections. On 12 February 1958, for instance, Ludovic Kennedy polled 17,603 votes in a by-election for the Liberals, pushing the Conservatives into third place, and on 27 March 1958, the Liberals won the Torrington by-election, their first gain since 1929.

Two days previously the British public had heard 'The Election Candidate', in which Tony Hancock is being asked to stand for the Liberal Party in a by-election. He exclaims that he knows nothing about politics and is told that it doesn't matter because he has appeared on television, this one sentence parodying the contemporary political scene in Britain. (The repeated broadcast had to be slightly rewritten to remove the reference to the Liberal Party and Tony Hancock was made to stand as an independent, which, whilst not harming the main plot in any way, did remove the sting from that particular tail.)

However, there is much to look out for in this script – the sub-plot of the collection of plastic guardsmen from cornflakes packets for instance (at this period of time, with the influences of commercial television's advertising, there was an abundance of free gifts with all manner of products, especially breakfast cereals), and the pondering over whether the model in the newspaper is really seventeen.

The newspaper itself becomes the sole topic of conversation, tracing everyday life reality and pre-empting the 'Sunday Afternoon at Home' dialogue, as Hancock reads out the headlines which have a special importance to a man of culture and enlightenment who likes to keep abreast of the world events. Even the very fact that he is reading one of the cheaper dailies is indicative of the Hancock character.

Watch out, too, for the moment when Hattie Jacques answers the door to Kenneth Williams as the Liberal Party Representative. He asks, quite naturally, 'Mrs Hancock?' – the reply is written by Galton and Simpson but could only be delivered so aggressively by the wonderful Hattie.

The end, once realised, is inevitable but sweet in its delivery. This script portrays so many aspects of the Hancock character: he is rude, arrogant, obstinate, childish

and childlike, pompous, incredibly vulnerable yet smugly resilient and helplessly but lovably innocent.

Much later, in the *Face to Face* interview with John Freeman for BBC Television, Hancock said, 'The character I play isn't one that I put on and off like a coat. It is part of me and a part of everybody I see.'

Avoiding the one and very conspicuous 'joke' in the script, you will be able to enjoy one of the best half-hour comedy scripts ever written for any medium.

THE ELECTION CANDIDATE

Script by
ALAN SIMPSON AND RAY GALTON

Recorded: 23 March 1958
Broadcast: 25 March 1958
Starring:
TONY HANCOCK
SIDNEY JAMES
BILL KERR
HATTIE JACQUES
KENNETH WILLIAMS
ALAN SIMPSON

Produced by
TOM RONALD

(*chink of crockery*)

HATTIE   More cornflakes Mr Hancock?

TONY   Yes please.

HATTIE   I'll have to open a new packet.

TONY   No, no I want to open it.

(*cardboard cornflake packet being opened*)

TONY   There. Oh isn't it annoying. Doesn't it make you sick. I've got him.

HATTIE   You've got what?

TONY   This little plastic soldier, I've got him. Why can't you buy packets with ones in I haven't got?

HATTIE   How do I know what's inside them?

TONY   It tells you on the front. Free all this month, plastic Guardsmen. Make your own Guards band up. Look at this, a trombone player, I've got him. I've got him six times. Daft grin on his face, look at him, I've a good mind to break him.

BILL   I haven't got him Tub.

TONY   What have you got to change?

BILL   I've got a spare drummer.

TONY   I've got him. The only one I'm missing is the trumpet player. Miss Pugh, go down and buy another packet of cornflakes, with a trumpet player inside.

HATTIE   Oh really. I bought forty-three packets last month just to find the flute player. They're all opened, a sheer waste, they'll never get eaten.

TONY   Yes they will. The next party we have, put some salt on them, and tell everybody they're crisps, that'll get rid of them. I must have my complete band.

BILL   Let me have one of your spare trombone players.

TONY   No.

BILL   But you've already got him.

TONY   I don't care, I'm saving them for swops. That kid next door might have a trumpet player he doesn't want. If he gets his set before me, I'll never hear the last of it.

HATTIE   Honestly. Grown men fighting over plastic soldiers.

TONY   Oh don't you start. It's all your fault we've had to buy so many packets. You could easily poke your finger under the lid and see which they've got inside.

HATTIE   Strangely enough when I buy a packet of cornflakes, I buy it for the cornflakes.

TONY   Oh well that's a typical woman's attitude. No imagination. It's the thrill of the hunt. Getting your set together. Look at them up there on the mantelpiece. Marching along there. What a stirring sight. A complete band . . . minus a trumpet player. (*emotional*) I've been waiting three weeks for that trumpet player. Breakfast is making me a nervous wreck, I don't mind telling you. I come down here every morning full of hope and anticipation, fingers trembling as I open a fresh packet and what happens . . . trombone players all over the place. It's very soul-destroying.

BILL   Let me have your trombone player Tub.

TONY   No.

BILL   I've only got a drummer.

TONY   That's your fault. You've been eating cornflakes as long as I have.

BILL   Yeah, but you always open them. You whip it before I get a chance.

TONY You should get up in the morning. You're not having my trombone player.

HATTIE Oh shuttup. I don't know what you're fighting about, next week they'll probably finish with the Guardsmen and start an entirely different set.

TONY Oh will they. Miss Pugh take a letter to the makers. Dear sir. I hereby warn you that if you discontinue putting Guardsmen in your cornflakes before I've got my set, I shall in future eat porridge. Yours sincerely, A. Hancock. Age seven and a half. There, that'll frighten them. I'm ready for my bacon and pease pudding now Miss Pugh. If there's any left. Look at her plate piled up there. You can't see her, just her arms coming round the sides. Are you there?

HATTIE Of course I am.

TONY Well come on then, shovel it out, whack some on the plate. Two rashers and a dollop. That's enough. Go on, get back behind your breakfast. I'd rather look at that than you. Haven't you finished with that paper yet Kerr?

BILL Won't be long. I'm just finishing the last bubble in 'Garth'.

TONY Well hurry up. He's been two hours reading that comic strip. Sitting there with his dictionary. Show me, where are you up to, what can't you manage?

BILL That bubble in the last picture there.

TONY Oh you great oaf. That's a question mark coming out of his head. That means he's puzzled.

BILL Oh. I thought I didn't recognise the letter.

TONY You've been a half hour trying to find that in the dictionary haven't you? I've been watching you. Give us the paper, I want to have a read.

BILL No, wait a minute, I haven't read it all yet.

TONY I'm not waiting for you to read it. By the time you've stumbled through it, it'll be yesterday's. Give us it here.

(*rustle of newspaper*)

TONY Hallo, Hallo, they're at it again, you can't trust them can you? (*pause*) Oh this man does talk some rubbish. (*pause*) Hallo, I see he's got three years. I knew he was guilty when I saw his photo last week, he had a moustache, that was enough for me. (*pause*) Butter's going up in China. (*pause*) Here, it was snowing yesterday in the north of Scotland. (*slight pause*) It was lovely down here wasn't it? (*pause*) Noel Coward's got a cold. (*pause, reads*) Man denies weekend in caravan. (*pause*)

(*rustle of paper*)

TONY Oooh she's nice. (*pause*) Seventeen year old model from Gateshead. (*pause*) No ring on her finger. (*pause*) Record crop of rice in Tibet this year. (*pause*) Vicar punches driving instructor. (*pause*) She doesn't look seventeen does she? (*pause*) Oh, look at this kitten sitting in the wellington boot, isn't that lovely? (*pause*) She's got a nice figure hasn't she? (*pause*) Hallo, I see Mr X has been had up again. He's in every week, he'll overdo it one day. (*pause*) Seventeen years old, eh, I don't know. (*pause*) Oh there's a good film south of the river this week. *I Was a Teenage Rock and Roll Vampire*, and *Kiss the Blood off My Washboard*. Marvellous. (*pause*) Have to get there early, before the schools come out. (*pause*) I bet she's nearly eighteen.

HATTIE Your pease pudding and bacon's getting cold.

TONY Do you mind.

HATTIE If you don't want . . .

TONY You're not having it. Look at her plate Bill. Scraped half the willow pattern

off she has. There's only half the bridge and the leg of a Chinaman left. Now shuttup and let me read my paper in peace. (*pause*) If she's seventeen, I'm a Dutchman. (*pause*) I see there's another by-election coming in East Cheam.

HATTIE   Oh. What happened to that nice man who was in before?

TONY   He's applied for the Chiltern Hundreds, and I'm not surprised. A right mess up he made of it. They made him Minister of Transport, what did he do? On his first job, he's £10,000,000 out on his estimate. On a £40,000 bridge.

HATTIE   He was very nice-looking though wasn't he?

TONY   Nice-looking, that's all that matters to you isn't it? I suppose you voted for him.

HATTIE   Of course.

TONY   Of course. He kissed her outside the polling station and she never got over it. She went back six times in disguise. A right smarmy he was.

HATTIE   He was a very sincere man.

TONY   Sincere. He was up there three years and not a sound out of him. He woke up once and yelled out resign, and even then he was had up on the carpet.

HATTIE   Why?

TONY   It was one of his own side speaking. It's just as well he's out of it. They're all the same these politicians. They're either flying out somewhere, flying back, ringing bells, or having eggs chucked at them. I have no time for them.

BILL   I've been thinking, if you break the end off the trombone, it'll look like a trumpet.

TONY   Pardon?

BILL   The trombone man. If you chop his trombone off . . .

TONY   I'll chop your trombone off if you don't shuttup. We're discussing politics. [Our MP has applied for the Chiltern Hundreds, which means there has to be a by-election to elect somebody to take his place in the House at Westminster. Besides, I'd always know it was a trombone with the end chopped off, I'd always be conscious of it. I'm going on for the trumpet.]

BILL   Yeah, OK. It was just a thought. I was just looking at it while it was standing there and I thought to myself, if you broke the end off the trombone, it would look just like a trumpet, and then you wouldn't have to buy any more cornflakes because you've got the trumpet player even if it is a trombone with the end broken off which you wouldn't notice unless you looked close and saw where it was broken if you were a musician.

TONY   Vote for Kerr. Independent idiot. He'd be a cert, he explains things so beautifully. He'd have the opposition confused after three lines.

HATTIE   Who's standing this time?

TONY   The usual rubbish. Sir Worthington Grape Conservative, and Arnold Biggs Labour. Or is it the other way around, you can't tell these days.

HATTIE   Which one's the best looking?

TONY   What does it matter what they look like? Honestly, if women had their way there'd be six hundred and twelve Robert Taylors up there. Show a bit of responsibility, woman. When I think of what Mrs Pankhurst and her mob went through to get the likes of you the vote . . . she must shudder when she sees the horrors you vote for. All teeth and hair oil.

HATTIE   It's not just their looks. I search in their faces for honesty and integrity.

TONY Honesty and integrity. What about the spiv you put in on the Council? A right Arthur English he was. When they put the chain of office round him, his shoulder fell down each side. You've always been a fool for a pretty face.

BILL Tub, have I got a vote?

TONY I shouldn't think so. Peers, clergymen and idiots don't get a vote over here. Anyway what do you want a vote for, what do you know about it?

BILL If there's anything going for nothing, I want it.

TONY That's the principle under which you've been living here for years isn't it?

HATTIE Take no notice of him, of course you've got a vote.

BILL Oh good. I think I'll vote for Worthington Grape.

TONY See, his two favourite drinks. The things people vote for. This is democracy gone mad.

HATTIE Who are you going to vote for then?

TONY · Neither of them. I don't hold with politics. They're both a waste of time. Sir Worthington Grape and Arnold Biggs. What a pair. A right couple of comics they are. Put a horse's skin over them, they'd do very well in pantomimes those two. I shall show my contempt by going down to the polling booth, taking my form, crossing both their names out and writing 'Get knotted' in. I have nothing but the utmost dislike for politicians.

(*door opens*)

SIDNEY Morning all.

TONY Hallo, Sid, come in. You're round a bit early this morning aren't you?

SIDNEY I'm just on my way home. Just popped in for some breakfast. What you got?

TONY What a liberty. Halfway house this. Hancock's pull-in for weary travellers. They wander in here for a cup of tea and a change of clothing. We had a bloke in yesterday for a hot dog, I've never seen him before. You come in here at seven thirty in the morning and ask for breakfast, I suppose you've been out all night again.

SIDNEY Yeah.

TONY What have you been doing?

SIDNEY Working. Do you mind if I put me sack down?

(*heavy clank*)

SIDNEY Now, what you got? I'm starving.

TONY What's in that sack?

SIDNEY Nothing. A few odds and ends that's all.

TONY Show me.

(*clinking of metal*)

TONY Odds and ends. Three hundredweight of assorted lead here. Sawn-off rainwater pipes, a few curly bits from under somebody's sink, all these bits of gas pipe . . . there won't be a lamp in the High Street working tonight.

SIDNEY I found it all lying on a waste-dump down the road.

TONY No you didn't. You've been creeping around Cheam all night with a hacksaw. Every night it's the same. Lead one week, brass the next week, copper the next week . . . this town will fall to bits if you don't turn it in.

SIDNEY No it won't, they're just odd bits I see sticking out of walls, I just trim 'em down a bit.

TONY You can't go around chopping bits of rainwater pipes off, it's not like pruning trees.

SIDNEY Are you going to give me any breakfast or not? I can pay for it. Here you are, two foot of waste pipe.

(*clonk*)

TONY Get that off my table.

SIDNEY That's worth seven and a tanner that bit.

TONY I don't care how much it's worth, get it off the table, you come in here trying to barter with your night's pickings, two foot of pipe for some cornflakes and pease pudding, whatever next! It's worth two curly bits and a section of guttering anytime that is.

SIDNEY You drive a hard bargain. There you are.

(*three clonks*)

TONY That's better. Miss Pugh give him some pease pudding.

SIDNEY What about the cornflakes?

TONY Oh all right.

SIDNEY Where's the little plastic Guardsman?

TONY They've all gone.

SIDNEY Oh blimey. I only need a trumpet player.

TONY So do I. You're the third one I know who only wants a trumpet player. Do you think they're still making them?

SIDNEY Yeah. I know a bloke in Epsom who's got six trumpet players. He's after a trombone player.

TONY Stone me, I've got a boxful of trombone players. It just shows you the distribution's all wrong. It's the sales manager, he doesn't know his job. They should have a certain number of each one sent to every area.

SIDNEY Of course they should.

TONY I didn't have this trouble with me fag cards. Complete set of footballers within the fortnight.

SIDNEY That's the way it goes. Anything in the paper?

TONY No. Nice bird from Gateshead on page two. Seventeen it says.

SIDNEY Oooh, let's have a look at that.

(*rustle of paper*)

SIDNEY Oooh yeah. She's never seventeen.

TONY That's what I said. Didn't I say that? Didn't I say she wasn't seventeen?

SIDNEY (*pause*) I see butter's gone up in China.

TONY Yes. I could see that coming. There's so many of them that's the trouble. Half a pound goes nowhere.

SIDNEY Yeah. (*pause*) He got three years then.

TONY Yes stood out a mile. He had a moustache you know.

SIDNEY Oh well. (*pause*) I reckon this bird's nearer twenty-one you know.

TONY As old as that?

SIDNEY Yeah.

TONY Well I said eighteen.

SIDNEY Could be. (*pause*) Why don't they eat margarine?

TONY Who?

SIDNEY   In China. It's just the same. 4302 people out of 5732 couldn't tell the difference in Cardiff.

TONY   No. Perhaps they don't like margarine in China.

SIDNEY   No, I expect that's it.

BILL   Sid.

SIDNEY   Yeah.

BILL   Why don't you chop the end off one of your trombone players so that he'd look like a trumpet player? You wouldn't be able to tell the difference unless you looked at it closely and . . .

TONY   Shuttup.

BILL   Well I just thought that maybe if he didn't have a trumpet player . . .

TONY   We know what you thought.

BILL   It just occurred to me that he could . . .

TONY   We know.

BILL   Well I just . . .

SIDNEY   (*pause*) Good cartoon today isn't it?

TONY   The political one?

SIDNEY   Yeah.

TONY   Very good. They always are, very good that bloke.

SIDNEY   Always gets straight to the point doesn't he?

TONY   Yes. Hits the nail right on the head. That needed saying that did.

SIDNEY   They ought to show that to every politician in the House.

TONY   Very satirical. Brings it right home doesn't he?

SIDNEY   Yeah. See, there's Khrushchev, and Dulles, and that Arab in between them and they're both giving him rifles.

TONY   Marvellous.

SIDNEY   Yeah (*pause*) I wonder what he's getting at.

TONY   I don't know. Very good drawing though isn't it? He's got old Dulles off hasn't he?

SIDNEY   That's Khrushchev.

TONY   Is it? It's very good of him anyway. (*pause*) They've got a nerve trying to kid us that bird's seventeen.

SIDNEY   It might have been a printer's error.

TONY   That's true. It does happen. They called me Tommy Hitchcock the other week. I wrote to them, and they put in an apology. They've got it in, look. Just there.

SIDNEY   Oh yeah. We apologise for any embarrassment caused last week when we wrote about Mr Tommy Hitchcock. We were of course referring to that celebrated comedian Mr Terry Hancick.

TONY   Well it's near enough, you can't keep writing can you?

SIDNEY   Hallo, they're holding a by-election round here. I didn't know that.

TONY   Yes. The last one applied for the Chiltern Hundreds.

SIDNEY   Oh I see. Well if he gets it, I think the others ought to get a raise as well.

TONY   So do I, after all fair's fair.

BILL   No, that's not what it is, the Chiltern Hundreds is what they apply for when they want to give up their seat.

TONY   What do you know about it?

SIDNEY   Yeah, why don't you mind your own business?

TONY   You buffoon, you come over here, you don't know what you're talking about, trying to tell us how our Parliamentary system works. The Chiltern Hundreds is an ancient custom. They apply for it when they want promotion. They get a hundred pounds, a new suit and a badge allowing them to use the House of Lords canteen without being accompanied by the Black Rod. I think you'll find that's right.

SIDNEY   Candidates: Sir Worthington Grape and Arnold Biggs. Are they local lads?

TONY   No. Whoever heard of an MP living in the place he represents? They've been assigned. One's from up north, the other one lives in Ireland. They'll come here for the election, then when it's over we won't see 'em for five years.

SIDNEY   Who are you voting for then?

TONY   Neither of them. I want nothing to do with politics at any price. What do they do for the common man? My cat got stuck up a tree last month, I wrote and told my MP and what did he do, nothing. He didn't come down. The cat's still up there. I have to send a whiting up on a pulley every lunchtime. All out for number one. Well they're not getting my vote anymore. I'm withholding it. I'm going to be one of the 'don't knows' in future.

(*door bell*)

TONY   Miss Pugh, someone at the door!

HATTIE   Well?

TONY   Well go and open it then.

HATTIE   You've got legs haven't you?

TONY   Yes, and you'll feel one if you don't go and open it.

HATTIE   They'll just have to wait, I'm finishing my pudding, the too-good-to-hurry pudding.

(*door bell*)

TONY   Go on, it might be important. It might be the grocer, with the week's food. Look at that. Up out of that chair like a Vanguard rocket.

(*door opens*)

HATTIE   Yes?

KENNETH   Oh good morning, are you Mrs Hancock?

HATTIE   Do you want a punch in the nose.

KENNETH   Oh no, I . . . no . . . offence . . .

HATTIE   I'm his secretary and that's bad enough. What can I do for you?

KENNETH   Do you think I might speak to Mr Hancock?

HATTIE   Won't you come in? That's him over there. The fat one in the red nightshirt.

KENNETH   Oh yes thank you. Ahem. Good morning Mr Hancock.

TONY   I'm sorry, mush, there's no breakfast left.

KENNETH   Oh thank you, but I've had breakfast. I don't know whether you are aware of it, but there's a by-election being held in this borough shortly.

TONY   Yes, we've just been talking about it.

KENNETH   Oh good, then you no doubt know that it is a straight fight between Conservative and Socialist.

TONY   No, no it says here Tory and Labour.

KENNETH Yes, well of course it's the same thing.

TONY Oh they're cunning, hiding under another banner, you see you can't trust them. They're after the floating voter.

KENNETH You don't support either of them I take it.

TONY I do not.

KENNETH Capital. I'm from the East Cheam Liberals.

TONY Isn't that an ice hockey team? Didn't you play Richmond Royals last week?

KENNETH Er no. We're a political party.

TONY Oh well, no, no I wouldn't know you.

KENNETH The Liberals, we're sometimes known as the Whigs.

TONY No I'm sorry, Bill might be interested. His head's been poking through a bit lately.

KENNETH No no you still don't understand, we are a political party, we follow a middle-of-the-road course. We put up candidates for election at Westminster.

TONY What you mean, like the other two mobs?

KENNETH Well our sympathies lie somewhere in-between the two extremes. I have a few pamphlets here that might help you to understand our policy.

TONY No you're wasting your time, I'm not voting this time. If you were an MP would you come down and get my cat out of that tree?

KENNETH Well I . . . no . . . er hardly . . .

TONY Well there you are, I'm not voting for the Liberaces either.

KENNETH The Liberals.

TONY Yes.

KENNETH That's not what I've come to see you about. At the present time we do not have a candidate for East Cheam, and we must have one. I'll come straight to the point. Will you be the Liberal Candidate for East Cheam?

TONY Me?

KENNETH Yes.

TONY But I don't know anything about politics.

KENNETH That doesn't matter. You've been on television haven't you?

TONY Yes.

KENNETH Good, that's all we demand of any candidate.

TONY But I don't know anything about you, shouldn't I know something about your policy?

KENNETH No, it doesn't matter. Your programme was quite popular wasn't it?

TONY Not bad. Here and there. It had its flashes.

KENNETH Well that should be all that's necessary. A pity you weren't a news reader, but still we can't have everything can we?

TONY But why pick on me?

KENNETH Well you're the only television personality living round here. And we couldn't poach any from other boroughs. They're all being earmarked for the General Election. Lou Preaker's being approached for Hammersmith, Jimmy Wheeler for Battersea South and Billy Cotton for Kensington. And I have heard that one borough are trying to get Matt Dillon over, but I think they're being rather optimistic.

TONY Have you thought about one of those chimpanzees for Bournemouth?

(*continued on page 106*)

Over page 'The Boys'—scriptwriters Alan Simpson (at typewriter, as he was the only one that could type) and Ray Galton at work
Above This picture, taken in 1957, shows Sid James and Tony Hancock enjoying rehearsals
Opposite above All eyes on Bill Kerr, during a recording of *Hancock's Half-Hour. Left to right*: Kenneth Williams, Tony Hancock, Bill Kerr and Sid James
Opposite below Hattie Jacques and Tony Hancock 'messing about' during a break in rehearsals

The Lad Himself, and scriptwriters Alan Simpson and Ray Galton, surrounded by images of life in the fifties

MOON ROCKET

COLIN
DUCK
AND HIS
QUARTET

Opposite A 1954 shot of Sid James, Bill Kerr, Moira Lister and Tony Hancock taking a read-through. Note the large hat that Sid James used to pull down over his eyes when appearing 'live' before the studio audience
Above Bill, Moira, Tony and Sid in action at a recording
Below Tony, Moira and Bill posing for a BBC publicity shot

Above left The young Tony Hancock
Above right A thoughtful moment
Below Tony making his point

KENNETH (*laughs*) I say that's an idea, I'll put that up to Head Office. What do you say Mr Hancock?

TONY Well I don't know . . .

KENNETH You leave it all to us. You just sit in at the meetings, the agent'll answer all the questions, you just nod a few times, sign a few autographs, that's all we require from you. You don't happen to have a beautiful wife . . . a ballet dancer possibly?

TONY No.

KENNETH Perhaps your secretary might lend herself.

TONY Her? Ballet dancing. You'd need six blokes to do a duet with her. One dancing and five lifting. I think we'd better keep her out of it.

KENNETH Well never mind. We'll bill you as Tony Hancock, star of stage, screen and the Liberal Party.

TONY But I'm not a Liberal. I'm not anything.

KENNETH Mere triviality. Don't you realise what it would mean to be an MP?

TONY Yes. I'd have to go up and get me own cat down.

KENNETH Yes but apart from that. You could be one of the country's leaders. You might even become Prime Minister.

TONY That'd be good. I could step out of aeroplanes waving me hat couldn't I?

KENNETH Exactly. And go straight through the Customs.

SIDNEY Take it boy. The pay might not be all that, but think of all those watches we could get through.

TONY All right. I'll do it.

KENNETH Good man. Now if you'll excuse me I'll pop back to HQ and prepare the campaign. Thank you and . . . I say, a cornflake packet.

TONY Yes.

KENNETH You don't happen to have a . . .

TONY No. Only trombone players.

KENNETH Oh bother. I only need a trumpet player. Never mind, I'll keep in touch. Goodbye now.

(*door shuts*)

TONY Well what do you think of that? Me an MP.

HATTIE You're not in yet, Bighead.

TONY Just a formality. I'll carry the saloon bar of the Hand and Racquet for a start. They'd sell their souls for a pint of mild and bitter.

SIDNEY I think it's marvellous son. We'll clean up.

TONY Here we are, again. What do you expect to get out of it?

SIDNEY I hear there's a lot of lead on the House of Commons roof.

TONY You'll do no roof lifting while I'm in the House.

SIDNEY Well, perhaps you can get me in the Cabinet somehow. Chancellor of the Exchequer, in charge of the loot. Or how about Home Secretary? There's one or two of the lads I'd like to let out of the pokey.

TONY Sid, being an MP means having a lot of responsibility towards one's country.

HATTIE Oh dear, he's gone all patriotic now.

SIDNEY Forgetting his friends already. They're all the same. Power mad. Well I'm not going to vote for you.

TONY   I don't care. There's enough people liked my television programme who'll elect me. I shall put the issue before the electors purely and simply. Bluntly. Vote for me or I won't go on television again. I think I shall go and change into my frock-coat. I feel quite important. This is a far far better thing I do now than I have ever done. Rembrandt.

(*door shuts*)

HATTIE   If he gets in, what disaster! All the parties will be at it, putting TV stars up as candidates. I can see it now. First Lord of the Admiralty . . . Wee Willie Harris.

(*music*)

TONY   Voters of East Cheam. In asking you to send me to Westminster I have no need to remind you of my record. Seventy-eight editions of *Hancock's Half-Hour* on radio and twenty-five on television.

(*crowd cheers*)

TONY   Thank you, thank you. And what have my two opponents got to match that record? Twenty years as a trade unionist. Twenty-five years on the council. Service in the diplomatic corps. Between them forty-five years in politics. All very nice, but has one of them ever been before the cameras at Lime Grove? No. Vote for Hancock, Ronnie Waldman's choice. Now are there any questions? Any questions you would like to know about my policy? Any points that are of vital interest to the nation?

KENNETH   Yers.

TONY   Over there. Yes sir?

KENNETH   Do you know Sylvia Peters?

TONY   I do sir.

KENNETH   What's she like?

TONY   A charming lady sir. Next question.

ALAN   Does Gilbert Harding really suffer from indigestion?

TONY   Never free from it. Has him doubled up. But I understand he'll be all right if he's needed at the next General Election. And the next question.

KENNETH   What do you intend to do about England entering the European Common Market thus bringing about a more sound economic structure of Europe without endangering our interest in Commonwealth trade and imperial preference?

TONY   Come now sir, this is no time for frivolous questions.

ALAN   Oi.

TONY   Yes sir?

ALAN   How big's Sabrina?

TONY   A very good question sir. How big is the prospective candidate for Leamington? I'm afraid sir they are official party figures which cannot be released until after the General Election.

ALL   Shame, shame. Answer, answer.

(*music*)

HATTIE   For you Mr Hancock, I haven't opened it.

TONY   Thank you Miss Pugh, the swordfish letter opener please.

(*letter being opened*)

TONY Curse. Another trombone player. I give up. When I get in I'll nationalise that lot. I'll be Minister of Cornflakes, I'll get that set somehow. I'll have them sent out with nothing but trumpet players in.

SIDNEY Well it's polling day today, what do you reckon your chances are?

TONY I shall landslide. I've got the House of Commons badge on the front of me bike already.

SIDNEY What do they think the poll will be like?

TONY We're expecting 100 per cent turn out. I'm providing transport for the old people who can't get down there. I'm taking them on me crossbar. Will you do some knocking up for me Sid?

SIDNEY Certainly.

TONY And if there's no answer you know what to do.

SIDNEY Yeah. Nip inside and break open the gas meter.

TONY You don't. You poke a pamphlet through the door.

SIDNEY Do you want me to do anything to the other two candidates for you?

TONY What sort of things?

SIDNEY Well . . . lay them up or something. I've still got a bit of that lead pipe I haven't flogged yet.

TONY Sidney this is a democratic election, you can't go around laying people up. I careth not for what they say but I will defend with my life their right to say it. Beethoven.

SIDNEY All right then, perhaps I can be of some help down the Town Hall tonight while they're counting the votes.

TONY What have you got in mind?

SIDNEY I thought perhaps fuse the lights in the middle and whip their bundles.

TONY No Sid, we won't be needing any of those methods. I have complete faith in the wisdom of the people of East Cheam. Today will be the turning point in the destiny of this borough. What is to be will be.

HATTIE Who said that?

TONY I did. Why don't you listen when people are talking.

(*music*)

TONY Switch the radio on Sid, the results should be in now.

(*click*)

KENNETH . . . said that he would look into it. Here are the results of the East Cheam by-election. Arnold Biggs, 29,348. Sir Worthington Grape, 28,903 Anthony Hancock, 1.

TONY I demand a recount. This is ridiculous.

HATTIE Well at least you got one.

TONY That was me. Didn't you two even vote for me?

HATTIE No. I voted for the gentleman with the moustache.

TONY Sid?

SIDNEY Well I played it safe. I put a cross by all the names and permed any one from three.

TONY What a farce. Why did I let them talk me into it? I can't understand it, they said I'd walk it, why didn't they vote for me? How did Arnold Biggs get all those votes? What happened to the power of television?

SIDNEY Oh it was there all right. The trouble is you haven't been on for a few months, whereas Arnold Biggs did *This is Your Life* last night.

TONY Oh well, if at first you don't succeed, try try again. Jack Hylton.

HATTIE Still, the election wasn't a complete waste of time. You have got something out of it.

TONY What?

HATTIE The local Liberal Party have sent you fifty packets of cornflakes as a consolation for losing.

TONY Oh how nice of them. See, every cloud may have a silver lining. I think I'll have some now. Pass me the top of the milk. Ah lovely. (*mouth full*) Mmmmm, delicious. (*he chokes*)

SIDNEY Quick, he's choking. Thump him on the back.

(*music*)

KENNETH Well, we've developed your X-ray Mr Hancock, and you did definitely swallow something.

TONY What was it Doctor?

KENNETH It appears to be a little plastic Guardsman.

TONY Can you get it out?

KENNETH No . . . I'm . . . I'm . . . afraid he's wedged, I'm terribly sorry old chap.

TONY Doctor, you can tell me, I can take it, I don't want you to lie to me, I want you to give it to me straight. What instrument was he playing?

KENNETH (*grave*) He was a trumpet player.

TONY Stone me, isn't it marvellous!

(1953)

5.0 AT YOUR REQUEST
(Continued)
The music you have asked for
introduced and played by
Sandy Macpherson
at the BBC theatre organ

5.15 GEOFFREY WALLIS
at the piano

5.30 News Summary
ROUNDABOUT
News, views, and music
Tuesday edition
Introduced by
McDonald Hobley
with
Bill McGuffie
Records from the Theatre:
' Oklahoma! '
Topic for Motorists: Phil Drackett
A Sporting Memory: John Arlott
Woman's Page: Josephine Douglas
6.29 Weather and News Headlines
followed by Tonight's Topic
BBC West of England Light Orchestra
(Leader, Frederick Lunnon)
Conductor, Frank Cantell
Produced by Denys Jones
Shipping Forecast at 5.58 on 1,500 m.

6.45 'THE ARCHERS'
A story of country folk
Written by
Edward J. Mason and Geoffrey Webb
Edited by Godfrey Baseley
Produced by Tony Shryane
(BBC recording)

7.0 Greenwich Time Signal
RADIO NEWSREEL

7.25 SPORT

7.30 News Summary
Wilfred Pickles in
HAVE A GO !
visits
the village of
Thornton-le-Dale, Yorkshire
with Mabel 'at the table'
and Harry Hudson at the piano
Presented by Stephen Williams
To be repeated on Sunday at 11.0 a.m.

8.0 Tony Hancock in
HANCOCK'S HALF-HOUR
with
Sidney James
Bill Kerr
Patricia Hayes
Wilfred Babbage
Anne Lancaster
Elizabeth Fraser
Written by
Alan Simpson and Ray Galton
Produced by Tom Ronald
(BBC recording)
To be repeated on Sunday at 5.30 p.m.

BOXING
Promoted by Harry Levene

Davey Moore v. Bobby
(U.S.A.) (SCOT
(World Featherweight (British Feat
Champion) Champ

Commentary by Eamonn Andrews on the
contest with inter-round summaries by W. Barring

FROM THE EMPIRE POOL, WEM

at 9.30

8.30 News Summary
'THE
DREAMING SUBURB'

A serial in twelve parts
adapted from his novel
by R. F. Delderfield
EPISODE 2
Miss Baker........Dorothy Holmes-Gore
The Carvers:
Jim.....................Malcolm Hayes
Louise....................Beryl Calder
Archie.....................David March
Judy.....................Sheila Grant
Bernard..................Tony Craze
Boxer...................Sam Jephcott
The Frasers:
Eunice..................Joan Matheson
Esme.....................Simon Lack
The Friths:
Edgar.................Godfrey Kenton
Esther....................Ella Milne
Elaine.....................June Tobin
The Piretas:
Toni....................Eric Anderson
Maria..................Sheila Manahan
Harold Godbeer.........John Bryning
Edith Clegg.........Catherine Salkeld
Frances Hopkins..............Eva Stuart
Edited by Cynthia Pughe
Produced by Norman Wright
(BBC recording)

9.0 Alan
DATE WI

9.30 News S
INTERNA
BOX
See top

10.15 RECENT
on gramop

10.30 Greenwi
NE

10.40 SERE
IN THE
feat
Hill-Bowen an
Henry
and the Montr
The William I
and Belle
Introduced by
Produ
James Dufour an

News Summ

11.55 LATE

12.0 Big
Close
follow
Shipping Forec

SUNDAY AFTERNOON AT HOME

'You watch, it'll go dark in a minute and we'll have to switch the lights on.'

The most talked about radio comedy show of all time, 'The Sunday Afternoon at Home' was a deliberate experiment by the writers and would have failed miserably had they not known and understood their cast and their characters so well. 'It was very risky,' recalled Alan Simpson, 'using so much "dead time" [radio silence] which was totally acceptable on the Third Programme [now Radio Three] but absolutely taboo in a light entertainment show.'

I was prepared to write 'There is no plot' but I suppose the plot exists around there being no plot, just four characters waiting for something to happen.

The pauses were timed and the timing was perfect. Robin Boyle, the BBC continuity announcer, talking of Hancock, recalled: 'I have never known anyone extract quite so much from a simple sigh or a pregnant pause. One of his silences would have the audience anticipating his next crushing line, like children waiting to open Xmas presents.'

Robin Guthrie (of The Cocteau Twins), talking in an NME interview, said, of Hancock, 'He used to say nothing for thirty seconds and a third of the population would be in hysterics.'

Although there is much more entertainment available on Sundays today, with wider access to television, videos, football matches, sport complexes, public and personal transport etc, all of us, at some time or another, must have suffered just such a Sunday afternoon – and if not, then let us go back to 1958.

It was the year of the first Aldermaston march (although they marched the wrong way; they got it right the following year); it was the beginning of the property boom; it was the year in which television became the chief broadcasting medium and when advertising was at a new and unprecedented height; it was the year of traffic wardens and parking meters; of new and thriving striptease joints; of the Boeing 707; of new-fangled 'stereo' records.

There was a tremendous consumer boom with the rapid introduction of American-style supermarkets (only four years after food rationing had finally been withdrawn), and the year of John Bloom's cut-price washing machines.

With all this active spirit about in 1958, it is not difficult to see why the inmates of 23 Railway Cuttings should be wondering why it was all passing them by on Sunday afternoon, producing a comedy blend of frustration and apathy, at not having the commitment to actually do anything about it.

I will analyse no further. Yes, I'm sorry, I didn't mean to begin any depth of discussion, but there is so much here to discuss; it's distilled life – it's Galton and Simpson at their best.

What do you do when you're bored? The television's broken, the piano locked, the car's broken down, it's pouring with rain . . .

'Oh, so that's what's making the roads wet . . .'

SUNDAY AFTERNOON AT HOME

Script by
ALAN SIMPSON AND RAY GALTON

Recorded: 20 April 1958
Broadcast: 22 April 1958
Starring:
TONY HANCOCK
SIDNEY JAMES
BILL KERR
HATTIE JACQUES
KENNETH WILLIAMS

Produced by
TOM RONALD

TONY (*yawns*) Oh dear. Oh dear oh dear. Cor dear me. Stone me, what a life. What's the time?

BILL Two o'clock.

TONY Is that all? Cor dear oh dear me. I don't know. (*yawns*) Oh, I'm fed up.

SIDNEY Oi.

TONY What?

SIDNEY Why don't you shut up moaning and let me get on with the paper?

TONY Well, I'm fed up.

SIDNEY So you just said.

TONY Well so I am.

SIDNEY Look, so am I fed up, and so is Bill fed up. We're all fed up, so shut up moaning and make the best of it.

TONY Are you sure it's only two o'clock?

BILL No, it's er . . . one minute past two now.

TONY One minute past two. Doesn't the time drag? Ooh I do hate Sundays. I'll be glad when it's over. It drives me up the wall just sitting here looking at you lot. Every Sunday it's the same. Nowhere to go, nothing to do. Just sit here waiting for the next lot of grub to come up. There must be something we can do. Bill, haven't you got any bright ideas?

BILL No.

TONY It was a waste of time asking really, wasn't it? (*Pause. Yawns*) Oh I'm fed up.

HATTIE Why don't you men go out for a walk while I wash up the dishes?

TONY (*mimics her*) 'Why don't you men go for a walk?' Why don't you go for a walk? Go on, hoppit. It'll be one less to look at all day. (*pause*) Have you finished with that paper yet?

SIDNEY No.

TONY Well hurry up, I haven't seen it yet. I want to know what my stars say.

SIDNEY What are you?

TONY June the twenty-first.

SIDNEY What sign is that?

HATTIE The crab.

TONY And what of it?

HATTIE I didn't say anything!

TONY The delight with which you said it implied an opinion. Watch it. I can't help being a crab. I had no choice about which day I should be born on; the matter was entirely out of my hands. I could easily have been a Leo, or a Gemini, or even an Aquarium, but fate decreed that I should be a crab.

SIDNEY Cancer the Crab, where are we? . . . ah, here it is.

TONY What does it say?

SIDNEY It says, 'Today looks like being a very exciting day.'

TONY Well good luck to *him*. Who is he? Arnold the Gipsy. Look at him, spotted handkerchief round his head, great cartwheel ear-rings. A right fake if I ever saw one. The nearest he's ever been to a caravan was at the Motor Show. Very exciting day indeed. Two o'clock gone and what's happened? The cat ran away with a sardine. The milkman left only one pint instead of two, and Mrs Crevatte next door crept home at nine o'clock this morning after being out all night. Moments of

high drama all that lot. What's going to happen next? The tension's killing me.

SIDNEY   Why don't you turn it in?

(*Pause. A few clearing of throats, sighs etc*)

HATTIE   Oh look, it's started raining.

TONY   That's all we wanted. You watch, it'll go dark in a minute and we'll have to switch the lights on. I think I'll go to bed.

HATTIE   You've only been up an hour!

TONY   That's by the way and nothing to do with it. I might just as well be in bed: there's nothing else to do. I wish I hadn't got up now. Your dinner wasn't worth getting up for, I'll tell you that. Sunday dinner is usually the meal of the week, the one thing that makes Sunday bearable. But not here. On Sundays in this house we get the same rubbish as the rest of the week, dished up on the best china, that's all.

HATTIE   What was wrong with the dinner?

TONY   Now be honest, it wasn't very good was it?

HATTIE   Well, I don't know, I ate all mine.

TONY   That's neither here nor there. You also ate Bill's, Sid's and mine. How you got your teeth through that roast beef I shall never know. I can only assume you sharpened them up on the Yorkshire Pudding.

HATTIE   It wasn't my fault, it was frozen meat.

TONY   That joint was harder when you took it out of the oven than when you put it in. That meal, whichever way you look at it, was a complete fiasco. I thought my mother was a bad cook, but at least her gravy used to move about. Yours just lays there and sets.

HATTIE   That's the goodness in it.

TONY   That's the half-pound of flour you put in it! I saw you shovel it in there; I thought you were going to plaster the room out. There's something wrong when you have to ask for another slice of gravy. It's not right.

SIDNEY   Here, there's a bloke here who can cure gallstones by just putting his hands on your forehead.

BILL   That's a funny place to have gallstones.

SIDNEY   No, no. He's got a box, you see, and he transmits life waves. You see, everybody's got life waves, and it says here this box tunes into your life waves and the waves travel through his fingertips into your forehead and smashes your gallstones up.

TONY   Charming.

SIDNEY   Well, it makes you think, don't it? He says he can cure anything so long as he gets on the right wavelength.

TONY   I know, and for an extra five bob he'll tune both your earholes into Family Favourites. What a load of rubbish. You don't believe everything you read in a Sunday newspaper do you? I would have thought you had more intelligence. It's a lot of silly nonsense. I find it incredible that after thousands of years of civilisation we, in this day and age, the twentieth century, still find ourselves surrounded by silly superstitious nonsense swallowed avidly by supposedly educated, intelligent beings. Bill, what do my stars say in your paper?

BILL   Huh? Mmmmm?

TONY   What are you doing pressing your stomach in?

BILL   I've been thinking about those gallstones. I think I've got them.

TONY How do you know?

BILL Well look, you feel. I've got two lumps, see. One just here and one round there.

TONY Lift your pullover up. You buffoon. They're the metal bits on your braces. Great oaf. I was asking you what my stars say in your paper. Romany Jim on page four.

BILL It's not here. I tore that bit out to put in the toe of my shoe because it's too big.

TONY There's all yesterday's papers to do that with, but no. You have to tear out Romany Jim. I want to know what he said. Take your shoe off.

SIDNEY You've heard what Arnold the Gipsy said.

TONY I've got no faith in Arnold the Gipsy. I want a second opinion.

BILL Well you can't have it. I'm not taking my shoe off.

SIDNEY Why don't you sit down and relax. It's a day of rest. Have a kip or something, anything, but do me a favour and shut up. Here, have a couple of pages of my paper. I'll keep the racing results and the gallstone smasher; you can have the court cases and the woman's page.

TONY Oh dear. What a life. It's Sunday, I've had a rotten dinner, it's raining, Romany Jim's been torn up and I've got nothing to do.

HATTIE There's plenty of odd jobs you can do around the house.

TONY Oh shut up. It's a day of rest. I'm not mending your bed again.

SIDNEY (*wearily*) Read the paper will you?

TONY Well . . . it makes you sick. I hate Sundays.

SIDNEY So do I, but there's one a week, there always has been, and there's nothing we can do about it.

TONY It's not like this on the Continent, it's their big day over there. All the cafés open, football matches, race meetings, everybody's gay. Not over here though. Everything's shut up.

SIDNEY I wish you would.

(*Long pause. Clearing throats. Humming. Sighs. Papers rustling*)

TONY Get your feet out of the way, put them over there. (*pause*)

TONY That's it, go on, take all the fire up. Don't let anybody else get a look at it, will you?

HATTIE I'm sorry, I'm just trying to get warm. (*pause*)

TONY What's the time?

BILL Er . . . the little hand's on two and the big hand's on three. That's . . . er . . . three minutes past two.

TONY It is a quarter past two.

BILL Oh yeah, that's right.

TONY Quarter past two. Another nine and three-quarter hours before it's Monday. Depressing isn't it? I don't care very much for Monday either. And me Saturdays are always spoilt thinking about Sunday. You know I sometimes think, what's it all about? What are we here for? Don't you sometimes think that?

BILL No.

TONY No, of course not.

(*Pause. Tony smacks his lips. Sighs. Hums a bit*)

SIDNEY Here. He can get rid of malaria as well.

TONY Who can?

SIDNEY The bloke with the radio set. It says Mr D. of Huddersfield had malaria for years, but this bloke tuned into his wavelength, switched on, put his hands on his forehead, and it was gone.

TONY How very uninteresting.

SIDNEY It makes you think, though, don't it?

(*Long pause. Rustle of newspaper. Little bit of singing from Tony which tails off and dies away into an embarrassed silence. Pause*)

TONY Have you noticed, when you look at that wallpaper long enough you can see faces on it?

BILL Honest?

TONY Yes, yes you can, you can see faces after a time. It's the pattern, it makes little faces. There's a lovely one of an old man with a pipe.

BILL Where?

TONY Come over here. Look at it from where I'm sitting. Screw your eyes up, now stare hard, squint a bit, that's it, now concentrate on that bit by the serving hatch. See it?

BILL No.

TONY Yes look, it's there, plain as eggs. Look see, there's his nose, that's his pipe, and there's his hat. See it?

BILL No.

TONY (*gets a bit annoyed*) Of course you can see it. There's dozens of them all over the room. Look, there's Churchill over there, Charlie Chaplin over the mantelpiece, concentrate, squint man, squint . . . don't shut them . . . can't you see them?

BILL No.

TONY Oh go and sit down. You wait till you want me to see anything.

HATTIE All I can see on the wallpaper are bunches of grapes.

TONY Who's asking you? Of course you can see bunches of grapes, that's the pattern. You've got to use your imagination to see the little faces. (*pause*) What's the time?

BILL The little hand's on . . .

TONY Oh not you, somebody else.

HATTIE Seventeen minutes past two.

TONY Seventeen minutes . . . doesn't time drag? (*pause*) I can't see that little old man with a pipe now. What angle did I have my head at? Oh yes, there he is. He's got a dog with him now. (*Pause. Sings*) Only a rose I bring you, only a rose to you . . . (*pause*)

SIDNEY & TONY (*together*) Here's a funny thing . . . I was just thinking . . .

TONY Pardon?

SIDNEY No, no, after you.

TONY No, no, go on, what were you going to say?

SIDNEY Oh nothing, nothing.

SIDNEY & TONY I was just going to say . . . I was just going to say . . .

TONY (*little laugh*) What were you going to say?

SIDNEY It doesn't matter, nothing important. What were you going to say?

TONY I've forgotten now.

SIDNEY Oh.

TONY (*sings*) Bom, bom, bom, bom, bom, bom, bom . . . (*Pause. Changes the tune*) Da, de dum, da de dum de da . . . what's that called, Sid?

SIDNEY What's what called?

TONY This tune. Da de de dum, da de dum de da.

SIDNEY I don't know.

TONY Don't you remember the film, old Anton Walbrook on the piano?

SIDNEY No.

TONY Oh. (*pause*) Let's go to the pictures.

HATTIE They don't open till half past four. It's Sunday.

TONY Well never mind, we'll go at half past four. What's on?

HATTIE Let's see, the Royal Cheam. Bette Davis and George Brent in *Little Foxes*, and *The Battle of Little Bighorn*.

TONY Oh. I've seen them. I've seen both of them. It's always the same on Sundays. They always put on old films that you've seen before. Makes you sick. What's on at the other place?

HATTIE It's closed down.

TONY Oh. So much for the pictures. (*pause*) What time do the pubs open?

SIDNEY Seven o'clock.

TONY Oh cor. Even that's an hour later than weekdays. And they close earlier. There's no one up there Sunday nights anyway. Except the barmaid. And she's a bit off. I told Harry, I said to him, what did you get rid of Gladys for? She was a fair piece. Her arms were a bit thick, but what can you expect when she's pulling pints all day long? But this one . . . oh dear oh dear, puts you right off beer, *she* does. You want to get it down quickly and get out. I told Harry straight, I said, 'Harry, you've done wrong there, getting rid of Gladys. There's no attraction coming in here now, cos your beer's rotten.'

SIDNEY Did you tell him that?

TONY Certainly. He didn't deny it. It's fallen right off that place. Well, the dart club's moved down to the Bull.

SIDNEY Why don't he get rid of her then?

TONY I think there's something going on between those two. He had a black eye the other day and he's been drinking more.

SIDNEY Shame. I like Harry.

TONY So do I. But there you are, these women, once they get hold of you mate. There you are. That's the way it goes.

SIDNEY Yeah.

TONY Yes. That's life. It's always the same. There you are. Up one minute, down the next.

SIDNEY Yeah.

TONY You never know when it's your turn next.

SIDNEY No.

TONY That's the way it goes. You never know what's round the next corner, do you?

SIDNEY True. No matter how bad off you are, there's always somebody worse off than yourself.

TONY That's very true. I was just thinking about poor old Albert in hospital. He's

been there a month, and no one's been to see him.

SIDNEY   Haven't they really, poor old devil.

TONY   No one's been near him. He's just laying there.

SIDNEY   Oh dear, makes you feel rotten don't it?

TONY   Poor old Albert.

SIDNEY   Well look, why don't we go and see him this afternoon? We haven't got anything to do.

TONY   (*pause*) No, it's a long way, isn't it? He's probably asleep. We'll go next week.

SIDNEY   Yeah.

(*pause*)

HATTIE   I wonder what I'd look like in the new fashions. I think I'll buy myself a trapeze dress.

TONY   I hope you fall off it.

(*pause*)

BILL   What about a game of Monopoly?

TONY   Yes. Bags me be the boot.

BILL   No, I want to be the boot. You can be the top hat.

TONY   I'm always the top hat. I'll be the boot, you can be the steamship. Sid can be the racing car.

BILL   I don't want to be the steamship, I want to be the boot.

TONY   You'll get my boot if you don't stop arguing. You are the steamship, Sidney is the racing car, Miss Pugh is the top hat and I am the boot. Right, who starts?

HATTIE   No one. You lost the board.

TONY   We lost the board. So we can't play Monopoly either.

HATTIE   No.

(*Pause. Humming etc*)

TONY   What's the time?

HATTIE   Twenty past two.

BILL   Well, the time's gradually going isn't it?

TONY   Mmmm. (*pause*) Here, I've just thought. When do you alter the clocks?

HATTIE   Today.

TONY   Do you put them forward or back?

HATTIE   Er . . . forward.

TONY   Ha ha. That'll get rid of another hour. Quick, give us the clock. There, twenty past three. That's better. Soon be Monday.

SIDNEY   Well, I've finished the paper. Now *I've* got nothing to do. (*pause*) Have you got a pencil?

TONY   Why?

SIDNEY   I thought I'd fill in the O's, the D's, the P's and the G's on the front page. You know, shade them in. I always do that when I've got nothing to do.

TONY   Do you do that as well? I sometimes make faces out of them.

SIDNEY   Getaway.

TONY   Yes, quite often. I put a pair of ears on the O's and a couple of eyes and a mouth; I get quite Annigonish at times.

SIDNEY   Have you got a pencil then?

TONY   No. I've got a pen.

SIDNEY   No, ink spreads on newspapers. I'll have to think of something else.
BILL   (*pause*) Let's play Beat Your Neighbours Out Of Doors. (*pause*) I said, let's play Beat Your . . .
TONY   We heard what you said.
BILL   Oh. Well, do you fancy playing?
TONY   Look, we are grown men. We are not that desperate for something to while away the time with. There are much more intelligent pursuits we could engage in. How do you play it?
BILL   I don't know.
TONY   Well, what did you suggest it for then?
BILL   Well, I thought you might know how to play it.
TONY   Well I don't.
BILL   It was just an idea.
(*pause*)
HATTIE   I think I'll knit myself a sweater.
TONY   Well that should solve the unemployment problem in the wool industry. That reminds me, you said you were going to knit me a string vest.
HATTIE   I haven't got any string.
TONY   You could unravel that shopping bag.
HATTIE   It wouldn't be any good. I haven't got any needles.
TONY   Use your fingers, they're thick enough.
SIDNEY   What's on the telly?
TONY   The dinner plates. Why don't you clear them off, Miss Pugh? Too lazy to take them out to the kitchen. You'll ruin that veneer.
SIDNEY   What programme's on?
TONY   Gardening Club on one and Free Speech on the other.
SIDNEY   Oooh good, let's have Free Speech on.
TONY   No. I want Gardening Club on.
SIDNEY   What's wrong with Free Speech?
TONY   I prefer Gardening Club.
SIDNEY   Why? You never do any.
TONY   I intend to do some.
SIDNEY   How? You haven't got a garden.
TONY   I have a window box, and a few pots of cacti hanging about somewhere.
SIDNEY   There's nothing in the window box.
TONY   I know that. I'm letting it lie fallow this year. Obviously you know nothing about farming. Have you never heard of soil exhaustion and the rotation of crops? You keep planting stuff in that it'll become a dust bowl. I saw *The Grapes of Wrath*, I know what I'm doing.
SIDNEY   I want to see Free Speech.
TONY   No. Leave that knob alone. Go and sit down. You'll have me flying ducks off the wall in a minute.
SIDNEY   I want to see Free Speech.
TONY   You're not seeing Free Speech. We're having Gardening Club.
SIDNEY   We'll toss for it.
TONY   All right.
SIDNEY   Heads Free Speech. Tails Gardening Club.

TONY   Tails. Gardening Club. Well done. We're having Gardening Club.

HATTIE   You're not.

TONY   I beg your pardon?

HATTIE   Didn't I tell you? The television set's broken.

TONY   You've been sitting there listening to us arguing about what programme to see and you knew it was broken. Why didn't you say so?

HATTIE   Well, I was getting quite interested in who was going to win. It passed a few minutes, didn't it?

TONY   Stone me. No television, it's raining, a rotten dinner and it's only twenty-five past three. Ooh I'll hit somebody in a minute.

(*pause*)

BILL   Let's play Murders.

TONY   If you open your mouth once more, we won't be playing murders mate, they'll be investigating one. I vote we all go to sleep. Right, heads down.

(*Pause. Smacking lips etc*)

TONY   Hallo . . .

SIDNEY   What?

TONY   Over the road's going out. Ssh, say nothing. Look behind the curtain, don't let them see you. That's the first time they've been out together for ages. I wonder where they're going?

HATTIE   She found out about him and that girl you know.

TONY   Never.

HATTIE   Yes. He said he had to work late and she saw them that night in the pictures. Shocking row.

TONY   Was there?

HATTIE   Yes, she was with the milkman.

TONY   Our milkman? The one with the big nose?

HATTIE   Yes.

TONY   He gets around doesn't he? There was that trouble with number twenty-eight last month, and the punch up with the husband at thirty-one. You wouldn't think he'd attract women with a hooter like that. It must be the uniforms, women love uniforms. Look, he's opening the gate for her, dear me, times have changed. He always used to slam it and try and fetch her shins a wallop. Look at them smiling at each other, love's young bloom. Makes you sick at that age, doesn't it?

HATTIE   He's got his Sunday best on.

TONY   So he has. Don't like it much. He shouldn't have shoulders that size with a small head like he's got. Here, come here, quick look, oh swipe me look, he's wearing gloves. Look at him carrying one. Oh my word, aren't we posh? It's her that's pushing him you know, she wants him to get an office job. Which way are they going? Down the street or up the street?

HATTIE   Up I think, aren't they?

TONY   Oh yes up. Let's see, up. They'll be going to see his sister in Acton. They always go that way. If they were going the other way it'd be her mother in Tooting. Oh, they're gone. Oh well, that's about all the excitement we can expect today. Come on, all sit down again. (*sighs*) Oh dear.

(*Pause. Odd hummings etc as before*)

TONY   (*sings*) Freight train, freight train, freight train going so fast. Freight train,

freight . . . where's me liquorice allsorts? I had a quarter of liquorice allsorts here. In a paper bag on the mantelpiece; where are they?

HATTIE Oh I am sorry, I've just eaten the last one.

TONY You gannet. They weren't even open ten minutes ago. You've shovelled the lot in. You know how much I like the square ones with the black and white layers. Oh pass me the nuts over. Oh yes, wonderful. A dishful of shells and a banana skin. Oh no, here's one, the last one.

(*nut being cracked*)

TONY Where did that nut go, it flew out of the crackers, where did it go?

BILL It went in the fire.

TONY Oh I give up. I'm not coming downstairs next Sunday. I'll have one of me pills on Saturday night and wake up on Monday.

BILL (*Pause. Starts singing to himself*) A wild Colonial boy.

TONY Do you have to?

SIDNEY (*pause*) Put the gramophone on.

TONY That's an idea.

(*Old recording of 'Elmers Tune'. It slows down to a stop*)

HATTIE The spring's gone. Why don't you buy one of those new three-speed hi-fi autochange radiograms?

TONY What's the point of having an autochange when you've only got one record?

HATTIE You could buy some long players.

TONY I don't hold with this modern stuff. Boogie Woogie. It's not right, all these youngsters jumping about like animals. I like Hutch.

(*pause*)

SIDNEY Who can play the piano?

TONY No one. Besides, the lid's down and we've lost the key.

(*pause*)

BILL Let's play Twenty Questions.

TONY What do you want to keep playing things for? What's the matter with you? Sit still.

(*Pause. Humming etc*)

BILL If we had a dog we could take him for a run.

TONY Why don't you go and clean your shoes or something? Scrape the inside of the oven out. (*pause*) What's the time?

HATTIE Twenty-five to four.

SIDNEY What time's Children's Hour on?

TONY What do you want to see Children's Hour for?

SIDNEY Well I thought 'Bill and Ben the Flower Pot Men' might be on. I like them.

TONY Oh, you mean skobollob. Yes, very good. Better than that 'Sunday Night at the Palladium' anyway. Anyway, they're not on on Sundays.

HATTIE (*pause during which we hear the usual noises*) Oh, look at this dress Elsa Martinelli's wearing. I think I'll send off for the pattern.

TONY I wouldn't bother.

HATTIE It'll only need a few alterations.

TONY Look dear, that dress cost Elsa Martinelli a hundred and fifty pounds. You wouldn't get away under a thousand. Forget it dear. You stick to your slacks.

(*Pause. Tony sings 'I Lift Up My Finger and I Say Tweet Tweet'. Doorbell rings*)

TONY   Who's that? Look through the window, who is it?

HATTIE   It's the man next door.

TONY   Oh dear, as if Sunday's not bad enough without him. Pretend we're not in.

HATTIE   He saw me pull the curtain.

TONY   Oh let him in then.

(*door opens*)

KENNETH   Oh, good afternoon all.

(*half-hearted hallos*)

KENNETH   Not a very nice afternoon is it?

TONY   No.

KENNETH   It's raining you know.

TONY   Oh, so that's what's making the roads wet.

HATTIE   (*sotto*) Stop it.

TONY   Well, of course it's raining. We've got eyes haven't we?

KENNETH   I've brought your Sexton Blake book back, Mr H.

TONY   Oh, thank you, put it down there.

KENNETH   I thought you might like to borrow my *Biggles Flies West*.

TONY   Thank you.

KENNETH   Yes.

(*pause during which Ken and Tony cough embarrassedly*)

KENNETH   Terrible weather for the chest this, isn't it?

TONY   Yes, yes, shocking.

KENNETH   Of course, the wife's in bed with a cold you know.

TONY   Oh I am sorry. Here, take a lemon into her.

KENNETH   Oh thank you. (*slight pause*) Er . . . you didn't mind me calling in did you?

TONY   No, no, no, no, no.

KENNETH   Oh good. (*pause*) Of course, the real reason I came in is because, well . . . it gets a bit boring sitting in there on a Sunday afternoon by yourself, there's nothing much to do is there? And Rosita said, don't you sit down there by yourself, Clark, you go in and see Mr Hancock and have a chat with him. I know it's always so lively in your house on a Sunday compared with the rest of the street.

TONY   Oh yes, madly gay. We have quite a ding-dong going on here some weeks. The table wine flows like water.

KENNETH   You're sure you didn't mind me popping in?

TONY   No, no.

KENNETH   [Yes. (*slight pause*) I er . . . I know it seems silly but it's quite thrilling for me to actually come into your house and talk to you like I am now, I mean you being on the stage and that . . . how glamorous it all must be . . .

TONY   Oh you've no idea, backstage at Barnsley, Derby, Northampton, it's sheer magic.

KENNETH   Yes it must be, that's why I was a little apprehensive.] You're such interesting people with such a lot to keep you busy, never a dull moment . . . I thought that you might be bored by someone like me, just an ordinary sort of chap.

TONY   Oh no, no, you're terribly fascinating.

KENNETH   Oh no, well I wouldn't say that, I mean the sort of life you lead is a lot

different to mine. I mean on the stage you meet all those pretty young ladies, and I suppose you sort of wine and dine them in all the big clubs in town.

TONY   Oh yes, unceasingly. It's a wonder you found me in.

KENNETH   Quite, quite. (*pause*) I always listen to your radio programme.

TONY   Really.

KENNETH   Oh yes, Rosita and myself never miss it. I heard last week's. I wasn't so keen on it as some of the others.

TONY   Weren't you?

KENNETH   No. I didn't think it was as funny. I thought Ted Ray had the edge on you last week. It must be very worrying for you trying to keep it up, week after week, especially with so many good newcomers arriving on the scene.

TONY   Yes, quite.

KENNETH   The week before could have been better as well, the actual jokes were funny enough but you sounded a bit tired. You must feel the strain, week after week, it's probably the BBC's fault for working you too hard. Of course I wouldn't tell you all this if you weren't one of my favourites.

TONY   No, no, of course not.

KENNETH   One or two of the lads at the office don't like you so much these days either.

TONY   They don't?

KENNETH   No. Of course they're very fickle. Rosita and I, we think you were at your peak five years ago. You were very funny in those days. Still I don't suppose you're bothered, you've made your pile I expect.

TONY   Oh yes, yes, I'm rolling in it. I've no need to work again for a fortnight.

KENNETH   Well you can't keep it up for ever can you?

TONY   Yes, well, I'm so sorry you've got to go now.

KENNETH   Oh no, I haven't got to go. I'm all right for an hour or two.

TONY   I thought I heard Rosita calling. Perhaps she's fallen out of bed.

KENNETH   No, no, she'll be all right. Er . . . may I sit down? Thank you. (*Long pause. Clearing of throats*) I was reading in the paper this morning that a man has invented a little box that can cure gallstones.

TONY   We read it.

KENNETH   Oh yes. (*pause*) I do impressions you know.

TONY   Oh really?

KENNETH   Yes. (*honks like a pig*) That's a pig.

TONY   And very good too.

KENNETH   I just do them for my own amusement you know.

TONY   Obviously.

KENNETH   (*Pause. Loudly*) Moooooooooo.

TONY   (*jumps*) Cor dear oh dear. Not in my ear, please. You frightened the life out of me.

KENNETH   I'm sorry. Moooo. Bow wow. Mooo. Bow wow. That was a cow being worried by a sheepdog.

TONY   Yes, well, I'm sorry you can't stop for tea but we haven't got enough fish paste to go round.

KENNETH   Oh I don't mind, you go ahead. I'll just sit here.

TONY   We need your chair.

KENNETH Oh very well, I don't mind standing. You go ahead and have your tea. There's no doubt about it, when you have friendly neighbours like this, it makes Sunday well worth while waiting for, doesn't it?

TONY Yes, yes, just think we might have sat here all day bored stiff. Ugh.

(*slow funereal link*)

KENNETH Quack, quack. Quack, quack. That was the lesser spotted corncrake.

TONY Oh yes, wasn't that good, eh Sid? Wasn't it good, Bill? Oh of course, I forgot, they fell asleep hours ago.

KENNETH Awk. Awk. Awk. Awk.

TONY Are you choking?

KENNETH No, no.

TONY What a pity.

KENNETH No, that was the Splayed Footed Moorhen.

TONY Well well, isn't that marvellous? That's six hundred animals you've done and you haven't even started on Africa yet.

KENNETH Yes, it's amazing the number of different impressions one can do in seven hours isn't it? Did you realise it's nearly twelve o'clock?

TONY Is that all? I thought it was at least Tuesday.

KENNETH Well, I think I'd better be going now.

TONY What, so soon?

KENNETH Yes, I'm sorry, but I can't stop here entertaining you for ever. Good night Mr Hancock, and do try and make your show funnier next week.

(*door shuts*)

TONY Either he moves or I do.

(*clock starts striking twelve*)

SIDNEY (*yawns*) Cor blimey, twelve o'clock. It's Monday at last. That must be the most miserable day I've ever spent in my life.

BILL Me too. We didn't play a single thing.

TONY Well it's the last day I ever spend like it, I'll tell you.

SIDNEY We've got to get organised.

TONY Definitely. We can't go on like this. Frittering away our lives like we've done today. We've got to do something constructive. Time's valuable.

SIDNEY I agree.

BILL So do I.

TONY We only live once.

SIDNEY Of course we do.

TONY There's a million things we could do.

SIDNEY Certainly.

TONY Yes. (*long pause*) I'll see you next Sunday then.

SIDNEY & BILL Yeah.

TONY Goodnight.

SIDNEY & BILL Goodnight.

Light Programme

1,500 m. (200 kc/s)   247 m. (1,214 kc/s)   VHF : Wrotham 89.1 Mc/s

MUSIC MIXTURE
Strings in Rhythm
Southern Serenade
phie Terné and Val Doonican
(Continued)

News Summary at 5.30
pping Forecast at 5.55 on 1,500 m.

The Band Waggon
this Tuesday presents
ERIC WINSTONE
AND HIS ORCHESTRA
with Ray Merrell, Joan Small
and Colin Prince
and featuring
The Roy Marsh Trio
The Alan Moorehouse Singers
and
The Dennis Walton
Saxophone Quintet
Introduced by Eric Winstone
Produced by Geoffrey Owen

News Summary at 6.30

5   'THE ARCHERS'
A story of country folk
Written by
ffrey Webb and Edward J. Mason
Edited by Godfrey Baseley
Produced by Tony Shryane
(BBC recording)

0   Greenwich Time Signal
RADIO NEWSREEL

25   SPORT

0   News Summary
Wilfred Pickles
in
HAVE A GO!
visits
Stornoway
in the Outer Hebrides
with Mabel at 'The Table'
and
Harry Hudson at the piano
Presented by Stephen Williams
Repeated on Sunday at 11.0 a.m.

8.0 The BBC Light Programme
presents
the fourth annual
FESTIVAL OF
DANCE MUSIC
PART 1
See foot of page

.30   News Summary
Tony Hancock in
HANCOCK'S HALF-HOUR
featuring
Sidney James, Hattie Jacques
and Kenneth Williams
Written by
Alan Simpson and Ray Galton
Produced by Tom Ronald
(BBC recording)
Repeated on Thursday at 9.0 p.m.

9.0   FESTIVAL OF
DANCE MUSIC
PART 2

10.   Stephen Grenfell
is the storyteller in
OUR DAY AND AGE
True stories of
the world we live in
18—'MISSION OF MERCY'
In the early hours of the morning a
child awakes in her father's croft in a
remote island of the Outer Hebrides.
The pain has grown much worse. Her
brother is hurriedly dressed and sent
for the doctor, who says an operation
within the next few hours can save her
life; but equipment and facilities for
such an emergency operation lie far
away on the Scottish mainland. One
phone call and the Scottish Air Ambu-
lance Service swings into action. Within
the hour a B.E.A. aircraft carrying a
nursing sister from the Southern General
Hospital, Glasgow, takes off from
Renfrew Airport. Another mission of
mercy has begun.
Script by Stephen Grenfell
Produced by Archie P. Lee
in the BBC's Glasgow studios
(BBC recording)

10.30   Greenwich Time Sig..
NEWS

10.40   BBC
DANCING CLUB
You are invited to danc
to the music of
Victor Silvester
and his Ballroom Orche
featuring all that is be
in ballroom dancing
Produced by David Mille

11.30   News Summary
LATE NIGHT
RENDEZVOUS
with
Sidney Bright and his M

11.55   LATE NEWS

12.0   Big Ben
Close Down
followed by
Shipping Forecast on 1,500 m

NNUAL BBC LIGHT PROGRAMME
OF DANCE MUSIC
STARRING
e King   Alma Cogan
Dene and the Dene-Aces

Ronnie Aldrich
and the
Squadronaires
with Ken Kirkham, Joan Baxter
and Peter Morton
The Johnny
Dankworth Orchestra
incorporating
the Johnny Dankworth Seven
The Stargazers

THE PICNIC

'So that's what they look like in daylight . . .'

And a right bunch of likely lads they are too; three men in a car, all with one thing on their minds! The Casanovas of East Cheam, the Don Juans of Railway Cuttings, Sid, Bill and Tony, are planning a day out in the country and it's not the scenery they're after.

The summer of 1959 had been the hottest and longest summer yet recorded that century; there were more cars taking to the open roads than ever before. Cliff Richard was at number one with 'Travellin' Light' and every gay young blade worth his Levis had a bright shining new Ford Anglia with upholstered seats and a radio aerial. There were just over 1,500,000 car licences issued in 1959, compared with nearly 18,000,000 in 1986, and yet even then the roads to the coast were becoming congested, which is probably why these three musketeers chose to go inland!

And travelling light? With a hundred-odd plum jam sandwiches? At least, it is suggested, they could swap some for some 'rubber' cheese – referring to the newly introduced 'processed' and pre-packed cheeses that were so much more convenient and easy to sell at the new supermarkets. And when I think of my mother, standing at the cheese counter at Sainsbury's, tugging away at that thin bit of wire and trying to cut off two ounces of the best Scottish Cheddar without chopping her fingers off . . .

They've got the car, they've got the food, so where are the birds? It was part of the youth ritual, and although Bill, Tony and especially Sid could by no means be classed as 'youth', it didn't seem to matter because they knew what the ritual entailed: it was part of the 'youth' scene to hit the dance floor on a Saturday night, as much to find a date for the Sunday as to actually partake in the physical exercise.

'It wasn't half crowded on the dance floor, wasn't it?'

'Yes, very comfortable.'

And watch out for the running-board . . . no, it wasn't a forerunner of the skateboard, it was a very functional part of cars in the thirties and forties, thus dating the Hancock car and Hancock himself, at the same time. Even at this late stage in the developing talents of Galton and Simpson, there is a 'joke' in there somewhere – you won't miss it. The scripts had become so refined by now that the contrived 'joke' sticks out like a sore thumb.

But there you are, I'm not telling you any more. I will now leave you to your own devices and to the mercy of 'The Picnic'.

'Wake up, Sid, we're breaking out . . .'

THE PICNIC

Script by
ALAN SIMPSON AND RAY GALTON

Recorded: 10 June 1959
Broadcast: 20 October 1959
Starring:
TONY HANCOCK
SIDNEY JAMES
BILL KERR
WILFRED BABBAGE
PATRICIA HAYES
ANNE LANCASTER
ELIZABETH FRASER

Produced by
TOM RONALD

TONY (*singing*) 'Oh what a beautiful morning, oh what a beautiful day, I've got a beautiful feeling, everything going my way . . .' Oh dear, oh dear, it's good to be alive. Six o'clock in the morning and all's well. (*sniffs*) Oooh, smell that air! (*coughs a little*) I'm not used to it yet, it must be good though. Just do my exercises . . . Touch the toes – up down, up down, up down. Down the sides of the leg now – up over down, up over down, up over down, get-the-hand-down-by-the-calf-of-the-leg, up over down . . . aaah! Now chest expansion. Shoulders back – get the blades touching at the back – that's it. Now – arms out, stretch. Round in out. Round in out. Round in out. Round in out. Finish up with some press-ups. Up down, up down, three down, four down, five down, six down. Ooh that's a hard one, that is. Oh well, I think I'll get out of bed now. Ooh, that lino isn't half cold! Oh dear, oh dear. I'll have to get that carpet mended, it's ridiculous, holes that size. Oh well, I'd better get those other two lazy so-and-sos out of bed.

(*rapping on door*)

TONY Bill, come on, six o'clock, rise and shine! Come on, get out of bed!

(*door opens*)

TONY Now come on, come on, get up. Look at him, not a movement. What a terrible sight to come across first thing in the morning! How can anybody sleep like that? Two feet and an earhole poking out. Oi, wake up!

BILL (*stirs & goes back to sleep again*)

TONY Completely oblivious. I wish I could sleep like that. He's the only man I've ever met where rigor mortis sets in the minute he closes his eyes. I know what I'll do. Roll the newspaper up into a funnel . . .

(*rustle of paper*)

TONY . . . place the pointed end in his earhole . . . Now, where's the water jug?

(*pouring of water*)

BILL (*yells*) Take to the boats, I'm drowning!

TONY His other ear's wet! It's gone straight through. Oh no, must have gone round the back.

BILL What did you want to go and do a thing like that for?

TONY Well, get up, you lazy oaf! I've been calling you for five minutes . . . don't wipe your face on my sheets, what do you think the curtains are there for? Now come on, get out of bed. It's picnic day. I want to get an early start before the roads get crowded.

BILL Oh, I don't want to go on a picnic. You go, I'll go back to sleep.

TONY You will not. Now come on, get up, there's a lot to be done. What's the matter with you?

BILL I'm tired.

TONY You should go to bed early, like Sid and I did.

BILL You wouldn't let me. You made me stay up all night, cutting sandwiches.

TONY All night! How many did you cut?

BILL Let's see, twelve loaves – about 140.

TONY 140? This is a picnic, not a safari. Who's going to eat 140 jam sandwiches? I suppose they're plum.

BILL Yes.

TONY I thought so. I hate plum. I always have done. I've always hated plum. And we've got 140 of them. 140 plum jam sandwiches. A fine picnic this is going to be.

What can you do with 140 plum jam sandwiches? Oh well, we'll just have to call in at the railway station buffet, see if they've got any swops. I know the girl behind the counter, she'll be all right for some meatloaf and a few slabs of rubber cheese. Well come on, don't sit there swinging your pyjama cord, get up!

BILL But I didn't get to bed till five o'clock.

TONY Well, that's an hour you've had, that's enough. What's the matter with you? Good grief, during the war, in the Commandos, I went days without any sleep at all. I didn't complain. There was a job to be done, and by heavens, we did it.

BILL You were in ENSA.

TONY Well, we did sketches about Commandos, I know what they went through. Now get up, and go down and wash the lettuces. And get the grit out of them. I do hate gritty lettuce. I'll go and wake Sid up. Plum. 140 of them. Plum mad he is.

(*knock on door*)

TONY Sid. Sid. Oh, it's hopeless. I know!

(*soft knocking on the door*)

TONY (*hoarse Cockney*) Wake up, Sid, we're breaking out.

(*door opens*)

SIDNEY I'm ready, got the rope, I – oh, it's you. I wish you wouldn't play about like that. (*yawns*) What's the time?

TONY Ten past six. Come on, we want to be out by half past seven.

SIDNEY Oh, of course, the picnic. What's the weather like?

TONY Marvellous. Not a cloud in the sky. Get the old sun-roof open in the car, it'll be glorious.

SIDNEY It's always open. It's trying to keep the thing on that's the trouble. Where's Bill?

TONY He's in the kitchen, washing the lettuce. Here, do you know what he's done?

SIDNEY What?

TONY He's cut 140 plum jam sandwiches.

SIDNEY Oh cor bli . . . I'm not going.

TONY It doesn't matter, we can swop them at the railway station.

SIDNEY They're not much better. As soon as she takes the glass dome off those things, they start crumbling.

TONY Never mind. What are you going to wear?

SIDNEY Oh, I don't know. Sweater, cycling shorts, and my Italian sandals, I reckon.

TONY Shorts eh? You're going to flash the legs. Do you think that's wise?

SIDNEY Why not? We've got the three birds coming, haven't we?

TONY That's what I mean, we don't want to put them on their guard straight away, do we?

SIDNEY Well . . . I haven't got anything else.

TONY Yes, you have. You've got a big wardrobe in there. What about that pair of policeman's trousers you had dyed? I've always liked you in those. I'll take the toothbrush round your white plimsolls while you get washed, eh?

SIDNEY All right then.

TONY Do you reckon those girls will turn up?

SIDNEY Of course they will. Blimey, we only met them last night, look how keen

they were. The best night I've had at the Palais for a long time, that was. It wasn't half crowded on the dance floor, wasn't it?

TONY   Yes, very comfortable.

SIDNEY   How old do you reckon they are?

TONY   Difficult to tell really. It was a bit dark, wasn't it, they only had the crystal ball going round, didn't they? I should think they were anything between, what . . . seventeen, and . . . forty-five.

SIDNEY   I liked Ethel.

TONY   Did you? Oh, I'm surprised, I rather preferred your one. What was her name?

SIDNEY   Hermione.

TONY   Yes, her. Very smartly done up, you know. Oh yes. That blue hair, it's very fashionable, you know. All the ladies in the West End have it. It costs money to have hair that colour.

SIDNEY   Yeah, well, they're on good money, those girls at the tanning factory. You preferred Hermione, eh?

TONY   Certainly.

SIDNEY   All right then, we'll have a change round. You take Hermione and I'll take Ethel.

TONY   What about Bill? He hasn't seen them yet. He doesn't know anything about it. He left before we picked them up, if you remember.

SIDNEY   Yeah. The girls are bringing along one of their mates for him.

TONY   Did we see her?

SIDNEY   Yeah. She was slumped across the bar, remember?

TONY   Oh, I know. The little one who was sponging the stout off her dress.

SIDNEY   That's her. The one with the ears.

TONY   Oh dear. How very unfortunate. Still, old Bill's nothing to write home about, is he? It's a pity though, because she's going to spoil it. She's a bit common in comparison with the other two.

SIDNEY   Oh yes. The other two are class.

TONY   Oh yes, you can tell that. They know how to dress, class always tells, they've got taste, you see. I hope they wear those stockings again, with the black diamonds up the legs, they're marvellous. I think we can look forward to a very enjoyable day. Come on then, get dressed.

SIDNEY   What are you going to wear?

TONY   Oh, my picnic set, of course. Straw hat, striped blazer and white flannels.

SIDNEY   Cor blimey. That's a bit *Three Men in a Boat*, isn't it?

TONY   Oh, I don't know. It's very young-looking, you know. It's the real stuff, it's dead Varsity. I got it from the railway lost property, it must be genuine, it was found on a train from Harrow.

SIDNEY   Oh well, you wear it if you feel good in it.

BILL   (*off*) Tub.

TONY   Yes?

BILL   (*off*) I've finished washing the lettuce, what shall I do now?

TONY   Turn the tap off . . .

BILL   (*off*) Yes.

TONY   Take it out of the sink . . .

BILL (*off*) Yes.

TONY And put it in the spin dryer. Give it three minutes, same as when you scramble the eggs.

BILL (*off*) Right.

TONY Oh, and tear a bit of newspaper off, wrap some salt in it, and put it in your pocket. Oh, and take the shells off the eggs.

BILL (*off*) Right.

TONY We'd better go down and give him a hand, or we'll never get out.

(*footsteps down stairs*)

TONY It shouldn't take long. I made the potato salad last night. I boiled them, and wrapped them in a bit of lettuce, is that right?

SIDNEY Sounds all right. Can I borrow your talcum?

TONY It's all gone. I used it last night when we mended the puncture on the car. Might still be some on the garage floor if you'd like to get the brush and pan out.

SIDNEY No thanks, I don't want bits of nails and sawdust under my arms.

(*Footsteps stop. Door opens*)

BILL Oh, morning, Sid.

SIDNEY Plum jam sandwiches.

TONY How are you getting on?

BILL Nearly finished.

TONY Oh, for crying out loud.

BILL Now what's wrong?

TONY When I said take the shells off the eggs, I meant the ones we boiled. Look at all that mess on the floor.

BILL Well, I didn't know which ones were which. They all look the same. What shall I do now?

TONY Nothing, go out and sit in the car. And don't play with the steering wheel. We'd better hurry up, we've got to pick the girls up soon.

BILL Girls, what girls? You didn't tell me there were girls coming.

TONY Aha, that's livened you up a bit, hasn't it?

BILL What are they like?

TONY Well, ours are all right. Well, yours isn't bad really, if you like ugly women.

BILL It's not fair, I always get the ugly ones.

TONY You're lucky to get one at all. Since when have you started being fussy?

BILL I prefer to choose my own girls, thank you.

TONY Don't you be unpleasant to her. If she gets annoyed at you, she'll tell the others, and then we've all had it. I've got too much money invested in this to take any chances. By the time the day's out, what with the petrol, this little jaunt is going to set me back the best part of thirty bob. It's a good job that car does sixty-five to the gallon.

SIDNEY I'm ready. How do I look?

TONY Very nice. I'm not sure about the Royal Artillery tie.

SIDNEY There's nothing wrong with it.

TONY I just happen to prefer braces to keep trousers up. Apart from that, I think you'll be a knockout. Right then – tactics. When we get to the bluebell woods, after we've had the grub we've got to try and separate them, right?

SIDNEY & BILL Right.

TONY They probably won't be keen on this at first, girls never like separating, so we have to use our loaves. I've always found the best gambit is to play hide and seek.

SIDNEY Cor . . .

TONY Ah, wait a minute. The object of my game is all hide and no seek. So if all goes according to plan, at ten o'clock I'll blow the hooter of the car, and you all make your way back, right?

SIDNEY & BILL Right.

SIDNEY Very clever.

TONY Right gentlemen, synchronise your watches, and here's a compass each. We're meeting the enemy outside the Town Hall at eight o'clock. Oh, and by the way, Bill.

BILL Yeah?

TONY Just for safety's sake, in case we don't want to see them anymore after this. I'm Harry, Sid's Herbert, and you're Clarence. Right gentlemen, let battle commence.

(*Engine starts up. Car drives off*)

(*picnic music*)

(*Car chugging along. Backfires half a dozen times, irregularly*)

TONY She's running well today, isn't she?

SIDNEY Well, she's moving, that's something I suppose.

(*clang, as a mudguard falls off into the road*)

TONY What's that?

BILL The mudguard fell off.

TONY Back or front?

BILL Both of them, with the running-board. Shall we stop and pick it up?

TONY No we can't, we're late. Besides we never use it, we can't get out that side anyway.

SIDNEY Hey look, on the steps outside the Town Hall. There they are, all three of them. (*laughs*)

TONY Oh yes. So that's what they look like in daylight.

SIDNEY Yeah.

TONY Let's turn round and go home.

SIDNEY We can't, they've seen us. They'll be all right once we've got a few drinks inside us.

BILL Which one's mine?

TONY The ugly one.

BILL They're all ugly.

TONY Well, yours is the ugliest, now shut up.

BILL I want to go home.

TONY You stay where you are. They're probably very nice girls.

BILL They'd have to be, with faces like that.

TONY Don't be so rude. Try and behave like a gentleman for once. Pull into the kerb.

(*car draws to a halt*)

TONY Hallo there. So glad to see you, lovely day for a pickers, what?

HERMIONE You're late.

TONY Yes. Well, we were unavoidably detained. My stockbroker was on the phone about my takeover bid for ICI. Well, shall we get under way?

ETHEL What's this then?

TONY What's what?

ETHEL This heap of old rubbish.

TONY That's the car.

ETHEL I'm not getting in that thing. You said last night you had a new one.

TONY Well, it was once.

ETHEL Yes, but blimey, there's only half of it there.

TONY Look dear, this is a very expensive vintage car. Gents like us always drive cars like this. If you want a flash American one, you'd better go somewhere else.

ETHEL What do you reckon, Hermione?

HERMIONE Well, it's a bit late to make any other arrangements now, isn't it?

ETHEL Yes, I think we've backed a loser here.

TONY Are you coming or not?

HERMIONE We'll ask our friend. What do you think, Dolores?

DOLORES I don't fancy it myself.

HERMIONE Well, I'm not coming if Dolores don't come.

ETHEL Well, I'm not going on my own.

TONY This is a good start, isn't it?

HERMIONE Well, that's it then, we're not coming.

TONY You've got to come. Stone me, we've got 140 plum jam sandwiches stacked in the boot, what's the matter with you?

HERMIONE There's no need to adopt that tone of voice.

TONY Oh, of course, I beg your pardon, I forgot my breeding for the moment, it's just that you promised to come last night, and . . . well, we've lashed out a fair amount of loot to entertain you good ladies.

ETHEL Oh well, we don't like to let people down. What do you think, Herm?

HERMIONE Well . . . it is a nice day, and we haven't got much else to do, have we?

ETHEL No. What about you, Dolores?

DOLORES I don't mind, if you two want to go, I'll come along for the ride.

TONY Ah well, it's all settled then. Come on, jump in . . .

HERMIONE Before we go, no funny business.

TONY I don't know what you mean.

SIDNEY I don't think I want to go now.

ETHEL And we want to be home by nine o'clock.

TONY Of course you will be. Have no fear on that score, dear ladies. I give you my word as an officer and a gentleman. Now jump in, it'll be a lovely day out in the country, I'm sure you'll enjoy yourselves. Oh by the way, introductions. As you know, I'm Harry, this is Herbert . . .

SIDNEY Hallo.

TONY And this is our friend you haven't met yet, Clarence.

BILL Hallo everybody.

TONY This is Hermione, and Ethel . . . and none of us have had the pleasure of meeting the other young lady . . . Dolores, is it not?

DOLORES That's right.

TONY Dolores, Clarence.

DOLORES Charmed, I'm sure.

BILL Likewise.

SIDNEY Hallo Dolores.

DOLORES Hallo Herbert.

TONY Well now, now the ice has been broken and all the formalities have been taken care of, we all know each other, all nice and friendly so to speak, I suggest we set off into the country and commune with Mother Nature.

HERMIONE What do you mean?

TONY Nothing dear. Stone me, this one's going to be a hard nut to crack. All aboard then.

ETHEL Where are we going to sit?

TONY Well now, Bill – er, Clarence is driving . . . I suggest Dolores sits next to him, and Herbert next to her. And me, Hermione and Ethel in the back.

SIDNEY You've done all right for yourself, haven't you?

TONY It's my car.

SIDNEY (*sotto*) What do you reckon?

TONY (*sotto*) They're not so bad after all, are they? We've known worse.

SIDNEY Yeah, I reckon if we play our cards right . . .

TONY Quite, quite . . .

HERMIONE What are you two whispering about?

TONY We're discussing the route. Clarence . . . Clarence.

BILL Oh, that's me . . . yes?

TONY I think we'll head for Cobham, and get on the A3. Okay, let her rip. Do you like going fast, girls?

GIRLS Ooh yes.

TONY (*to himself*) Hard luck.

(*car revs up & painfully staggers off*)

(*picnic music*)

(*car going along*)

HERMIONE Oh, how much further?

TONY (*to himself*) Don't they keep on? I don't think they've stopped moaning once since we've left. (*aloud*) Not far, my little pigeon. Ha ha. My goodness, look at that countryside stretched out before us.

ETHEL Oh, I've seen it.

TONY You haven't seen that bit.

HERMIONE Oh, it isn't half cramped at the back here. Can't he move the seat forward?

TONY No, he can't.

HERMIONE Why can't he?

TONY Because his feet'll be in the fan belt if he does. Now please, one car one driver, let the man alone. He's doing his best. What about a sing-song to cheer us up? What about a rollicking song of the road?

DOLORES I'm hungry.

TONY Oh, she's off now. We're nearly there, we'll get the food out in a minute.

ETHEL We've been driving for hours.

TONY It only seems a long time.

ETHEL   Well, we've passed lots of open country, why can't we stop there?

SIDNEY   Because we're not looking for open country.

TONY   Sssh . . . ssh . . . ssh. Oooh, look!

HERMIONE   What?

TONY   Two big wooden men carrying a ladder across a field.

DOLORES   Little things please little minds.

SIDNEY   And bigger fools look on, there.

TONY   Now, now, Herbert. Don't let's degenerate. Keep above it all.

ETHEL   I wonder what Frank and Joe are doing?

TONY   Well, that's a nerve, isn't it? You're out with us, never mind about Frank and Joe. The girls of today, honestly . . . Do you mind, dear, throw your dog-ends out of the window, don't tread 'em out on the carpet.

HERMIONE   You call this a carpet? My dog sleeps on better stuff than this.

TONY   You don't like me, do you? Or my car.

HERMIONE   Not particularly.

BILL   I see. Well, as long as I know where I stand. If you fancy my friend, we'll have a change round.

HERMIONE   I don't fancy any of you much.

TONY   Quite frankly, I'm at a loss to understand why you came at all.

HERMIONE   Well, if you must know, Mr Clever Dick, it was to teach Frank and Joe a lesson. They've gone to Southend on the boat, and we're not going to let them think they're indispensable. We're using you.

TONY   There's nothing like being honest, is there? When I think of all the bread this lot's cost us . . . you're very ungrateful, madam.

ETHEL   Oh, stop quarrelling, you two. We're here now, so we may as well make the best of it.

SIDNEY   Hear hear, good girl Ethel, that's the spirit.

ETHEL   Who said you could put your arm round my shoulder?

SIDNEY   Oh cor . . . it was just resting on the top of the seat. Clarence, stop the car at the next railway station, I'm going home.

TONY   No, no, Herbert, if you go home that's no good, we might as well all go home.

HERMIONE   That's an idea.

TONY   No, no, look. Let's start again. It's the drive, our nerves are getting frayed, we've been in the car too long. We're nearly there, let's all be friends, come on, little fingers. That's better. Ah, here we are, Clarence. Turn right here, that's it.

DOLORES   Here, this is a little road, isn't it? Where are you taking us?

TONY   A delightful spot, madame, idyllic is more the word.

DOLORES   *(screams)*

BILL   What, what did I do, I was changing gear.

DOLORES   You touched my leg.

BILL   I didn't notice. It felt like the gear stick.

DOLORES   Are you insinuating I've got thin legs?

BILL   No, I just didn't notice . . . I'm sorry, I won't change gear again. We'll finish the journey in bottom.

TONY   You change gear whenever you have to, you're not ruining my engine just for the sake of her skinny legs.

ETHEL   Where's this idyllic spot you were gabbing about?

TONY   Just round the corner. A running stream, a mill pond, leafy willow trees, lush green grass, secluded glens, clusters of bluebells in the thicket of the woodland . . . a paradise cut off from the rest of the milling throng.

HERMIONE   I don't like the sound of it.

TONY   You haven't seen it yet. I sat up for three hours with a survey map choosing this spot. The sort of scene exiles weep over, this is. Here you, Clarence, pull in over there.

BILL   Shall I leave the car on the road?

TONY   No, take it right through under the trees in the field. We don't want anybody to know we're here.

HERMIONE   Why?

TONY   Where do you usually go for picnics, Wembley Stadium? Right, this'll do. Stop here.

(*car stops*)

TONY   That's it.

BILL   Right. Let's play hide and seek.

TONY   Not yet. Hang on a minute, we haven't had the plum sandwiches yet. Ah, what a lovely view, dead tranquil this is. Look at that scenery, doesn't it make one feel at peace.

SIDNEY   Yeah. Where's the boozer?

TONY   There isn't a boozer. I deliberately chose a place completely devoid of boozers.

SIDNEY   Where are we going to get a drink then?

TONY   The stream. The crystal clear stream.

SIDNEY   Oh . . .

TONY   Don't you start. You're as bad as they are.

SIDNEY   We passed enough boozers on the way down, I would have got tanked up then if I'd known. What about the birds? They're not going to forget Frank and Joe on two glasses of crystal clear stream water.

TONY   I know that. Which is why I called in at my mother's yesterday afternoon.

SIDNEY   Why?

TONY   I scrounged a couple of bottles of her potato wine. Scalp raiser, that stuff is. Just leave everything to me.

HERMIONE   What are you two whispering about now?

TONY   Discussing the most convenient place to lay the tablecloth.

HERMIONE   On the ground.

TONY   Of course. Why didn't I think of that? All right ladies, be seated. We'll have the feast laid out before you in no time at all.

(*picnic music*)

TONY   Have another jam sandwich.

HERMIONE   No thanks.

TONY   You've only had one. We've got another 120 in the car.

HERMIONE   I don't want any more. I thought we'd have chicken and salmon and things like that.

TONY   Chicken? At three and six a wing? You must be mad. Go on, get the plum jam down you. There's people in Europe who'd be glad of that.

BILL More lettuce anyone?

DOLORES No thanks.

BILL Hard boiled eggs?

ETHEL No thanks.

BILL Potato salad?

HERMIONE No thanks.

BILL Everybody finished?

DOLORES Yes.

BILL Well, what about a game of hide and seek?

TONY Not yet. After the wine.

HERMIONE What's this hide and seek he keeps talking about?

TONY Nothing, nothing. Have some wine. Here you, hold out your tin mug.

(*pouring of wine*)

TONY There, look at that beautiful amber liquid. French that is, you know. Comes from the best vineyards in Calais, that does.

ETHEL Oh, I wouldn't know, I like Scotch myself.

TONY Well, we haven't got any. This is better than Scotch. You don't really get the benefit of the bouquet until you've had about three mugfuls. Drain that one, go on, down the hatch, there's plenty more.

HERMIONE Well, come on then, fill it up. No short measures.

TONY By all means, hoo, hoo . . .

SIDNEY Here come on, go easy, what about my bird? Here you are, love, pull the cork out with your teeth.

ETHEL Aren't you men drinking?

TONY No. 'Tis but a small sacrifice for such charming company.

HERMIONE Ooh blimey, get him!

TONY Three charmers we've got here. I'll stick to Bohemians in future, much more understanding. Half a page of Bertrand Russell and they're putty in my hands.

SIDNEY Come on, girls, drink up.

DOLORES It's all gone.

ETHEL What do we do now then?

TONY Well, er . . . let me think now, what could we do . . . what would be amusing for you. . . ? I know, I've just thought of something. Do you know how to play hide and seek?

HERMIONE Yes, but we're not splitting up.

TONY That's it then, fold the tablecloth up, all back in the car. All go home.

ETHEL We've only just got here. It's only two o'clock.

TONY Well, *I've* had enough. I've never spent such a miserable day in my life. What's the matter with you girls? You were quite keen in the Palais last night.

HERMIONE You're a bit touchy, aren't you?

TONY I'm sensitive, madam. You can't ride roughshod over people like me, 500 years of breeding have gone into me, I'm like a sensitive racehorse, a violin string . . .

SIDNEY You've upset him now, look at his nostrils flaring.

HERMIONE Just because we said we didn't want to play hide and seek.

TONY Yes.

HERMIONE Well, that's kids' stuff. I'd rather go into the woods and pick bluebells.

TONY Pardon? Pick bluebells?

HERMIONE Yes, I love bluebells. Brightens the old front room up at home.

TONY Oh, they do, they do. I never thought of the bluebells, much too corny.

HERMIONE Mum asked me to bring her a bunch back anyway.

TONY And we wouldn't like to disappoint your dear white-haired old mother. What a lovely girl you are. I take back any uncharitable comments I may have made in the heat of the moment. I've never had the pleasure of such delightful and charming company in the whole of my natural. Well then, to the bluebells. How shall we do it, spread out a bit, I reckon. What, ten acres to each couple?

HERMIONE Oh no, we don't want to separate.

TONY You don't?

HERMIONE No.

TONY Oh.

SIDNEY Well, the only trouble is the bluebells are very scarce round here, we stand a much better chance of finding them if we spread out a bit.

TONY Oh, definitely. He knows what he's talking about. A great bluebell man is Herbert. International authority on bluebells, aren't you, Herbert?

SIDNEY Yeah.

TONY Oh yes, whatever else he may be, he knows his bluebells.

ETHEL Well, I don't know . . .

TONY Look, I tell you what we'll do. We'll all spread out in pairs, and when one pair finds any, they yell out and we all come running. Right? Cheerio, see you at ten o'clock.

HERMIONE Wait a minute, why do we have to go in pairs?

TONY Protection, my dear. We couldn't let you wander through the woods on your own. It's dangerous. Notorious bandit country, this part of Surrey. Come on, my dear, the bluebells are waiting. (*sotto*) Don't forget, lads, listen for the ten o'clock hooter.

(*music*)

TONY Oh, you lovely creature, you primitive product of nature, sitting there with your bare feet stuck in a rabbit hole . . . Oh, if only I was a painter, I would immortalise this moment for the whole world.

HERMIONE What about these bluebells?

TONY Never mind the bluebells, this moment is ours. From the moment I first saw you last night at the Palais, I've thought of nothing else but you. How my heart cried out for you in the spot waltz. How desperately unlucky you were, not to be the first one up to the bandstand with a gentleman's left boot. And then I didn't sleep a wink last night, thinking of today when I would see you again. Don't torture me anymore, look at me, look into my eyes, what can you see?

HERMIONE Myself, in those two little black bits.

TONY Just one kiss, one fleeting kiss, just one intoxicating touch of your lips, and I will be your slave for ever, oh, my little woodpigeon, my Aphrodite, how I . . .

HERMIONE I wonder how the others are getting on.

TONY Better than I am, I hope. Pay attention. Look at me. Can't you feel the magnetism that draws us inescapably together, the voice within you that cries out

to be heard . . . the voice of womanhood, saying, now, now, now . . .

HERMIONE Yes, I can, yes, yes . . .

TONY Har har . . . at last on the home stretch. Oh, Hermione, Hermione, it is Hermione, isn't it?

HERMIONE Yes.

TONY Oh, Hermione, Hermione, there is so much unhappiness in the world, so many rules, conventions, so many people to tell us what to do, and what not to do, what fools we are to listen, we are free, rules have no meaning for us . . .

HERMIONE You're right, you're right.

TONY Of course I'm right, oh Hermione . . .

(*scout's whistle*)

SCOUTMASTER Over here, boys, rally rally rally . . . Beaver Patrol, attention! Right everybody, we'll make camp here.

TONY Oi.

SCOUTMASTER Yes?

TONY Push off.

SCOUTMASTER Oh, I beg your pardon, I didn't see you down there.

TONY This bit's taken, push off.

SCOUTMASTER I'm sorry, old man, we Scouts have rented all this area from the farmer for our Jamboree. Unload the cart, boys, get the tents up. Jenkins and Blower, start foraging for wood.

TONY Oh, this is ridiculous. What chance have you got? Come on, you. Get your shoes on.

HERMIONE Aren't you going to help me up.

TONY You've got legs, haven't you? Come on, get your foot out of that rabbit hole, we haven't got all day.

HERMIONE We did have a minute ago.

TONY Well, we haven't now. I'm fed up. We're going home. If you think I'm going to sit here kissing you, with half a dozen spotty-faced Cubs poking their heads through the bushes, you've got another think coming. (*angry*) Come on, stop dragging behind, pick your feet up. What a fiasco! Go on, get in the car. I'll call the others.

(*car hooter*)

TONY Here they come, ploughing their way through the undergrowth.

SIDNEY (*approaching*) What's up? It's not ten o'clock yet, we've only been gone five minutes.

TONY Baden-Powell's mob's arrived. Hundreds of them.

SIDNEY Oh cor . . . I was just getting up to the bit about what fools we are to listen, 'cos rules have no meaning for us.

TONY So was I. Doesn't it make you sick? Well, come on let's get off home, there's not much point in hanging round here. Come on, all in the car, and if one of you women so much as opens your mouth on the way back . . . out!

ETHEL You're not in a very good mood, are you?

TONY No I am not. And let it be a warning. Come on, Clarence, what are you waiting for?

BILL We've got a puncture.

TONY Oh no, that's all I needed. Where's the spare wheel.

BILL   In Cheam High Street. It was on the running-board that fell off.

HERMIONE   Oh well, we're not stopping here with you lot, we're going to walk to the station and get the train.

TONY   Good luck to you. We'll see who gets home first. We'll have this mended, and as we roar past you, don't expect us to stop and pick you up. Hurry up and mend the puncture, Bill.

HERMIONE   (*calls*) Rotten old car, anyway, I knew it would break down.

TONY   Oh, go home. I hope you get blisters. Stupid women. I don't know why I bother with them, I really don't, you're better off on your own. Votes for women, I wouldn't give them a bone to gnaw, some of them. Come on you, hurry up with that tyre.

(*music*)

(*owl hoot*)

TONY   Haven't you mended that tyre yet?

BILL   No.

TONY   Good grief, it's two o'clock in the morning. You've been at it eleven hours.

BILL   I haven't got any tyre levers, I'm trying to use my fingers.

TONY   Haven't you even got the tyre off the wheel yet?

BILL   No. I can't see what I'm doing and I'm tired.

TONY   It's your own fault, suggesting picnics, I've got no sympathy with you.

BILL   I didn't know anything about it, it was your idea. You made me sit up all night cutting jam sandwiches.

TONY   And I'm sitting up all night eating them. Now come on, get your fingers down that tyre. Sid and me are going to have a sleep in the back of the car. And when you've finished, don't wake us up, just drive us home nice and quietly. Picnics? Never again.

DALY
lly (soprano)
ajna (piano)

omb (Sadly rustles the (Suppressed tears); A

(Transylvanian sorrow); n coeur comme il pleut itaphe; Széckely Song , 11)

38 (Love song); Kocsi, girl's song); Ludaim,); A bubánat keserüség of grief); Asszony, s dialogue) ecording)

WORLD
OBSERVER

Russell, O.M.
heory which he s some of the lexities about our e world

nd, he says, that this ved; but he contends of physics, it cannot at no prudent person n this for any theory. roadcast of Feb. 2)

GER
m 100
. 106
ir and
ic Orchestra
Nederlandsche
o-Unie
Carl Caraguly
available by cour- ederlandsche Radio-

LAINE
GLAND

account of the poet's years in shire, and Bourne- is briefer stays in ford, and Salford

nd produced
nce Tiller

rine Salkeld
John Bryning
rion-Crawford
, Frank Duncan
James McKechnie
, Eric Phillips
Arthur Young
ecording)
on Friday at 8.0

ZART
flat (K.498)
ed by
vsky (clarinet)
ovsky (viola)
hofer (piano)
hone records

THE FOURTH ANNUAL BBC LIGHT PR

FESTIVAL OF DANCE

Ted Heath
AND HIS MUSIC
with Bobbie Britton and Peter Lowe

Mick Mulligan
AND HIS BAND
with George Melly

Ke
AN
Kay

Jo
AND

VOCAL STARS

Dickie Valentine **The Fraser Hayes Four** **Ma**

STAR INSTRUMENTALIST

Petula Clark **Betty Smith** **Jim**
(tenor sax)

Master of Ceremonies: Brian Matthew
Produced by John Hooper and Geoffrey Owen
THE FIRST OF THREE CONCERTS FROM THE
Royal Albert Hall
8.0 to 8.30 and 9.0 to 10.0

5.0 MUSIC MIXTURE
(Continued)

News Summary at 5.30
Shipping Forecast at 5.58 on 1,500 m.

6.0 The Band Waggon
each Tuesday presents
RONNIE ALDRICH
AND THE SQUADRONAIRES
with
Ken Kirkham, Peter Morton
Joan Baxter, and Andrew Reavley
Cliff Townshend and his
singing saxophone
and the
Dixieland Group
Produced by John Burnaby

News Summary at 6.30

6.45 'THE ARCHERS'
A story of country folk
Written by
Edward J. Mason and Geoffrey Webb
(BBC recording)

7.0 Greenwich Time Signal
RADIO NEWSREEL

7.25 SPORT

7.30 News Summary
Wilfred Pickles in
HAVE A GO!
visits
The Burgh of Ballater
on Royal Dee-side
with the great sweep
of the Grampians lying behind
with Mabel at 'The Table'
and
Harry Hudson at the piano

8.0 The BBC Light Programme
presents the fourth annual
FESTIVAL OF
DANCE MUSIC
See above

8.30 News Summary
Tony Hancock in
HANCOCK'S HALF-HOUR
featuring
Sidney James
Bill Kerr, Hattie Jacques
and Kenneth Williams
Written by
Alan Simpson and Ray Galton
Produced by Tom Ronald
(BBC recording)
Repeated on Thursday at 9.0 p.m.

9.0 FESTIVAL OF
DANCE MUSIC
(Continued)

10.0 Wilfrid Thomas presents
DATE WITH A DISC
A choice of gramophone records
for the family circle

10.30 Greenwich Time Signal
NEWS

10.40 BBC
DANCING CLUB
You are invited to dance
to the music of
Victor Silvester
and his Ballroom Orchestra
featuring all that is best

11.30
T
D

Si

11.5

12.0

Shipp

B
Engi
If yo
nical
micr
ders,
used
casti
apply
TECH
The
in Lo
with
perio
for p
tiona
over

Male
or equ
have
betwe
apply

THE POETRY SOCIETY

'My aura of perception didn't even wobble!'

Tony Hancock's frustration in the bluebell woods ('The Picnic') brought forth the marvellous lines: 'I'll stick to Bohemians in future . . . Half a page of Bertrand Russell and they're putty in my hands.' Here, in 'The Poetry Society', we witness that great desire for intellectual acceptance taken to the nth degree, with Galton and Simpson submerging him headfirst in a basinful of culture.

The rock 'n' roll craze was all but over; Teddy boys became shop assistants and the pop culture had fallen back on the standards that had always worked so well in the past. The Top Ten hits of the period, following the Tin Pan Alley ballads of 'moon in June' phraseology, were softly sentimental. 'Dream Lover', 'Livin' Doll', 'Only Sixteen' and 'Travellin' Light'.

The *avant-garde* movements of the mid-fifties had burnt themselves out and the 'angry young men' had merged into the obscurity of the very establishment against which they had once rebelled.

A new wave had lashed the edges of the universities, colleges and polytechnics, though, as ever, Hancock was a little late in discovering them; they were the Beatniks, forming part of what was known as the 'Beat' generation.

The music was jazz, albeit light and processed traditional jazz (Trad), and the poetry was the 'Beat' – a strained, hard and often depressing type of verse extolled by such poets as Allen Ginsberg and Lawrence Ferlinghetti.

I knew nothing of this when I first heard the show, but I loved it just the same. Now, in retrospect, one realises just how cleverly Galton and Simpson had satirised the contemporary poetry scene, and, more importantly, what a brilliant script this is because it remains an incredibly funny show, even if you have no knowledge of what was being satirised.

As if spurred on by this brilliant script, the cast honoured it with excellent performances all round. Warren Mitchell's character 'Gregory', for instance, was totally believable and perfectly cast. Without giving too much away, there is a moment when Gregory explains how members of the poetry group should prepare themselves to receive a poem, and pours forth a long and deadly serious monologue. Hancock pauses, and you can almost hear him scratching his head. His reply is simple – two words: 'I see.' Only Tony Hancock could have said those words in exactly the way that Galton and Simpson wanted them spoken, and only they could have predicted it.

The show opens with Hancock dressed as a Beatnik, and a few words of explanation might not go amiss for those of us too young to remember. Like the Punks, the Teddy boys and the Mods, the Beatnik craze was most easily identified by dress, but while it out-lived the skiffle craze, the Beatnik movement failed to gain any real ground outside the campus. With long hair, beards and 'fisherman rope sandals', Beatniks were the intellectual fore-runners of the Flower Power era; aloof and spacial, but not spaced out. They congregated, uniformly clad in heavy duffle coats, in darkened coffee bars very similar to the one described in the script. One such group would huddle together for hours of philosophical pontification over one glass of Coke or a cup of frothy coffee, and it always surprised me that the proprietors of such places ever made a profit but then, as the craze wasn't very long in existence, perhaps they didn't!

On the subject of payment, I had better explain that the 'National Assistance' spoken of here does not refer to any governmental loan for new enterprises but was the predecessor of the Social Security benefits.

It is interesting to note that while this newly emerging youth culture followed the American 'Beat' poets, the established 'literary' societies preferred John Betjeman,

winner of the 1959 Queen's Gold Medal for Poetry, Robert Graves, winner of the 1959 Foyle Prize, and John Masefield, then Poet Laureate.

It is not surprising that, when all Hancock's attempts to get 'hip' with this 'cool' intellectualism fail, he reverts – not to contemporary establishment, not to the classics – but to his roots, the music-hall.

'What about our aims for improving the world?'

THE POETRY SOCIETY

Script by
ALAN SIMPSON AND RAY GALTON

Recorded: 25 June 1959
Broadcast: 8 December 1959
Starring:
TONY HANCOCK
SIDNEY JAMES
BILL KERR
FENELLA FIELDING
FRASER KERR
WARREN MITCHELL

Produced by
TOM RONALD

TONY I want a word with you two.

SIDNEY (*bursts out laughing*)

TONY What are you laughing at?

SIDNEY (*laughing*) Oh dear, oh dear . . . cor dear . . . what does he look like?

TONY I fail to see any cause for undue hilarity.

SIDNEY You want to stand where I am. If you're wearing those clothes for a bet, you've won. What a twit you look.

TONY I don't know what you mean. If you're referring to my slightly unconventional mode of dress, I'll admit it must seem a little different to you bourgeoisie, but to we Bohemians it's quite normal, everyday run-of-the-mill clobber.

BILL You're not going out in the street like that, are you?

TONY I see no reason why I shouldn't. As it happens I'm not going to, but I see no reason why I shouldn't.

BILL Well I'm not going out with you like that.

TONY I can't understand what all the fuss is about. There's nothing out of the ordinary in this lot. Blue and white striped stocking cap, home woven vegetable fibre shirt, canvas trousers, and fisherman rope sandals. Not exactly shipping clerk gear I admit, but nevertheless indicative of my new state of mind. My friends and I are rebelling against conformity.

SIDNEY Well what do they wear?

TONY Same as this of course. We are the avant-garde of the new culture. We are dedicated to setting up a new order of things, determined to establish a new set of values, to break away from the bonds that threaten to stifle the cultural and creative activities of man's mind.

SIDNEY Oh blimey, another lot of layabouts.

TONY We are not layabouts. We are artists, mush. Writers, poets, thinkers, all men who are seriously perturbed about the state of the world at the moment.

SIDNEY And what are you lot going to do about it?

TONY We are going to show the world the real truth, by setting them an example, developing our superior intellects. Culture mate, that's where the hope of the world lies. And a more cultural mob than us you wouldn't find outside of the Chelsea Embankment . . . twenty-seven throbbing intellects raring to go.

BILL Can I join?

TONY No you can't. This isn't a ping-pong and darts club. This is a group with lofty ideals, a cultural discussion group dedicated to the betterment of mankind.

SIDNEY Well why can't he join then, he's mankind?

TONY Well . . . only up to a point. He's not far enough advanced for us.

SIDNEY Well you said it was for the betterment of mankind.

TONY Yes, but stone me, you've got to have something to start on. Look at him. You can't expect us to go that far back. We're only interested in modern shaped people.

SIDNEY What exactly do this mob do?

TONY Well . . . we meet every night down the coffee bar and we chat.

SIDNEY I haven't seen you.

TONY Not that one you go to . . . El Castanetto. That's bourgeois that is. We go to the one done up like a graveyard. We sit on the old cardboard tombstones, round

the plastic coffins and we indulge in philosophical analysis. We formulate our plans for our brave new world. Gladys takes it down in her notebook, then when she's filled it up we're going to publish it. We're calling it *A Thesis on the Reconciliation of Homo Sapiens in Relationship with his Natural Destiny and the Theory of Selective Evolution.*

SIDNEY   Sounds all right, they might make a film of it.

BILL   Yeah, that'd be good. A musical. I can just see it . . . (*sings to tune of 'Friends and Neighbours'*) When you've got Ho . . . mo . . . Sapiens, and selective evolution, da da de da . . .

TONY   Are you taking the mickey?

SIDNEY   Well I ask you, what a load of old rubbish you talk sometimes.

TONY   I wouldn't expect you to understand the outlook of an intellectual like me. I mean, let's face it, you've never been one for new movements, have you? You've always been complacent, haven't you? You're not particularly bothered about the impending stagnation of Western Civilisation, are you?

SIDNEY   No, not really. As long as my horses don't stagnate, I don't care what happens.

TONY   Exactly. The struggle of the Human Race is nothing compared with your struggle up to the two bob window at Cheltenham, is it?

SIDNEY   No it's not.

TONY   Exactly. Reactionary you are. Dead reactionary. You epitomise the very people the East Cheam Cultural Progressive Society are fighting against.

SIDNEY   Who?

TONY   The East Cheam Cultural Progressive Society. That's us. The E.C.C.P.S. Or the Ecpers, as we are known locally. We are a breakaway from the Society for Nuclear Disarmament, allied to the Society for Moral Rearmament, and affiliated to the International Committee for the Exchange of Cultural, Artistic and Intellectual Information, the World Fellowship of Progressive Thinkers and the East Cheam Football Club. Actually we haven't got much in common with them, but we had to have somewhere to meet, and they're the only ones who'd lend us their shed.

SIDNEY   Really when you add it all up, its all a bit tatty, isn't it?

TONY   Tatty? We're the hope of the world, mate.

SIDNEY   What else do you do?

TONY   Well, during the day we pursue our various artistic sidelines. Some of us make pots and jugs, and then there's Adelaide, she's very good in the raffia mats, there's Percy and his Welsh bedspreads, and some of us paint, and sculpt, and the rest of us lay in bed thinking.

SIDNEY   You're one of the layers in bed thinking, of course.

TONY   We must all do what is best suited us. You see, Sidney, we are a collection of kindred spirits who are all revolting against the Establishment.

BILL   How long have you been at it?

TONY   Three days. I was lost like you two . . . a useless vacuum wandering in the wilderness of futility, no purpose in life. Then it happened . . . last Thursday night it was, I heard the group talking in the coffee bar and it was like opening a new door, everything seemed to suddenly fall into place. These are the people I've been looking for, I thought, and I asked if I could join them. They weren't keen at

first, they weren't sure if my intellect was of a sufficiently high standard, but I bought them a cup of coffee all round and they let me join.

SIDNEY Now come on, let's be honest, we know why you joined . . . you fancied the sandals, didn't you?

TONY That had nothing to do with it.

SIDNEY I know you of old, you'd join anything if the clobber suited you. You're pretentious.

TONY I am not pretentious.

SIDNEY You can't stand anybody thinking you're ordinary. You have to be different to other people. You've always seen yourself as a bit of a weirdy haven't you?

TONY What do you mean, a weirdy?

SIDNEY Well . . . all these hairy shirts, tight trousers, and bare feet.

TONY I am not a weirdy. My dress is merely a symbol of my hatred of convention.

BILL Tub, can I borrow your razor?

TONY You can keep it. I won't be needing it any more, I'm growing a beard.

SIDNEY Oh, cor blimey. And you're letting your hair grow long, of course.

TONY One inch below the shoulders, regulation length, unless you're a female, then you can have whatever length you want. Most of them have crew cuts.

BILL Please let me join, Tub. I'll grow a beard and let my hair grow long. I'll provide my own sandals and shirt, you won't have to buy them for me. I don't expect to be allowed to join in the intellectual discussion, I'll be the caretaker, I'll be the man what looks after the shed for you, while you're making your pots.

TONY No.

BILL I'll comb your beards for you.

TONY No. We don't want you. We'd be conscious of you.

BILL I wouldn't make a noise.

TONY We'd know you were there. It'd put us right off our contemplating. How could we concentrate on reshaping the world with you sitting there scratching your head? I'm sorry, both of you would be completely out of place, which is why I want you out of here by seven o'clock.

SIDNEY What for?

TONY It's Thursday night.

SIDNEY Well?

TONY Thursday night . . . our poetry reading classes.

SIDNEY Oh no, you're not having that bunch of toerags round here.

TONY May I remind you this is my house. I shall invite just who I like. And if you don't approve you can load your horse and cart and leave.

SIDNEY Why can't they hold it round one of their houses?

TONY Because I'm the only one in the group who's got a house.

SIDNEY Haven't got houses? Where do they live?

TONY Ten of them live in a basement under the pet shop, there's seven live on a boat on the canal, and the other fifteen of them live with *them*.

SIDNEY Don't they do any work?

TONY Oh please Sidney, work. Work is the biggest restricter of men's minds. They can't allow themselves to be hampered by the menial soul-destroying labour of

everyday jobs. Work to them represents the Establishment, and they're against that.

SIDNEY What do they live on then?

TONY The National Assistance.

SIDNEY They're not against that part of the Establishment then?

TONY Won't you ever understand?

BILL Who's providing the food and the drink for the poetry reading classes?

TONY I am of course.

SIDNEY They've got no objections to you going out to work and owning a house and having money then?

TONY Well . . . the question has been raised, my having money is a bit of an embarrassment to their aims . . . they've suggested I get rid of it.

SIDNEY Well they're certainly doing their best to help you.

TONY It's no good you trying to disparage them, Sidney. I know these people. They're geniuses, every one of them. Oh, we don't expect plebeians like you to appreciate our motives. We're outsiders you see, scorned and mocked by the mass but whether they like it or not, vital to the progress of future generations.

(*knock on front door*)

SIDNEY Open the door, the outsiders are outside. Well I'm off, I'm taking my bottle of brown ale out the sideboard, I'm not letting any outsiders get outside that.

TONY No, don't go, I'd like you to stay. I'd like you to listen to the poetry reading . . . it might convince you that these people have a great talent to offer the world.

BILL Yeah, let's stay Sid, it might be a giggle.

SIDNEY Oh all right then, but don't blame me if I get in a punch up with a few of them. You know me, a word out of place and I'll get stuck into them.

TONY You'll learn something from these people Sidney, this'll be the most instructive evening you've ever spent in your sordid life. I'll go and let them in.

SIDNEY One word, that's all, one lip curled up and there won't be any teeth left under it.

(*door opens*)

(*A crowd of people. About twenty coming into the room*)

TONY Ah welcome brethren. Come in, come in, welcome to my home.

GREGORY Ah Anthony dear boy, so this is where you live.

TONY Yes. Do you like it Gregory?

GREGORY Yes. Yes I think I do. I'm definitely getting turquoise vibrations.

SIDNEY What's he talking about?

BILL I don't know.

GREGORY The vibrations. The house is giving off definite vibrations.

SIDNEY It's the trains going by.

GREGORY Who are these persons?

TONY They're friends of mine Gregory. Sidney James, William Kerr, this is the leader of our group . . . Gregory.

SIDNEY Gregory what?

GREGORY Just Gregory. We never use surnames in our group. They're very bourgeois. I suppose you'll be leaving shortly.

TONY Well actually no . . . I've asked them to stop for the poetry reading. They live here with me you see.

GREGORY Good heavens. Still, I suppose it's quite an interesting experiment actually living with these people.

SIDNEY He's getting up my nose, this bloke.

GREGORY I suppose you sort of watch them and make notes . . .

TONY Well I . . .

GREGORY You're working on a thesis on the mental workings of the lower order of the species.

SIDNEY Oh dear . . . he's going to get my fist right through his beard in a minute.

TONY Sid, Sid, please, no punch ups, not yet . . . he doesn't mean anything, he's the most advanced member of the group . . . I mean he thinks Bertrand Russell's a bit of a charlie, you can't blame him for not reckoning you. Come and meet the other members . . . this is Greta.

GRETA (*low and husky*) How do you do . . .

SIDNEY Oh blimey, I've seen some birds . . . look at it. All lank hair and wooden beads. How do you do, pleased to make your acquaintance.

BILL Hiya doll, how about you and me sloping off down the pub? There's a piano down there, it's talent night tonight in the saloon bar . . . are you musical?

GRETA I only listen to Bartok and Weber.

BILL Well that's all right, sing a couple of their songs, the lads won't mind.

GRETA What an intriguing little savage you are.

TONY Bill, come away . . . I must apologise Greta, he's not one of us, he's very suburban in his musical taste . . . he doesn't appreciate the finer points of classical music like we Gilbert and Sullivan fans. By the way dear, I know it's against all group ethics to consider such things important, but I must say I like your turn-out tonight.

GRETA Oh thank you, do you like it?

TONY Oh yes, very individual. The elongated eyebrows touching the earholes certainly gets me going I might tell you. And the blue lipstick sets it off marvellously. I think without a doubt you are the weirdest looking one here tonight.

GRETA Oh that's very kind of you. I do my best.

GREGORY Well shall we start? We have many important new works to read.

TONY By all means . . . I'll get some chairs.

GREGORY That won't be necessary. We don't use chairs, chairs are a symbol of unproductive work, the furnishings of a decadent society.

TONY Of course, of course, I hadn't realised . . . Bill, take the chairs out and burn them, horrible suburban bric-a-brac. Well then, what do we do, stand around?

GREGORY My dear fellow, haven't you read your handbook? It definitely states, at cultural meetings of the group such as poetry reading, the members shall adopt postures in keeping with the intellect of the individual without sacrificing the mood of the work. We are thus irrevocably united as a group in relationship to the poem being read.

TONY I see. Well you start, and I'll sort of stand loosely so I can sort of slide into something as it comes over me.

GREGORY We will commence with a work by myself. This I consider to be the

most significant contribution to the art of this century. It is an abstract poem in which I have successfully transferred into words the emotions which the abstract painter expresses on his canvas.

TONY   Oh, I shall look forward to this.

GREGORY   I have entitled it *Tin-can*.

TONY   *Tin-can*. Hm . . . let's see, I think I'll lean up against the fireplace with one arm up suggesting the lid's been opened.

SIDNEY   Look at them. Three on the window-sill, two under the table, three upside-down against the wall and seven on top of the bookcase. I think we'd better phone for the hurry up wagon, have them taken away.

GREGORY   Quiet please. I can't get in the mood with talking going on. Right. *Tin-can*, by Gregory.

> Splish splash, splonk,
> Wooden shoes, red socks,
> Coffins, tombstones and tranquillisers.

TONY   Very good, very significant that is.

GREGORY   I hadn't finished had I?

TONY   Oh, I'm very sorry.

GREGORY   Aspirins and driving tests,
> Jet planes and skeletons,
> Frog singing to egg timer,
> Calendars and candles, upside down,
> Plastic apples on coconut,
> Splish Splash, splonk.

TONY   Is that it?

GREGORY   Yes, that is it.

TONY   Marvellous, I wish I could write like that. Are you all right? By jove, you look washed out.

GREGORY   It's just the emotional strain of reading it. The vibrations sap my energy.

TONY   Yes, I know how it is, it's a pity we burnt the chairs, we could have had a sit down.

GREGORY   Did you like the poem?

TONY   Sensational. What an emotional experience. I haven't heard anything like that since *The Road to Mandalay*. Who's next?

GREGORY   Rupert.

SIDNEY   Oh we haven't got another one. Let's get the booze out.

TONY   Do you mind. If you can't appreciate the delicacy of the works, you might at least have the courtesy to keep your cakehole closed. Bill, what are you doing?

BILL   I've adopted a pose. In readiness for the next one.

TONY   Very funny, now come out of the sideboard before I clout you one. Carry on Rupert.

RUPERT   My piece is rather more spiritual. It is an outcry from the soul of my grandfather.

TONY   Ah . . . that should be good. I feel definite octogenarian tendencies coming over me. I think I'll lie on the floor with my feet up. Oh, hallo Greta, I didn't see you under the carpet. I hope this is as good as the last one. (*whispers*) I couldn't

half do with a cup of tea couldn't you?

GREGORY Quiet. If you please Rupert.

RUPERT This poem I am sending to UNESCO for translation into eighty-four different languages. But for the purposes of this reading, I shall render it in the original English.

SIDNEY If it's anything like the other one it won't really matter.

GREGORY Do we have to have this troglodyte here?

SIDNEY What does he mean? What did he call me? Where's that dictionary? Troglodyte. T-r-o-g- . . . Trog . . . here we are Troglodyte. Cave dweller of Western Europe . . . an anthropoid ape. Here, anthropoid ape . . . that's insulting isn't it?

TONY Well, it all depends on what context it's used in. In this case, it's intended to indicate a certain . . .

BILL Hit him Sid.

TONY No don't. Please. This is my first day at home evening . . . don't spoil it please . . .

BILL Punch his nose in.

TONY I'll punch yours in if you don't keep quiet. This is a cultural evening, we've having no bounce ups in here. What must my friends think of you? . . . I must apologise for the behaviour of these two hooligans.

GREGORY Quite all right old man, we understand. This display of primitive vulgarity shows exactly why we've cut ourselves off from the mass.

SIDNEY Oooh, isn't he superior? I'd just like to get him inside a ring, one round that's all . . .

TONY That's right go on, show me up. It was a mistake asking you to stay.

GRETA Oh please be quiet, all this quarrelling is interfering with my perceptive aura.

TONY You see, you've upset Greta now. Her perceptive aura has gone for a burton. That can be very nasty that can. Now keep quiet and listen to Rupert. All right Rupert, let's have you lad. Poke your head out of your sweater.

RUPERT I've called this poem, *Blank Details*.

TONY Ah yes, *Blank Details*, I feel a sort of purple mood coming over me. I think for this I shall sit cross legged on the floor, yogi style with one foot tucked behind my neck. Proceed.

RUPERT *Blank Details*, by Rupert.

       Straw in the wind,
       Straw in the wind,
       Straw in the wind,
       Straw in the wind,
       Straw in the wind,
       Fly, fly, fly,

TONY Marvellous. That's got my vote for the Nobel Prize for a start. He's captured the mood completely. I don't know how he gets so deep I really don't. What an insight he's got into the nature of things. Well done Rupert, seldom have I been so moved.

SIDNEY Straw in the wind, fly, fly, fly, what does that mean?

TONY Look Sid, I can't be bothered to explain to you . . . if you have to ask what it

means, you'll never know. You've either got it, or you haven't got it, that's all there is to it.

BILL Can I read my poem now?

TONY Pardon?

BILL I've just written a poem. Can I read it?

TONY I somehow don't think the sort of poems you write will be suitable for this gathering. We are not interested in young ladies from various parts of the country.

BILL No, no I've written an abstract poem.

TONY Don't be ridiculous, one has to be sympathetic with the symbolism of existence to turn out that sort of stuff. Get back in the sideboard.

GRETA No, let's hear what the little savage has written. It might provide some light relief after the intensity of the last two offerings.

TONY Oh very well, make it quick, and don't take the mickey.

BILL Thank you. Ahem. *Incandescent* by William.

      Hic Haec Hock,
      Rinky tinky on purple grass,
      Shafts of light, hob nailed boots
      Tramping down the bamboo
      That grows upwards, downwards, sideways,
      into the concrete cosmos,
      Life is mauve, I am orange,
      Hic hac hoc.

TONY What a load of rubbish. You buffoon. Rinky tinky on purple grass. What does that mean? You're orange and life is mauve. I have never heard such unadulterated codswallop in my life. Get back in the sideboard this minute.

GREGORY Wait. How dare you speak to a genius like that?

TONY I beg your pardon?

GREGORY A genius.

TONY What him? A genius. He doesn't know how to spell it.

GREGORY That was without a doubt the most inspired stimulating piece of poetry I have ever heard. Transcending anything anyone in this group has ever created. I'll never be able to write such a masterpiece as that.

TONY Yes, but he's a dolt. He can't do anything.

GREGORY Can't do anything. In a few brilliantly conceived lines he has summed up the human capacity for suffering and its struggle for survival.

TONY Oh come now Gregory . . . surely it was empty, devoid of any symbolism . . . you made a mistake, he fooled you for a moment, analyse it, bamboo, hob nailed boots, well it doesn't mean anything to me. My aura of perception didn't even wobble. Greta, what did you think?

GRETA It was like a revelation. It transported me to another plane. For the first time I saw the fifth dimension. Like a golden flash cleaving the skies, I was transported to the heights of delirium.

TONY See what you've done now, she's off. Why don't you keep quiet when there's ladies present?

GREGORY Life is mauve, I am orange . . . it says everything, I suggest we call it *The Last Poem*, there's nothing left to write about now. How do you do it?

BILL Well, I didn't think it was that good. It wasn't one of my best.

GREGORY Oh this man. What an intellect. He has reached the Gates of Perception and he says it wasn't one of his best. Would you do us the honour of taking over the leadership of our group?

BILL Well I . . .

TONY Oh, this is madness. Look, I've written a poem.

GREGORY I am talking to the master.

TONY Don't make any hasty decisions. Listen to mine. A little gem this is. Taken me four years to complete this has. All my soul has been poured into this little number. Listen. Life is cream, I am puce . . .

GREGORY Maudlin sentimental rubbish.

TONY I object. You haven't given me a fair hearing. Mine's the same as his, I've just changed the colours round. Hang on, don't go. Don't crown him yet. The rest of it is a knock-out. Revelations you've never dreamt of, unfolding before your eyes. Cop this.

> Steel rods of reason through my head.
> Salmon jumping where jump I,
> Camels on fire, and spotted clouds,
> Striped horses prance the meadow, wild,
> and rush on to drink at life's
> fountains deep. Life is cream, I am puce.
> Ching Chang Chollah.

GREGORY How dare you revile the group with such shallow trivial nonsense?

TONY It was as good as his, what's the matter with you? It's too deep for you, that's the trouble.

GREGORY What does it mean?

TONY What does it mean? I should have thought it was obvious. It's a plea for the er . . . um . . . well it's more of an outcry against the er . . . well you take the camels on fire under the spotted clouds. There's a provocative line if ever I've heard one. In that I've summed up the whole situation in the Gobi desert . . . and life's fountains deep, well, that's a plea for more water holes, that's why the camels are on fire, they're gasping, they haven't had a drop to drink since they left Kabul . . . it's a very long trip.

GREGORY And Ching Chang Chollah?

TONY They're the drivers, you won't get any change out of them, they couldn't care less. As long as they've got their striped horses they're quite happy. Well? (*pause*) Well, ask him to explain his then, go on, see what rubbish he comes out with.

GRETA There's no need to ask him, the words speak for themselves in every throbbing line. William is telling us that life is a fraud, that we are merely insects existing on the tail of a turtle.

TONY Did you tell them that?

BILL You heard the poem, I would have thought it was obvious.

TONY Don't listen to him, he's having you on, you can't make a nitwit like him leader of the group. Sid, of course Sid, my only ally, now the truth will come out. Go on Sid, expose him, tell them what a poltroon he is.

SIDNEY Who?

TONY Well him . . . this witless wonder here. Hurry up, tell them before they

have the laurel wreath on his head.

SIDNEY   What him, William, the greatest intellect ever to come out of Australia?

TONY   Betrayed. Stabbed in the back in my hour of need.

SIDNEY   Yes, you couldn't have done better picking this intellectual giant as your leader. What a scholar he was. Teaching the professors he was when he was five . . . turned his back on society, disillusioned at nine . . .

TONY   It was the other way round. They tried to lose him in the bush.

SIDNEY   A legend at thirteen, this boy . . . the wandering Einstein of Queensland, they called him.

TONY   What are you hoping to get out of this?

GREGORY   This only confirms what his work has already told us. He is obviously a man of extreme literacy and learning. A worthy successor to me. All in favour say aye.

OMNES   Aye.

GREGORY   I, Gregory, hereby relinquish leadership of our group and invest you, William, with all the powers that go with all titles and privileges that go with it.

TONY   Titles and privileges, so that's what you're up to Mr James, you've been sitting there reading the rule book. Show me that. 'The leader of the group receives from levies from the other members a remuneration of no less than five hundred pounds per year so that he may be exempted from the need to work and may spend all his time on contemplation and intellectual pursuits.' Five hundred a year, is that right Gregory?

GREGORY   Oh yes, and his lieutenant gets three hundred and fifty.

TONY   Who's his lieutenant?

SIDNEY   It says here the leader has the privilege of choosing his own lieutenant.

TONY   At three fifty a year.

SIDNEY   Yeah.

TONY   And that's what you're after. Well you've had that, because it also says here that the leader can only choose for his lieutenant a man who has proved his intellectual qualifications by having produced an original cultural piece of work.

SIDNEY   Exactly, I shall now read an abstract poem I've just written. *Limbo*, by Sidney.

TONY   Oh this is getting farcical. I should have the job.

GREGORY   Quiet please, Sidney's going to read to us.

SIDNEY   *Limbo* by Sidney.
Mauve world, green me,
Black him, purple her,
Yellow us, pink you.

GRETA   Beautiful, beautiful.

SIDNEY   Lead pipes, fortune made,
Six to four, came in second,
Green country, blue Harringay and White City.
Hic haec hoc.

GREGORY   I can't take any more, all this sensuous excitement in one evening. What an experience to hear such beauty, such translucent symbolism. How you must know life, Sidney.

SIDNEY   Oh I do, boy.

GRETA   How you must have suffered to produce work like that.

SIDNEY   Suffered . . . I've been in agony sometimes.

GREGORY   We must have Sidney as our leader's lieutenant.

TONY   You don't know what you're saying. He's a fake. He's only after the loot. Why, before you came in he was saying what a load of idiots you are.

GREGORY   We are idiots compared with him.

GRETA   Sidney, Sidney, I feel the vibrations between us growing stronger and stronger, some red, some yellow . . .

SIDNEY   Yeah, all right love, we'll sort them out later, eh?

GREGORY   Sidney, will you do us the honour of becoming our second in command?

SIDNEY   Certainly, it'll be a pleasure.

TONY   Wait, he's taking you on, it's the cider you've been drinking, it's inflamed your senses . . . look I've written another poem, it's better than his . . . Jake was a coward, a great big fellow with a turned up nose . . .

GREGORY   Get out.

TONY   It's a funny old world we live in, but the world's not entirely to blame, it's the rich that gets the credit and the poor that gets the blame.

SIDNEY   Throw him out. He's a troglodyte.

GREGORY   Yes, throw him out.

TONY   It's my house. You can't throw me out. Here you are, here's one. *The Highwayman*. He wore a French cocked hat on his forehead, and a bunch of lace at his chin. And the Highwayman came riding, with his whiskers soaked in gin. No? All right. Here you are . . .

SIDNEY   Sling him out.

TONY   No . . . put me down . . . I'll have the law on you. Layabouts, get back to work. Useless members of society, parasites. There's a green eyed yellow idol to the south of Katmandhu, there's a little wooden cross up on the hill . . .

(*Door slams. Frantic banging on the door*)

TONY   Let me in. Let me in. I'm still a member. There's a little old log cabin across the great divide, where lives a grizzled old prospector, by the name of Andy Clyde. What about our aims for improving the world? It was pouring with snow on the Equator, the icebergs were melting fast . . . oh I can't be bothered with them. I'll go down the coffee house, there's bound to be another movement started up since yesterday. I'll start one of my own. How did that poem of Sid's go now? Mauve world, green me, black him, purple her . . . that's it, that'll get them. A breakaway group. We'll be anti-everything. The new intellectual movement to shake the world. Or shall I go to the pictures? Yes, I might as well, I think that's more my hammer. Taxi.

5.0 AT YOUR REQUEST
(Continued)
The music you have liked for
introduced and played by
Sandy Macpherson
at the BBC theatre organ

6.15 GEOFFREY WALLIS
at the piano

6.30 News Summary
ROUNDABOUT
News, views and music
Tuesday edition
Introduced by
McDonald Hobley
with
Bill McGuffie
Records from the Theatre:
' Showboat '
Topic for Motorcyclists:
Peter Arnold
Sporting Memory: Raymond Baxter
Films on Release: Gordon Gow

6.29 Weather and News Headlines
followed by Tonight's Topic
BBC West of England Light Orchestra
(Leader, Frederick Lunnon)
Conductor, Frank Cantell
Produced by Denys Jones

Shipping Forecast at 5.58 on 1,500 m.

6.45 ' THE ARCHERS '
A story of country folk
Written by
Edward J. Mason and Geoffrey Webb
Edited by Godfrey Baseley
Produced by Tony Shryane
(BBC recording)

7.0 Greenwich Time Signal
RADIO NEWSREEL

7.25 SPORT

7.30 News Summary
Wilfred Pickles in
HAVE A GO!
visits
the village of
Stanway, Gloucestershire
with Mabel at the table
and Harry Hudson at the piano
Presented by Stephen Williams
to be repeated on Sunday at 11.0 a.m.

8.0 Tony Hancock in
HANCOCK'S HALF-HOUR
with
Sidney James, Bill Kerr
Warren Mitchell
Fenella Fielding, Fraser Kerr
Written by
Alan Simpson and Ray Galton
Produced by Tom Ronald
(BBC recording)

8.30 News Summary
' THE
DREAMING SUBURB '
A serial in twelve parts
adapted from his novel
by R. F. Delderfield
EPISODE 9
Miss Baker........Dorothy Holmes-Gore
The Carvers:
Jim.....................Malcolm Hayes
Archie...................David March
Maria....................Sheila Manahan
Bernard...............Henry Davies
Boxer...................David Spenser
The Frasers:
Esme...................Simon Lack
Elaine.................June Tobin
The Hartnells:
Ted....................Trevor Martin
Margy.................Betty Baskcomb
Louise Strawbridge........Beryl Calder
Edith Clegg...........Catherine Salkeld
Sydney Frith..........Trader Faulkner
Jean McInroy..............Rita Staines
Mr. Hargreaves........Norman Claridge
Gloria.................Kathleen Helme
Other parts played by members of the
BBC Drama Repertory Company
Edited by Cynthia Pughe
Produced by Norman Wright
(BBC recording)

9.0 Alan Dell's
DATE WITH A DISC

9.30 News Summary
TUESDAY TUNETIME
presents
THE SHOWBOAT
A moving sound stage of
music and songs
from the world of entertainment
Sidney Torch
conducts the
BBC Concert Orchestra
(Leader, William Armon)
and the Showboat Singers
Olga Gwynne, Cherry Lind
Bill Newman
with contrasts from
The Dennis Wilson Trio
Research and script by Neil Stevens
Introduced by
Patricia Hughes and Jimmy Kingsbury
Produced by Charles Beardsall

10.30 Greenwich Time Signal
NEWS

10.40 SERENADE
IN THE NIGHT
featuring
Bill Bowen and his Orchestra
Henry Krein
and the Montmartre Players
The William Davies Quartet
and Renata
Introduced by Alexander Moyes
Produced by
James Dufour and Gareth Walters

Keeping his date
Alan Dell has a Date with a Disc at

11.55 LATE NEWS

12.0 Big Ben
Close Down
followed by
Shipping Forecast on 1,500 m.

HANCOCK IN HOSPITAL

'I'd give my plate of mince tonight for a pencil to stick down it.'

Everyone has, at some time or other, either been in hospital, or has visited someone in hospital, so we all know what it's about; the bunch of grapes, the bottle of barley water, the packet of boiled sweets, the smell wafting up the nose and permeating everything it comes in contact with, the noise emanating from the broken castor on the food trolley or the enamel dishes as they hit the floor just as it's all gone quiet. And then there's the silence.

The dreadful moment when the conversation, across the entire ward, stops dead. Eyes, no longer looking at people, fix upon the bed sheets or the tubes that wire the patient to Radio Two. Those wonderful moments at home, when silence between two people can say so much, do not seem to exist in the hospital situation; instead there is this panic-stricken urgency to say something, anything, rather than admit to the silence. It is then, in those singular circumstances peculiar to hospitals, that topics of conversation become more banal than meaningless. Richard Briers referred to this show as his 'favourite bit of nonsensical dialogue . . . where Sid and Tony are talking about the weather, and how difficult it is to get cold when you're hot.'

Another piece in this script that Richard loves is the dialogue – akin to the scene in *The Reunion Party* on television a few years later when Hancock is trying to remember the name of the man who was in the next bed to Dopey Kent – in which Bill is trying to communicate the name of some chap that he had met, but couldn't remember his name. And every hospital visiting time must feature the well-meaning and good-intentioned personality, as pictured here by Patricia Hayes, with her offer of 'would you like a biscuit?' This portrait of the lonely figure, with the only visitors being the unwelcome variety, was painted briefly in a much earlier script, 'The Matador', episode twelve of the second series. This show featured Hancock suffering from an advanced case of 'malingery', and Alan and Ray summed up the commitment to hospital visiting with these lines, spoken by Tony Hancock: 'It's always the same when you're ill. Lifelong friends . . . they come to visit you, knock back your chocolate biscuits, talk to the bloke in the next bed, and they've gone.'

That's it really, settle down for the last in the present series of *Hancock's Half-Hour* . . . with a packet of crisps and a pint of winkles . . . you can't whack it mate!

HANCOCK IN HOSPITAL

Script by
ALAN SIMPSON AND RAY GALTON

Recorded: 28 June 1959
Broadcast: 15 December 1959
Starring:
TONY HANCOCK
SIDNEY JAMES
BILL KERR
PATRICIA HAYES
JOAN FRANK

Produced by
TOM RONALD

(*slight chatter*)

NURSE O'HARA   Ah, good afternoon to you Mr Hancock, and how are we feeling today?

TONY   On not so bad nurse, sitting up and taking notice, like the weather, up and down. Keeping cheerful, looking on the bright side.

NURSE   Ah, that's the way. I wish all our patients were cheerful like you.

TONY   Ah well, that's all you can be isn't it? When you're in hospital you've just got to make the best of it. There's always somebody worse off than yourself. Count your blessings, that's what I always say. It's no good lying here moping, keep smiling, keep your chin up and remember, every cloud has a silver lining.

NURSE   Well, you're doing very nicely, doctor's very pleased with you.

TONY   Is he really? Oh, I am glad, for his sake. He's done his job and I've got to do mine. When do you reckon the plaster will be coming off?

NURSE   Now don't you go worrying about that, you've got to give that leg a chance to set properly.

TONY   Yes of course you're quite right. We mustn't rush things. It's just that one gets restless lying in bed like this . . . I notice it more than most people you see, an outdoor type like me. We athletes, we have to keep moving you see. It's purgatory being kept in one position all the time. It's like keeping a magnificent tiger in a cage. Oh dear, how they must be missing me at the White City.

NURSE   [Oh, do you go dog racing then?

TONY   Athletics dear. Throwing things, jumping about, running, all that lark. Tell me honestly nurse, you can be frank with me, I don't mind, I can take it . . . do you think I'll ever be able to do the three-mile steeplechase again?

NURSE   Oh, I wouldn't worry about it. Yesterday you were wondering if you'd ever play at Wimbledon again, and the day before who'd take your place at Twickenham, and last week you couldn't wait to get back to Wembley for the figure skating championships . . . not to mention the Grand Prix at Silverstone, and the Boat Race next year.

TONY   You've been talking to the other nurses haven't you. Bigmouths. That's all you ever do, stand around patients' beds chatting . . . know everybody's business don't you? Come on, get my pillow bashed up and hoppit.]

NURSE   Would you like your face washed?

TONY   No I wouldn't.

NURSE   It's visiting day today. Don't you want to look nice?

TONY   No I don't. I won't get any, and I'm certainly not going to have my face washed for all that lot of visitors.

NURSE   How do you know you won't get any visitors?

TONY   Because I've been here three weeks, and I haven't had any yet. Not a nibble. They've forgotten all about me, and don't think I haven't noticed. It's very embarrassing on Wednesdays and Sundays. I feel a right charlie sitting here sometimes. Every other bed in the ward piled high with visitors. And I have to sit up with my headphones on, smiling as if I don't care. I've heard them. Nobody visiting him again today, poor man, take a biscuit over to him.

NURSE   Oh come now, it's not as bad as that.

TONY   It is, mate. I'm unwanted. It's very sad. Nobody's been in, not even a doctor. It's very heartbreaking.

NURSE You've got a lot of company, all the other patients.

TONY Company. This lot. They don't talk to me. Haven't said a word to me since I arrived. They don't like me. [I've tried making friends with them, and what happens? As soon as I wake up in the morning and say hallo, on go their headphones and that's them finished till lights-out.] I'm a very lonely man. If it wasn't for you bringing my boiled egg round in the morning I'd go bonkers. You're a very comely young lady you know.

NURSE Now, now, stop that Mr Hancock, remember your temperature.

TONY No, no I mean it. You're on nights next week aren't you. I'll tell you what . . . you undo the weights on my leg, and about two o'clock in the morning, I'll climb on the bed trolley and drag myself down to the duty room for half an hour.

NURSE You'll do no such thing. Now come along, the visitors will be in in a minute. I'll run the flannel over your face.

TONY No, what's the point. (*splutters*) Oooh, that hospital soap, what do they use that for, stripping paint? Oh dear, here use some of mine. I've got a box full here, all different colours. Have a flannelful of gardenia. Oh dear, all this trouble just for other people's visitors. All I hope is there's something good on the headphones.

NURSE Oh you poor man.

TONY Don't you poor man me. I don't want your sympathy. (*airy*) I don't care if I don't have any visitors. I don't like visitors. Very boring. There's nothing to say to them. You just sit looking at each other for two hours . . . waiting for the bell to go. You're glad to see them go and they're glad to get out of it. Yes, I'm quite thankful I don't have anybody coming to see me. It's quite a nice change to be on your own. Bore me stiff visitors do.

(*bell, crowd stampeding, approaching*)

TONY Here they come. The Charge of the Light Brigade. Look at them, pounding up the ward, anybody would think there was a sale on. Stand by my leg, there's a good girl, they knock it about something horrible with their baskets.

NURSE You are in a bad mood.

TONY I have every right to be.

(*chatter of visitors*)

TONY Hark at them, rabbiting away. It sounds like the birdhouse at Regent's Park. Oh dear, where's my headphones?

NURSE Well, I'll be off then, get back on duty. Do you want anything out of your locker?

TONY You're joking, of course. There's nothing in there. Nobody brings me anything. There's just the stuff I brought in with me. A toothbrush, a flannel, and a plastic bag, and my box of coloured soap. Go on, clear off, leave me in peace. Look at it, same as always, the only bed with no visitors. Not that I care. They'll notice I'm on my own again in a minute. Here we go.

WOMAN Hallo.

TONY Oh, cor, it's her. Hallo.

WOMAN On your own again?

TONY Yes.

WOMAN How are you feeling?

TONY All right, yes.

WOMAN Would you like a biscuit?

TONY No thank you, I've got plenty in my locker. Piled high with stuff it is. I have to throw most of it away, I can't eat it all. I'm always getting parcels because my people can't get here you see, they live so far away.

WOMAN Oh well, so long as you're not lonely.

TONY Oh no, I'm not, I'm not.

WOMAN You wouldn't like me to come and have a little chat with you after I've . . .

TONY No thank you.

WOMAN I expect you want to listen to your headphones.

TONY Yes please. I don't know why she comes to see her husband if she wants to talk to someone else. [I wish she wouldn't do it. They're all looking at me now. I wonder if I'm going red. I'll get my pen out and pretend I'm writing a letter.] Roll on four o'clock, get them out of here. Dear oh dear, look at the parcels being opened. Look at the food being unloaded. It's like the Surrey Docks in here some afternoons. [Thirty-three bedfuls of grub, patients and visitors. Well I'm glad it's nothing to do with me. You're better off on your own. (*sighs . . . lip smacking*)] I wonder what's on the headphones. Oh, *Woman's Hour*. How madly interesting. Mrs Griselda Plunkett is going to tell us how to fillet haddock. I'd better listen to this, this'll come in handy. There's nothing I want to do more than laying in bed with my leg up, filleting haddock. What's on the other programme. Oh cor, 'Handel's Water Music'. We'll get back to the haddock filleting I think. Oh, it's changed, it must have been a little haddock. What's this then? Lady Pamela Pilkington is going to tell all us ladies how to organise an embassy ball. Oh swipe me, how glittering. There must be over five million housewives around Stoke on Trent who want to know how to throw embassy balls. Oh get off woman.

WOMAN Are you talking to me? Do you want a biscuit?

TONY No I don't want a biscuit. Oh I think I'll have a kip. It's sitting up that draws the attention. I'll slide down under the bed trolley, they won't notice me then. (*yawns*) Oh dear . . . what a life. No grub, no visitors, nothing to listen to, and my leg up. Oh well, that's the way it goes. (*yawns . . . smacks lips . . . settles down*) Oh dear my leg itches. I'd give anything for a good scratch. It's this plaster. It does irritate when it's hot. I'd give my plate of mince tonight for a pencil to stick down it. [Another hour and fifty minutes before this lot go home. (*yawns*) I must ask the Lady Almoner for a jigsaw puzzle to do on the bed table. (*pause*) I wonder what Bridie looks like without her uniform on. She's a lovely girl. It's those black stockings that get me going.] (*pause*) I wonder what we've got for tea. Fishpaste again I expect. Let's see, Wednesday . . . that'll be salmon and shrimp, two thin bits of brown bread and a slice of angel cake. Build me right up that will. Oh well, I think I'll doze off. (*settling down for a doze.*)

SIDNEY There he is. Third one along.

BILL Where? I can't see him.

SIDNEY That one there. That big bulge under the bed-clothes with his leg up.

BILL He's asleep.

SIDNEY Let his leg down, that'll wake him up.

(*pulley being let down . . . wallop at the end of it*)

TONY (*yells in agony*)

SIDNEY (*pleasantly*) Hallo Hancock.

BILL Hallo Tub.

TONY (*still groaning*)

SIDNEY How are you feeling?

BILL What's the matter with him, isn't he glad to see us?

SIDNEY He'd better be. After coming all this way just to see him.

TONY Wind my leg up. Wind it up.

(*pulley being wound up*)

TONY (*groans in relief*) Oh dear, you fools, fancy doing a thing like that.

SIDNEY It won't hurt it, it's in plaster isn't it?

TONY It came right down on my good one. Half a hundredweight of plaster of Paris plus a leg, and you know how much my legs weigh. If I have to have the other one strung up as well, I'll . . .

SIDNEY Oh shut up moaning. We've come all this way to visit you, you might at least be pleasant. (*calls*) What are you lot all staring at? Go on, turn round and mind your own business.

TONY That's it, thank you. I'll be very popular when you've gone.

BILL Well . . . how's it going Tub?

TONY Well, I suppose it's . . . you don't have to put a mask on, you won't catch anything, I've got a broken leg. You can't catch broken legs. What did you have to bring him for?

BILL I wanted to come and see how you were getting on.

TONY Oh thank you very much, very considerate of you. I've been here three weeks, and now you decide to drag yourself out of bed and come and see how I am. Five hundred yards away you are . . . not one head poked round the door, no enquiries, no postcards, nothing. Very hurt I am, I thought I had friends . . . well now I know where I stand.

SIDNEY Well, I don't like hospitals.

TONY [Neither do I, that's why I thought you might come and cheer me up. It's only for two hours a week.

SIDNEY Two hours? Oh blimey, I thought it was only half an hour.

TONY You don't have to stay that long, you can go when you like. Well now you're here you might as well sit down.

BILL There's only one chair. I'll sit on the bed.

TONY Well mind my leg. And when the sister comes round, get off, they don't like it.]

SIDNEY Don't they smell funny, hospitals?

TONY Disinfectant.

BILL See, I told you there were germs about.

TONY It's to stop us catching anything from you lot. (*sniffs*) You stopped at the Hand and Racquet on the way, didn't you?

SIDNEY We only had a quick one.

TONY Well, it's disgusting coming into a hospital smelling like that.

SIDNEY Don't he go on?

TONY I have every right to go on, I lay in here day after day, nobody comes to see me, on my own the whole time and . . .

BILL We brought you some things.

TONY Oh. Oh I . . . Have you? That's very kind of you, I'm sorry I was a bit niggly. I feel rather ashamed of myself going off at you. What have you brought me?

BILL We thought you might be hungry so we brought you something to eat.

TONY Oh, that's very nice of you, it really is.

BILL Here you are. A packet of crisps and a pint of winkles.

TONY A packet of crisps and a pint of winkles. You've really been to a lot of trouble haven't you? A lot of thought went into that. You staggered out of the pub and saw the winkle stall standing there.

BILL Well yeah . . .

TONY The fact that you know very well I can't stand winkles didn't deter you in the slightest.

BILL Well, we thought it would be nice to bring you something.

SIDNEY We brought some shrimps as well.

TONY Ah that's better, I like shrimps, where are they?

SIDNEY We ate them on the way over.

TONY You ate them. You ate the shrimps which I like and bring me the winkles which I can't stand.

SIDNEY Well, we didn't have a pin.

BILL Where do you want the crisps?

(*crisps*)

TONY Don't tip them on the counterpane.

BILL I thought if I tipped them out we could all dip into them.

TONY Get them off the bed. If I get one of them down my plaster I've had it. A writhing mass of unscratchable itch. A packet of crisps and a pint of winkles. [Who else would bring that into a sick man besides you two? All the other lads here get cakes and pies and cooked dinners and tins of stuff, and fruit and chocolate. I can't remember any of them ever having a packet of crisps and a pint of winkles.

BILL Well, the shops were shut.

TONY They haven't been closed for three weeks.]

SIDNEY Well if you don't want them, we'll eat them. Have you got a pin?

TONY What a liberty. If the doctor comes round and sees you two eating winkles across my bed, what's he going to think?

SIDNEY Oh here's one. Ah, lovely. Come out you little beauty.

BILL Well . . . how are you feeling?

TONY Oh not too bad. They're very pleased with me actually. I'm going along very well. I'm the best patient they've ever had so they tell me, yes, the rest has done me good, I don't think I've ever felt so fit.

SIDNEY You don't look too good to me.

TONY Oh cor . . . winkles, crisps and now the knockers.

SIDNEY I'm just telling you what I think. I don't think you look at all well.

TONY Well, the doctor does. He says I'm doing marvellously.

SIDNEY Ah well, they always tell you that. They wouldn't tell you the truth.

TONY What do you mean?

SIDNEY Nothing, nothing, if they say you're doing all right then you must be doing all right. They should know what they're talking about.

TONY Well of course they should.

SIDNEY They're clever blokes, they've studied long enough.

TONY Well exactly.

SIDNEY It's just that I've never seen you look so pale. Ashen is more the word.

TONY Oh dear, oh dear, what a couple of cheerful charlies you two are.

SIDNEY Still, it's probably because you're inside all the time.

TONY Yes, that's it.

SIDNEY But I've never seen him looking so ashen have you Bill, all the years you've known him, have you ever seen him looking so ashen?

TONY [Do you mind? Do you mind talking about something else? Eh? Do you mind changing the subject?

SIDNEY Oh I'm sorry, I'm sorry.

TONY I feel perfectly well. There's nothing wrong with me, so change the subject. Talk about something else.

BILL (*pause*) What are you in here for?

TONY I beg your pardon?

BILL What are you in hospital for?

TONY What am I . . . I've broken my leg.

BILL Oh. How did you do that?

TONY Well stone me, you ought to know, it was you who left the bucket of water on top of the stairs. Honestly, adding insult to injury. What am I doing here?

SIDNEY Have you lost weight?

TONY No, I haven't lost weight.

SIDNEY Oh, I just wondered, I thought you were looking thinner . . . you're certainly looking ashen.]

TONY Do you have to keep talking about my health? Can't we talk about something else? You're supposed to have lots to talk about when you visit somebody in hospital.

SIDNEY All right, what do you want to talk about?

TONY Well, tell me the news. What's been happening?

BILL Oh the news. Oh yeah. What's been happening. Nothing much at all.

TONY Well there must be something to talk about. Think, have a think, what's been happening outside?

BILL Well . . . um . . . er . . .

(*tapping on locker . . . rhythmic annoying tap*)

TONY (*after a fair pause*) Don't keep tapping my locker.

SIDNEY Oh I'm sorry. (*pause*) Want a fag?

TONY You can't smoke in here.

SIDNEY Oh blimey, that's going to be a drag . . . how much longer is there?

TONY Another hour and a half.

SIDNEY Hour and a half . . . without a fag . . . oh dear.

(*Pause during which they make various noises. Clearing throats . . . bored stiff noises*)

SIDNEY What's the time?

TONY Another hour and twenty-nine minutes.

SIDNEY Oh.

(*another pause*)

BILL Here, guess who I saw yesterday?

TONY   Who?

BILL   What's his name . . . you know . . . that fellow who used to live round the corner . . . what's his name . . . you know him . . .

TONY   Ginger Williams.

BILL   No, not him. The other one.

TONY   Oh I remember, the tall bloke with the dark hair, who used to go out with that bird from across the . . .

BILL   No, not him. Oh, what's his name . . .

TONY   Not that funny bloke who used to live with his mother?

BILL   No. More recent than him . . . you know him . . . what's his name . . .

TONY   Describe him to me.

BILL   Well . . . shortish . . . fairish . . . medium build . . . oldish . . . looks younger than that though . . . nice fellow . . . you know him . . . oh, what's his name . . . his brother went out with that girl . . . what's her name . . . you know her . . .

TONY   Hilda.

BILL   No . . . the other one. The little girl who lives down the High Street . . .

TONY   Ethel.

BILL   No, that's the one who got married. No, I mean the other one . . . what's her name . . . well anyway, I saw him yesterday.

TONY   How was he?

BILL   Oh just the same. He never changes does he?

TONY   Doesn't he?

BILL   Well you know him better than I do.

TONY   Do I? Well, what about him?

BILL   Oh nothing. Nothing. I just saw him, that's all.

SIDNEY   What's the time?

TONY   One hour twenty-six minutes to go.

(Pause, during which Tony hums a bit. They clear throats, yawn, etc.)

TONY   Stop drawing on my leg.

SIDNEY   Oh, I'm sorry. I was just working out my winnings. Nine bob to come.

BILL   It's been warm, hasn't it?

TONY   Oh yes, very warm, I should say so, yes. By jove, yes, it's been warm all right, my word yes indeed.

BILL   I expect you've noticed it, laying there.

TONY   I have. My goodness me I have. Yes indeed, very warm it's been. I should say so, oh yes.

SIDNEY   It's not so bad when it's cold 'cos when you're cold you can always get warm, but when you're warm it's very difficult to get cool.

TONY   You're right there. You're very observant. Yes, it's very difficult to get cool when you're warm . . . yes it's been very warm, my goodness it has.

BILL   It can't help with your leg in plaster.

TONY   It doesn't. It certainly doesn't. It's very uncomfortable.

SIDNEY   Well it must be.

TONY   Well it is. Always is when it's warm, and it's certainly been warm hasn't it?

SIDNEY   Yes.

(Pause. Noises as before)

SIDNEY   Pillow all right?

TONY   Yes thank you, yes, it's fine, yes, very comfortable, thank you, yes, it's fine . . . yes, just right.

(*pause*)

SIDNEY   Have they tested your heart since you've been in?

TONY   No. Why?

SIDNEY   Oh I just wondered. I thought they would have.

TONY   Well why should they?

SIDNEY   Well it's just a precaution. You never know, do you?

TONY   You never know what?

SIDNEY   Nothing, I just thought as you're looking so ashen.

TONY   I'm not looking ashen. You've got ashen on the brain, what's the matter with you?

BILL   Harry Curtiss.

TONY   Who?

BILL   Harry Curtiss. He was the bloke I saw yesterday.

TONY   I've never heard of him.

BILL   Oh. Well he hasn't changed anyway.

TONY   Good luck to him.

SIDNEY   What's the time?

TONY   I don't know, my watch has stopped.

SIDNEY   Oh well, do they ring a bell when it's time for us to go?

TONY   Yes.

SIDNEY   Oh that's all right then.

TONY   (*hums to himself*) Nothing's happened then?

BILL   No. Oh yes, the council changed the dustbin yesterday.

TONY   Oh good, I am glad, we needed a new one. They used to leave more up the path than they put in the lorry.

(*pause*)

SIDNEY   Do you want a winkle?

TONY   No thank you.

SIDNEY   (*whispers*) Here.

TONY   (*whispers*) What?

SIDNEY   (*whispers*) That old boy over there, what's wrong with him?

TONY   (*whispers*) Not so loud. He's in for a check-up.

SIDNEY   (*whispers*) Oh. What are they checking him up for?

TONY   (*whispers*) We don't know, they haven't told him yet.

SIDNEY   (*whispers*) Oh. He looks a bit ashen too, don't he?

TONY   (*whispers*) Yes, I've noticed that.

SIDNEY   (*whispers*) Perhaps he's got the same as you.

TONY   I haven't got anything.

BILL   Here what's that old lady crying for down there, by the side of that man's bed?

TONY   Where? Oh. He's going home tomorrow. (*pause*) So nothing else has happened then?

BILL   No.

TONY   Oh. (*Pause. He whistles. Hums a bit. Clears throat*).

BILL   Have you got any bananas?

TONY   Where am I going to get bananas from?

BILL   I just thought you might have some.

TONY   Well I haven't. I wish I did have. Instead of a packet of crisps and a pint of winkles.

SIDNEY   [What's the time?

TONY   I don't know. There's a clock on the wall.

SIDNEY   Blimey, it's half past three, the big race is on, can I borrow your headphones?

(*headphones rattle*)

TONY   You're supposed to be visiting me, not listening to the radio.

SIDNEY   Hallo, they're under starter's orders.

BILL   Unscrew one of those headphones and pass it over.

TONY   Isn't it marvellous? Give them to me.

SIDNEY   No I want to listen to the race.

BILL   So do I.

TONY   Give them to me. (*they struggle*)

(*loud snap of springy steel as the headphones break*)

TONY   Now look what you've done, you've broken them. I'll have nothing to listen to all week now. Why don't you leave things alone? That's the only thing I used to enjoy, my radio.

SIDNEY   We can't listen to it now either, can we?

BILL   And you haven't got any bananas.

SIDNEY   And I've eaten all the winkles.

BILL   And there's no crisps left.]

SIDNEY   Here, look who's down in the end bed.

BILL   Who?

SIDNEY   Old Arthur Phillips. I haven't seen Arthur in years.

BILL   Neither have I.

SIDNEY   I wonder what he's doing in hospital. Poor old Arthur. It must be rotten for him stuck in hospital. Let's pop over and cheer him up.

(*chatter and footsteps*)

SIDNEY   (*going off*) Hallo Arthur, what are you doing in here then?

TONY   Well of all the nerve. He's got twelve people round his bed already. (*calls*) What about me then?

WOMAN   (*off*) You on your own again . . . do you want a biscuit?

TONY   Oh go away.

(*Hancock music all going wrong*)

NURSE   Come along now, wake up Mr Hancock, it's tea time. Get your tray up.

TONY   (*yawns*) Oh hallo Nurse . . . the visitors haven't gone yet then.

NURSE   No, another ten minutes yet. You haven't got any visitors again then?

TONY   Oh yes I've got two. My two best friends. There they are down there laughing and shouting.

NURSE   Well here's your tea then. Bread and butter fishpaste and angel cake.

TONY   Oh thanks very much. Ah this looks very nice. A packet of crisps and a pint of winkles! Ah this is it . . . I'm going to enjoy this.

SIDNEY Ah hallo Hancock.

TONY Oh, you've decided to come back.

SIDNEY Yes well there's only another ten minutes, soon be time to go home. He's a lad that Arthur isn't he?

BILL Yeah it's a pleasure visiting him.

SIDNEY Hallo, tea up.

NURSE Would your two visitors like a cup of tea?

SIDNEY Yes please dear.

BILL Can we have something to eat as well?

NURSE Sorry, that's for the patients.

SIDNEY Oh never mind, we'll have some of his.

TONY You won't, that's my tea, I don't get anything more till the mince tonight.

SIDNEY You've got three slices there, that's one each.

TONY You're not having any, I'm hungry.

SIDNEY So are we. Don't be so selfish. We take the trouble coming to visit you, you can at least share your tea with us.

BILL We brought you a packet of crisps and a pint of winkles.

TONY I never touched them.

SIDNEY You could have done, we brought them for you.

BILL It wasn't our fault you didn't like them.

SIDNEY Come on, give us a slice of fishpaste.

(*clatter of china*)

TONY Get your hands off my angel cake. Let go . . . Mind the tray . . . take the angel cake out of the fishpaste.

SIDNEY Well, let me have a bit then.

TONY No.

(*Tray falls on to the floor. Crockery smashing*)

TONY Oh well that's it then. All over the floor. Now none of us get any. They won't come round again. And there's mince tonight, and I don't like that. And all you brought in was a packet of crisps and a pint of winkles.

SIDNEY Well never mind, don't worry about us, we'll get something in the visitors canteen on our way out.

TONY Oh dear, what a life. Two hours visiting time can put you back three weeks.

(*pause with the appropriate noises*)

SIDNEY What's the time?

BILL Another five minutes.

SIDNEY Don't time drag.

TONY Look, why don't you go. There's no point in hanging it out. It's been very nice. I'm glad you came . . . now hoppit.

BILL Oh no, we came here to see you, and we're not going till the bell rings.

TONY Oh cor . . .

BILL When you only get two hours a week you want to make the most of it.

(*pause as before*)

TONY (*quickly*) Was that the bell?

BILL No.

TONY Oh!

SIDNEY Old Grandad Perkins died last week . . .

172

TONY Do you mind? . . .

(*pause as before*)

BILL Have you got any books we could read?

TONY No I haven't. I was asleep when the librarian came round. She only comes round once a fortnight. I'm the only one in the ward who hasn't got a book to read.

(*pause as before*)

TONY Well don't just sit there. Say something. Stone me, you were talking to Arthur Phillips for an hour and a half non-stop . . . surely you've got something to say to me. Anything. Something that'll last five minutes.

SIDNEY I'm fed up with talking, I've got a sore throat laughing so much with Arthur.

TONY Oh I'm glad he's been cheered up by my visitors.

(*pause as before*)

(*telephone bell ringing in the distance*)

TONY There it is, the bell, all go home. That's it. Thank you for coming, it's been very nice . . .

SIDNEY It's the telephone in the duty room.

TONY Well, the bell will be going any moment now, I wouldn't bother to wait . . .

BILL No we're going to stop till four o'clock, it's the least we can do.

SIDNEY It'll look bad if the other visitors stop and we go before time.

TONY No, no I won't mind.

BILL No we'll stay.

TONY Oh.

(*pause as before*)

TONY Oh dear, I think a bit of that angel cake's got down my plaster. Oh I'll be in agony tonight.

BILL Shall I poke my fountain pen down and scratch it for you.

TONY No thank you. You've broken everything else round the bed, you leave my leg alone.

(*pause as before*)

SIDNEY [Have you had your liver examined?

TONY Pardon?

SIDNEY Your liver. Perhaps that's why you're looking so ashen.

TONY Is that all you've got to talk about? I'm quite all right.

SIDNEY Well you know best. But you're the dodgiest looking one in this ward.

TONY I am not the dodgiest looking one in this ward, I'm very healthy . . . well, I was until two hours ago.]

(*bell rings*)

TONY There's the bell. Ha ha ha. The bell. Going home time. Thank you for coming, it's been very nice. I have enjoyed your company, and if you feel like coming to see me again next week – don't.

SIDNEY Well ta ta then, look after yourself.

BILL Cheerio Tub. It's been nice chatting to you again.

SIDNEY Yeah, and I hope that ashen face of yours isn't anything serious.

BILL & SIDNEY Cheerio.

TONY Yes cheerio.

(*People chattering as they leave. Silence*)

TONY Oh thank goodness for that. Peace at last. (*sighs with pleasure*)

NURSE Ah there you are Mr Hancock.

TONY Where did you expect me to be?

NURSE Now now. Cheeky monkey. Did you have a nice visiting hour?

TONY Oh yes, hilarious.

NURSE Well, I've got some good news for you. The doctor's just phoned, he says I've got to take the plaster off your leg.

TONY What now, so soon?

NURSE Yes, it's healed faster than we expected. He's just had a look at the X-ray . . . the plaster can come off and you can go home in a couple of days.

TONY No more visiting days.

NURSE No, not for you.

TONY Well come on, then me little darlin', let's get at it.

NURSE Right, we'll get the knife under that little lot and have it off in a jiffy . . . (*knife cutting through plaster*)

NURSE . . . Ah, that's coming nicely . . . yes, there it comes . . . nearly done . . . there. That's it.

TONY (*while she's doing it*) Oooh . . . aaaah . . . ooh, the air's getting to it. Oooh, I can't wait to have a good scratch. Oh lovely.

NURSE There. How does it feel?

TONY Oh marvellous.

NURSE Ah yes, that's perfect. Would you like to try and put your weight on it.

TONY Oooh can I?

NURSE Sure. Come on, up you get. Don't put too much pressure on it. Stand up and take the weight on your good leg.

TONY (*straining*) Ah . . . I'm doing it, look, I'm standing. I'm standing up . . . Oooooowwwwwww.

(*terrific crash as Tony comes a cropper*)

NURSE Mr Hancock what's happened?

TONY I slipped. My leg. My other one. Get some more plaster quick.

NURSE How did it happen? What did you slip on?

TONY Empty winkle shells. Hundreds of them. Get the doctor . . . and get me a private room. And no visitors. Oh, why don't people leave you alone?

BIOGRAPHIES

by Chris Bumstead

ALAN SIMPSON and RAY GALTON

Scriptwriters

Alan Simpson was born in Paddington in 1930, Ray Galton in 1929 in Brixton, and prior to their meeting at the Milford Sanatorium, where they were undergoing treatment for tuberculosis, Alan had been working as a shipping clerk and Ray had been employed by the Transport and General Workers' Union.

At the hospital, Alan and Ray wrote and performed their own comedy scripts over the internal radio system. Their first professional engagement was for the comedian Derek Roy, and the first complete radio show was *Calling All Forces*.

Their television credits include *Hancock's Half-Hour* and *Hancock, Steptoe and Son, Casanova*, various series for Frankie Howerd, Sid James and Les Dawson, several *Comedy Playhouse* plays and *Galton and Simpson* series, and the dramatisation of *Clochemerle*.

The film scripts of Galton and Simpson include *The Rebel, The Bargee, The Wrong Arm of the Law, Loot*, and the two Steptoe films. They were also involved in supplying additional material for *Up the Chastity Belt* and *The Magnificent Deadly Sins*.

The Hancock scripts, both from television and radio, are now published in book form, and have also been translated into many languages, particularly in Scandinavia where the stage show has been a great success.

More recently Alan Simpson has been on a sabbatical, while Ray has worked with Johnny Speight on *Room on the Top*, and with John Antrobus on the stage farce *When did you last see your Trousers?* at the Garrick.

Their last work specifically for the medium of radio was in 1959, on the last series of *Hancock's Half-Hour*.

TONY HANCOCK

Comic genius

Tony Hancock was born on 12 May 1924, in a semi-detached in Southam Road, Birmingham. Jack Hancock, his father, was a semi-professional music-hall artist, who was suffering from ill health when four years later the family moved into the Railway Hotel, as proprietors, in Bournemouth.

Educated at Durlston Court Prep School, Swanage, and later at Bradfield College, Berkshire, Tony Hancock was described as a 'medium' scholar but a fine all-round cricketer.

Leaving school at fifteen, he tried his hand at a few 'jobs' but found the pull of the theatre too strong in his blood. After a few pitfalls, he established himself as a stand-up comedian, touring local theatres entertaining the troops, and he passed an audition to join Ralph Reader's *Gang Show*.

Tony Hancock's film credits include *Orders Are Orders, The Rebel, The Punch and Judy Man* and *Those Magnificent Men in their Flying Machines*.

On television he is best remembered for the *Hancock's Half-Hour* and the *Hancock* series that he made for the BBC, but other credits include *The Tony Hancock Shows, The Blackpool Shows* and a 'straight' role in *The Government Inspector*.

Though never really happy with long-running stage shows, Tony Hancock appeared in two very successful revues with Jimmy Edwards, *London Laughs* and *Talk of the Town*. Other stage appearances included pantomime, The Royal Variety Performance, and provincial tours with his own show.

Radio was the medium which gave him the most important breaks in the struggle for acceptance, and, as if to return the compliment, Tony Hancock gave some of his best ever performances to that medium. He appeared in numerous variety shows and comedy series, including *Educating Archie*, before getting his first solo radio show, *Star Bill*, wherein the working relationship with Alan Simpson and Ray Galton first began to flourish.

And on 2 November 1954 the British public heard the opening show of *Hancock's Half-Hour*.

SIDNEY JAMES

Comedy Actor

Sidney James was born in Johannesburg on 18 May 1913, the son of South African vaudeville actors. He began his working life as a diamond digger, was promoted to a diamond polisher, became a stevedore, and dabbled in amateur boxing, eventually making the ranks of the professional boxing circles.

Sid had enjoyed frequent but small successes on the stage in South Africa before coming to England in 1946, where his amazing adaptability enabled him to portray such a convincing Cockney character that very few people ever doubted that he was born within the sound of Bow Bells.

In 1947 he appeared in his first film, playing Eddie Clanton in *Black Memory*, and was to go on to appear in some 117 films, including *The Lavender Hill Mob, Miss Robin Hood, Orders Are Orders* with Tony Hancock, and, of course, the tremendously popular *Carry On* series.

Although more widely recognised as a comedy actor, Sid's early film career was centred around the rough Cockney character who wavered on the edge of a criminal existence, but he was not averse to displaying his talents in other directions: singing, for example, in the stage show *Wonderful Town* and *Guys and Dolls* and again, on film, in the Tommy Steele movie *Tommy the Toreador*.

On television, apart from the many reruns of the *Carry On* movies, Sid is best remembered for his long-running success in *Bless This House* with Diana Coupland as his much-suffering wife. *George and the Dragon, Citizen James* and, of course, *Hancock's Half-Hour* are just three further examples of his many TV appearances.

After his work with Hancock in *Orders Are Orders*, it seemed quite natural that when Hancock, Galton and Simpson were assembling the cast for the first series of *Hancock's Half-Hour* on radio, they should seek Sid to join the team. The character that he was to play was reminiscent of his earlier film appearances: a rough diamond with just a hint of the criminal underworld.

ANDREE MELLY

Actress

Born 15 September 1932, in Liverpool, to Francis and Edith Melly. Educated at Belvedere High School, Liverpool, and Mon Fertile, Switzerland. Married to Oscar Quitack.

Andrée's film credits include *The Belles of St Trinian's*, *The Horror of it All*, *The Secret Tent* and *Brides of Dracula*.

Making her television début with a major role in the 1950 series of *Just William*, Miss Melly's other TV credits include *Hot Summer Night* and *The Navigators*.

Andrée's stage début was in 1941, at the Little Theatre, Southport, as Thomas in *Quality Street*, and it was to the legitimate theatre that she devoted most of her energies, appearing in such diverse productions as *The Ghost Writers*, *Plaintiff in a Pretty Hat*, *Reclining Figure*, *Boeing Boeing*, *The Killing of Sister George*, *As You Like It* and *The Importance of Being Earnest*.

On radio, Andrée starred in the world première of *Rhinoceros*, appeared in numerous plays, the series *Petticoat Line*, *Woman's Hour*, and more recently *Just a Minute*, but her first venture into radio comedy was, of course, with *Hancock's Half-Hour*.

BILL KERR
Comedy Actor

It is much to my regret that I have been unable to contact Bill Kerr at the time of writing. Therefore, if the following biography appears a trifle sketchy – my apologies.

Bill, who really *was* born in Wagga Wagga, made his stage début in vaudeville in Melbourne at the age of seven. As a child he appeared in numerous Australian films, as well as singing and dancing on stage, and as time went on he began to build up a comedy routine on Australian radio.

Having worked his way to England in 1947, he was quick to make an impact on the British public with appearances on *Variety Bandbox*, opening his act with 'I'm from Wagga Wagga, I've only got four minutes!' Bill Kerr starred in several radio comedies before joining the 'H.H.H.' team, and was very successful in films such as *The Dam Busters, Appointment in London, You know what Sailors Are* and numerous *Carry On* films.

Going back to his vaudeville roots, perhaps, Bill turned to the musical stage productions and appeared in *Teahouse of the August Moon* and *Damn Yankees*.

On television, he did a *Doctor Who* series with Patrick Troughton in 1967, had a large and long-running role in the 'soap' opera *Compact* during the fifties, and appeared with Sid James in the BBC series *Citizen James*.

Bill has also toured with Spike Milligan in the show *The Bed Sitting Room*, and appeared in numerous films and television serials for children's television.

Returning to Australia, a few years ago, he had a starring role in *Gallipoli*, and is in constant demand by the Australian television and film circles as a well-established character actor.

JOSEPHINE EDWINA (HATTIE) JACQUES

Comedy Actress

Hattie was born on 7 February 1924, in Sandgate, Kent, to Mary Adelaide and Robin Rochester Jacques. Her father was an RAF pilot who was killed in an air crash when Hattie was only eighteen months old. As a child, she took ballet lessons and spent the greater part of her youth helping out at her grandfather's pawn shop in King's Road, Chelsea.

Educated at Godolphin and Latymer School, she left in 1939 and joined the Red Cross during the war, falling in love with an American Major. When he was killed in action, it took a long time for Hattie to recover from the shock.

After a short spell as an arc welder, Hattie landed a job at the Players Theatre, London, and in 1944, at the age of twenty, she took to the stage for the princely sum of £3.00 a week.

In 1949 she married actor John Le Mesurier, a marriage that brought forth two children, Robin (1954) and Kim (1958), and lasted for sixteen years.

Because of her size (she was apparently twenty stone at the age of fifteen) it seemed natural that the greater part of her career was to be devoted to comedy roles. In an interview for *TV Times* (3 June 1977) she joked, 'Can anyone be completely happy and fat? I can't; there's too much of me to worry about!'

Hattie's stage, film, television and radio credits are a positive kaleidoscope of the entertainment world in the fifties and sixties. On stage she loved pantomime and particularly the part of the Fairy Queen in *Sleeping Beauty*, but other appearances included: *The King Stage, The Bells of St Martins* and *Large as Life*.

On television Hattie Jacques is probably best remembered for her shows with Eric Sykes, but her credits also include: *Our House, The Tony Hancock Show, Catweazle, The World of Beachcomber* and *Frankie Howerd*.

In films, as a founder member of the *Carry On* series, she appeared in nearly all the *Carry On* films, plus *Oliver Twist, Pickwick Papers, School For Scoundrels* and many, many more.

On radio, Hattie appeared in *ITMA, Educating Archie, Calling All Forces* and, of course, *Hancock's Half-Hour*, where she played that marvellous character 'Griselda Pugh'.

KENNETH WILLIAMS

Comedy Actor

Kenneth Williams was born on 22 February 1926, in St Pancras, London, son of Charles George and Louise Alexandra Williams.

Kenneth was educated at Lyulph Stanley School and Bolt Court, London, and was trained as a lithographic draughtsman.

Following his army call-up, he was sent to India with the Royal Engineers, but soon got a desire for acting and was accepted for the Combined Services Entertainment.

Shortly after his return to England, Kenneth Williams made his stage début in *The First Mrs Fraser* with the Newquay Rep. Ken's London stage début was at the Scala, in December 1952, as Slightly in *Peter Pan*. Other stage credits included: *The Buccaneer, Gentle Jack, One Over the Eight, The Undertaking* and Joe Orton's *Loot*.

Apart from the numerous *Carry On* films, in which, incidentally, he appeared more than any other member of the team, Kenneth Williams' film career has been prolific and varied, including: *Trent's Last Case, The Beggar's Opera, Innocents in Paris, The Seekers, Raising the Wind* and *The Hound of the Baskervilles*.

Ken's appearances on television read like a roll-call of the most popular TV shows of the sixties and seventies. As well as having been interviewed no less than five times on the Michael Parkinson Show, he appeared in *The Eamonn Andrews Show, What's My Line?, Jackanory, Arena, Looks Familiar, Star Turn, International Cabaret* and *Hancock's Half-Hour*.

Ken, the author of several books, has also made many LP records including *The World of Kenneth Williams* and *The Best of Rambling Syd Rumpo*.

It is, however, radio that Kenneth Williams sees as his favourite medium and it was with radio that his name became associated most often, prior to the *Carry On* films. Such programmes as *Round the Horne, Beyond Our Ken, Stop Messing About* and *Just a Minute* are just a very small selection of his radio output, which, of course, included that ever popular *Hancock's Half-Hour*.

MOIRA LISTER

Actress

Born 6 August 1923, in Cape Town, South Africa, to Margaret and James Lister. Educated at Parktown Convent, Johannesburg. Married to Vicomte d'Orthez.

Moira's film credits include *Grand National Night*, *A Run for Your Money*, and *The Yellow Rolls Royce*, while on television she has appeared in *Major Barbara* and *Simon and Laura*, plus the long-running series *The Very Merry Widow*.

The greater part of Moira's career has been devoted to the theatre, and this work includes *Twelfth Night, She Stoops to Conquer, French without Tears, King Lear* and *Move over Mrs Markham*.

Her autobiography was published in 1969, entitled *The Very Merry Moira*.

Miss Lister's only concession to the medium of radio seems to have been her one-series appearances in *Hancock's Half-Hour*.

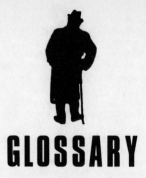

GLOSSARY

Being a poor attempt to explain the unexplainable
and to direct the serious student of East Cheam
Language (Lingo) towards a greater understanding
of the phraseology employed in the scripts.
Chris Bumstead

BIRD
A woman; attractive person of the female sex.

Originating from Edwardian days, when Robert Browning, played by Charles Laughton, would write secret love letters to his sweet-heart, Jane Austin-Rover, referring to her as his 'precious nightingale that doth write and sing, and shout and dance and do anything . . .' etc. Thus began the craze of referring to one's female partner or lover (or both) as being a particular species of bird (a craze, incidentally, recently revived for the purposes of the *Guardian*'s personal column on St Valentine's day). It was only when the myriad poets and thinkers of society had run through the entire *Observer's Book of Bird Names* that the usage slipped to being general to the species, i.e. 'bird'. Thereafter one referred to one's fiancée simply as 'one's bird', and the art of *l'amour* became 'the art of bird-pulling'.

In the mid-1980s the word is regarded as having chauvinistic overtones and is no longer used in the best circles, but is still, however, used in the stalls, as in 'the bird with the tray of ice-creams'.

BONKERS
Crazy; a trifle insane; mad.

In the gentle art of Cowley-waltzing (a forgotten breakaway routine from the Morris-dancing fraternity), a 'bonker' was the fool, comic or jester. He would often be played by the village idiot who would carry a stick of variable length, attached to which was a sheep's bladder filled with calf's foot jelly, and he would gaily strike his head with this implement until such time as either the dance had finished, or he had been knocked completely senseless. Very few 'bonkers' ever survived more than a few appearances before becoming deranged and ending up in a hurry-up wagon. The term 'bonkers' therefore, in the East Cheam colloquial, means 'mad', as in 'You must be bonkers!'

BUFFOON
A person of low intelligence fond of making low and coarse jests.

Another word for buffoon is 'merryandrew', meaning a person who makes low jests by employing grimaces and antic postures, and it is easier to define the words together. Many centuries ago a wayward spittle-splicer, with no spittles to splice, was called an 'andrew' after King Andrew of Gwent who, in AD 754, decreed that all spittles would be bound and not spliced. Thus a 'merryandrew' was an 'andrew' who was a little light-headed, and since the 'buffoon' was the implement, now rendered redundant, used in spittle-splicing, the two words became synonymous, with the original word, merryandrew, being lost in antiquity and the word buffoon becoming more generally used to describe someone of a seemingly low intellect. Its usage in the East Cheam vocabulary is one of contempt.

CAKEHOLE
Mouth; area of face containing tongue.
(*See also* Pudding Shute)

CHARLIE
A person who, by the actions of others and the stupidity of his own, is made to appear totally witless.

Lord Charles Fotherington-Grudge, 16th Earl of Thorpe, was the butt of a practical joke by some of his cricketing pals, in which they 'arranged' for Charles to make a speech on the subject of the bye-laws of cricket at a public meeting, but introduced him instead to the audience of the Wimbledon Hippodrome Music Hall Theatre as the new comic, 'A right Charlie'.
(*See also* Mug)

CLOBBER
1) To hit; to resort to physical violence.
2) Clothing; attire; articles of clothing.

1) Clobber, when used in the sense 'to hit', is a direct misderivation of the term 'to club' or 'to clubber', meaning to strike with a sharp instrument in a dull manner. To clobber, in the East Cheam vocabulary, refers to the fact that all hopes of normal communication are at an end and somebody is about to get a 'punch up the bracket'.
2) Clobber, meaning 'clothing', is derived from an eighteenth-century word used by shoe-repairers in the East Cheam Cobblers Lodge to refer to a paste used in cobbling to fill, or patch up, holes in leather. It came to mean any footwear that had been patched up and, eventually, to any article of clothing that was not perfect in every way.

COALBOXED
Finalised; completed, possibly ahead of schedule; stopped.

When an idea or process, having been thought through to its fullest conclusion, is then stopped because some obstacle renders the original idea impossible the phrase is often used: 'That's coalboxed that, then!' This is derived from Cheam itself, wherein dwelt the richer and more eminent persons of Sutton society. Coal used to be delivered to Cheam houses through the lounge or drawing room and into the yard, which caused much embarrassment to any visiting clergy etc. A Cheam bye-law was thus passed which stipulated that all coal delivered in the Borough of Cheam should be properly housed in a box fitted with a hinged lid. Thus the term 'coalboxed' came to mean 'got rid of', 'tucked out of the way', along with the more commonly used phrase, 'That's put the lid on that, then!'

No longer in everyday East Cheam usage, this pretty phrase is in need of resurrection.

COBBLERS (A load of 'old')

Rubbish; unqualified and unsubstantiated fact; cheap fiction.

'What a load of "old" cobblers' is a slang expression in common usage today, but actually originated in East Cheam during the East Cheam Apprentice Boys Riots of 1785. Incensed by low wages, poor conditions and continual harassment from their employers, the apprentices of East Cheam met secretly to plan an uprising, but were dismayed to find that the apprentice boot-makers would not join their crusade.

Thereafter, the Union of Shoe and Boot Repairers were hailed as 'blacklegs' and the apprentices took a solemn oath to totally discount any statement issuing from any collection of cobblers. Thus the phrase 'a load of "old" cobblers' was accepted into the East Cheam vocabulary as meaning 'unworthy of attention'.

CODSWALLOP

Nonsense; a load of old cobblers (*see* above).

A 'wallop' (*see* below) being a sudden blow, and a cod being a type of oblong fish encased in orange crumbs found in cardboard boxes in supermarkets, a 'Cod's Wallop' can be literally translated as 'a sudden blow from a supermarket fish product'. It has now become more widely used to describe any nonsense or ridiculous fantasy, in that a 'wallop' from a box of fish fingers has no effect and therefore something which is 'codswallop' is utterly pointless.

A similar derivation, put forward by the East Cheam Alternative Dictionary, is that a 'wallop' is a part of the fish roughly equivalent to the human appendix, in that it has no useful function, and therefore a 'Cod's wallop' is useless. This suggestion however has been discarded by the author as being a 'load of old cobblers'.

COR BLIMEY

Expression of surprise.

From the Hebrew 'Cor', meaning measure, and 'Bloymeh', meaning ambush, and hence meaning 'a measure of surprise attack', but used nowadays simply as an exclamation of amazement.

CREW CUT

A style of haircutting which removes all superfluous hair to within one quarter of an inch of the scalp.

The crew cut was initiated by Lord Nelson during the Battle of New Orleans in 1845 because of the severe hindrance that was caused to battle manoeuvres by his crew having to stop and pick up their wigs when they were knocked off by the low ceilings in the *Victory*. He insisted that the ship's barber, Sweeny Todd, cut all the crew's hair to within a quarter inch of the scalp and banned the wearing of wigs. This, in turn, resulted in the famous 'Caine' mutiny of 1846, wherein Michael Caine, played by Fletcher Christian, led the crew into mutiny because Oliver 'Kiss Me' Hardy was excused the new haircut regulations.

DOG-END

The butt, or filter tip end of a smoked cigarette. Origin unknown.

DOG'S DINNER (Done up like a . . .)

To be dressed formally; clothed in a fashionable and distinguished manner; smartly attired.

During the late forties and early fifties it became increasingly important to the inhabitants of Cheam to disassociate themselves from the lower classes now occupying the seedier areas of the district, and particularly the 'cave-dwellers' in East Cheam. To exhibit their obvious higher class, Cheam council arranged for the people of East Cheam to go on bus tours of Cheam itself, and to demonstrate their infinite superiority they arranged for these tours to coincide with their pets' feeding time. Thus, a coachload of open-mouthed East Cheamites would witness the butler preparing twelve-inch steaks, garnished with parsley and red wine sauce, for the dog of the house. The phrase 'done up like a dog's dinner' thereafter was applied to anyone in East Cheam who had taken any unusual care with their dress.

DOLT

Dull fellow; stupid person.

Corruption of 'bolt', a slang term in the East Cheam vocabulary of the 1920s and onwards used to describe any rare and often unique inhabitant who was particularly bright or fast (as in a 'bolt of lightning'). The opposite description, 'dolt', meaning slow-witted and dull, didn't enter the East Cheam language until much later and probably coincided with the appearance of a certain William 'Billabong' Kerr, a wandering Australian.

DUCKS (Flying)

A wall decoration, usually occurring in triplicate. The geometrical positioning of three china or alabaster representations of undistinguishable breeds of duck depicted in flying mode, on an interior wall, normally above the mantelpiece or fire was very popular in East Cheam in the 1940s. The status of the owner would be gauged by the size and quality of the flying ducks, and those of 23 Railway Cuttings were probably modelled on starlings, cast in modelling plaster and hand-tinted with wax crayon.

FAG

1) Cigarette; snout (*see* Snout).
2) Errand boy serving college prefect.

FLICKS

Building, with public access, for the exhibition of cinematographical works of art; a cinema.
So called because of the 'flickering' motion of the projected image upon a large screen. (*See also* Pictures.)

FLUFF (A bit of . . .)

A term of endearment used to describe a member of the female sex.
'A bit of fluff', according to the East Cheam Cultural and Philosophy Club, refers to the light and delicate nature of the female sex, likening them to the feathery down used in making soft bedding. This is not to be confused with the more contemptuous description, 'a bit of skirt', which has long since been deleted from the East Cheam Dictionary.

GAS POKER

A hollow, thin, pointed length of metal, through which town gas would pass. This would be pre-ignited and inserted into the heap of nutty slack piled carelessly in the fire grate and would eventually cause the coal to burn. Though thin and hollow, the gas poker could be of considerable weight and was often utilised by East Cheam inhabitants as a weapon. Since the gas poker was also attached to a flexible tube (which would normally be connected to a gas terminal), the weapon was very accurate when in the hands of a skilled user. Highly recommended was the 'Fatlegs Hancock Double Twirl and Drop Shot', which could render a victim unconscious for days.

GRUB

Food, necessary for the continuation of human existence.
From the Latin 'Grubus', God of Cabinet Puddings.

GUINEAS

Unit of currency pre-decimalisation with a value of £1.05p.
This unit was used exclusively by the BBC, it having been granted to them in the famous Charter of Independence, which was actually signed on Cheam Bridge in 1933.

HAMMER (That's not really my . . .)

Thought to be a variation of 'That's not really my cup of tea', but of unknown origin. The author assumes it to be Cockney rhyming slang of some description and would welcome enlightenment from any student of the East Cheam language who may have further knowledge.

HOOTER

Nose; protrusion on face with air-holes.
The word is actually pronounced 'OOTER', as in 'Cor Blimey, look at the size of 'is OOTER', with the 'H' remaining silent in everyday usage and only added when in the company of bishops, magistrates and other such dignitaries as one might be having to tea on a Sunday afternoon.
The term derives from the resemblance between the sound that is omitted in the process of blowing the nose and that of a hooter or car horn.
The more advanced student of the East Cheam Language might well wish to try out a more menacing usage, or, as it is known in East Cheam, the 'Sid James approach' and ask: 'Are you looking for a bunch of fives up yer OOTER?' but beware, this is *not* recommended for beginners as it may result in some personal discomfort.

HOPPIT

Term of non-affectionate farewell used to signify that the person addressed should make an early exit.
'Go on, HOPPIT' means, literally, go away, push off, leave now. It is a blatant corruption of the term 'Go on Hoppity', a medieval phrase brought back from the Crusades by Little John, when he went to relieve Mafeking from the skiffle craze of 1865.

KIP

To sleep; to indulge in instantaneous slumber.
Shortened from KIPPER, which is a species of sleeping fish.

LIVIN' DAYLIGHTS

Dire threat, as in 'I'll beat the LIVIN' DAYLIGHTS out of you'.
An expression deriving from Transylvanian mythology wherein anything that moved at night was undead and anything that moved during the day was either Peter Cushing or a Hammer film crew.

MICKEY (Taking the . . .)
To make fun of; to ridicule.

A word introduced into the East Cheam language and, eventually, English slang, from the criminal underworld wherein a 'Mickey Finn', named after the inventor, was a drugged drink given to an unsuspecting victim with intent to render the person unconscious of his or her actions, thus making the victim liable to ridicule or fun. The actual usage of the phrase today has been reversed because the person 'taking the Mickey' is usually the aggressor rather than the victim.

MOCKERS (Putting the MOCKERS on)
To downgrade; to criticise severely.

'To put the mockers on' means to cast a dark cloud over the proceedings in such a way as to bring them into disrepute.

The Mockers were a sixteenth-century band of wandering minstrels from the West Country who invented, according to legend, a new kind of doleful music which was referred to as 'Granite and Sandwich'. They were hired by mischievous young vagabonds to play their music at social functions, especially weddings, where the Mockers would almost certainly reduce the audience to tears. Thus, bringing the Mockers on to the stage (or 'putting the Mockers on') meant to dampen a previously happy atmosphere.

The use of the term slipped into decline after 1587 when the leader of the band, Alfredus Mocker, was attacked and killed by a group of angry choirboys. It was revived in East Cheam, in 1949, in the Dog and Duck Saloon Bar with the début of the 'Whistling Hillbillies'.

MUG
1) Face; that part of the body containing the ooter and cakehole.
2) A poltroon; a person of gullible nature.
1) Cockney rhyming slang (Toby jug, mug) derived from the 'face' portrayed on Toby jugs.
2) In Shakespeare's *Twelfth Night and All's Well*, the character of Toby Falstaff, played by George Arliss, was a bit of a charlie, and therefore a toby jug – mug.

MUSH (Rhymes with bush)
1) Facial features; the characteristics of the face.
Originally a term used to describe boiled maize, 'mush' has come to mean 'face' since it was used by Oscar Wilde-Hammerstein to describe the face of Harry Whistler, which appeared to him to resemble boiled maize.
2) A name of anonymity; a name called when the true name is unknown. 'Oi, mush', or more expressively, 'Oi! Mush!': from the East Cheam Preparatory School for Sons of Gentlefolk, where the term 'Mush' or 'Mushty' was used to denote a fag (*see* FAG (2)) – derivation unknown.

NIBBLE (Not a . . .)
Zero; nothing; nil.

A fisherman's term of apology to the patient spouse who is at home with frying-pan poised. It refers to the lack of interest displayed by the attendant fish on contemplation of the bait offered, whereby the fish did not attempt to nibble the hook. In East Cheam terminology, the phrase is more often used as an expression of failure after a long evening's attempted 'bird-pulling'.

OAF
A person of low intellect; an idiot.

The word is Anglo-Saxon in origin and was brought over by the Vikings in 1566 when they landed at Hastings and overpowered the Budes of Laburnum Road. It comes from ancient legends concerning the fairies who would spirit away young children from their beds and, so that their parents would not miss them when they got up for their cornflakes in the morning, the fairies would leave a substitute child of far lesser intellect – an oaf.

PICTURES
Place of entertainment where cinema films are exhibited.

The cinema was known as the PICTURES (an abbreviation of 'Moving Pictures') for some considerable time, though only when referring to cinemas outside East Cheam. The Roxy, Canal Walk, East Cheam, was more familiarly known as 'The Flea Pit' because of the amazing variety of wildlife which used to fly over from the canal during the hot weather. These small creatures tended to congregate in front of the projection lens and render the screen blank, bringing forth catcalls, ice cream wrappers and assorted peanuts from the stalls and empty chocolate boxes from the circle.

PUDDING (Cabinet)
Type of dessert.

Cabinet pudding was a mixture of suet, lard, raisins and stale bread with water or syrup, which was boiled slowly in an enamel bath-tub over six gas rings. It was so called because a strong box or cabinet was required to support the weight of the cooked dish.

PUDDING SHUTE
Mouth; part of the face below nasal apparatus; throat.

Describing the mouth, the throat, or a combination of the two, the 'pudding shute' is in essence that part of the digestive system which first comes into contact with food. The correct pronunciation is 'puddin' shute', and the usage is wide and varied: 'Stuff that down yer pudding shute'; 'Do you want a punch up the pudding shute?'

QUID
Item of currency – value £1.00.
Originally meaning 'a piece of chewing tobacco', this word came to signify instead the cost of the said tobacco. Thus six ounces (one quid) of Lionel Everymore's Fragrant Chewing Tobacco cost £1.00, so the term 'quid' came to mean £1.00.

RADIOGRAM
Piece of furniture incorporating a radio.
The RADIOGRAM, which was very popular among the affluent consumer society in the 1950s, was a vast mahogany cabinet which, depending on its cost, would contain a cocktail cabinet, a sideboard, a cutlery drawer, a knife grinder, a wind-up record player, a selection of Tommy Steele records and a radio. The latter would be attached to some VALVES, a tuner, which could receive Radio Luxembourg in three different languages (all inaudible because of the static), and some loudspeakers, which pointed inwards to deflect the sound from the opposite wall and stop your neighbours from listening to *your* records.

RATBAG
Term of great endearment.
The word is usually used to compliment someone of a lower intellect than oneself, as in 'Get to bed ya ratbag'. It derives from the Latin *Rattus Baggus*, meaning 'one of great feet'.

RATION BOOK
Method of restricting goods to a specified amount per person.
Introduced during the Second World War, ration books were little green books containing stamps. They had to be presented to the seller, when buying a rationed item, who would remove the appropriate number of stamps (coupons) for the item purchased. Goods sold at Sid James' Nylons and Fancy Goods Emporium, Cheam, were exempt from this scheme by order of the local magistrate, Edwardian Fred.

RAY (Ted)
A popular radio comedian of the late fifties who starred in the series *Ray's a Laugh*.

ROZZERS
Upholders of the peace; policemen.
Derivation unknown at the time of going to press as the East Cheam Constabulary were unable to comment owing to the Billiard Tournament in the Police Canteen.

SKOBOLLOB
Word of greeting used by 'Bill and Ben, the Flowerpot Men', a young children's television programme of 1958/59. Original derivation unknown.

SNOUT or SNOWT
A cigarette.
Term used by infantrymen during the Crimean War, starring Burt Lancaster and Robert Mitchum. Because of the extensive use of nerve gas during this conflict, each soldier was issued with an extra ration of cigarettes and ordered to keep one in his mouth at all times. This gave the effect of the soldier having two noses, or snouts, causing the Japs in the opposite trenches to call: 'Oy, Tommy, want a light for yer snout?' (in Japanese, of course).

SPATS
Coverings for a man's legs to prevent his trousers from being splashed with mud.
Essential attire in the days before main drainage was introduced in East Cheam in 1962. Also called spatterdashes, they could be worn over or under the gaiters, depending on colour and taste.

STONE ME
Announcement of surprise; exclamation.
Derived not, as was earlier thought, from biblical times, but from the sudden removal of the Coronation Stone (as stood upon by King Canute when he burnt the cakes at Trafalgar, thus giving Mr Kipling sole rights to the eccles trade) whereupon Queen Victoria was heard to whisper, 'Stone me – It's gone!'
The saying came into popular usage in the Royal Borough of East Cheam because of the local association with Her Majesty, who once stopped off at Bert Grundy's Shoe Repair Shop to get Prince Albert's boots mended.

SWIPE ME
Announcement of shock; exclamation.
To swipe; to whisk away; to take suddenly by surprise.

TATTY
Run-down; no longer of good report.
From the French, *tati*, after the character in the film *La Plume de Mon Oncle*, in which Jacques Tati played a person of the road.

TOSH
Anonymity proclaimed.
Name given to a person (a) when the real name is unknown, or (b) to score points from in denying knowledge of the real name. 'Oi, Tosh!' means 'hey you'.

TRAM DRIVER
Person who drove trams.
A most respected profession in Cheam and one aspired to by many a mere tram conductor. Privileges included being allowed to wire up your television set to the overhead conductor wires.

TWIT
A person of low or zero intellect.
So called because of such a person's tendency to 'twitter' like a bird, making much noise but not conveying any intelligible message.
   (The author wishes to deny the statement made in the *East Cheam Alternative Dictionary* that a group, or collection, of TWITS is called The Tony Hancock Appreciation Society.)

VALVES
Glass objects, slightly smaller than light bulbs, which were found in groups inside a radio or television set. They glowed and hummed when working and often over-heated. A common saying in the East Cheam Radio Repair Shop was 'Sorry Squire, yer valve's gone!'

WHOPPER
1) Unusually large.
2) Unfounded lie.
Used to describe anything surprisingly big, as in 'Look at that ooter, what a whopper!', comes from the Texas 'Whoppers', large bison with exceptionally large molars, and the word crept into the English language when brought to East Cheam with the American Air Force. In return they took Miss Griselda Pugh, who was once described as a large bison with . . .

WIRELESS
An instrument of torture.
Designed to whirr into action ten minutes after it had been switched on, wirelesses were employed with the greatest effect between the years of 1954 and 1959, when they brought enjoyment to listeners, young and old, who tuned in to the broadcasts of *Hancock's Half-Hour*.

ACKNOWLEDGEMENTS

My sincere thanks to everybody who helped in the preparation of this book, especially to the Scriptwriters Alan Simpson and Ray Galton (who wish it to be known that they disassociate themselves from the rest of the rubbish, which was written entirely by me), and Richard Briers, Andrée Melly, Freddie Hancock, Peter Goodwright, Roger Hancock, Tessa Le Bars and David Nathan. Also thanks to Dennis Main Wilson for taking time out, from researching his own 'History of British Comedy' for the World Service, to contact me. Help with the research came from Nick Smith and Dorothy Hunt of the THAS Archive Department, with extra material from George Brown and Frank Tuffin.

On a personal note, thanks to my family (*all* of them), with deepest thanks to Elisabeth and Pearl for the encouragement.

Chris Bumstead

PICTURE CREDITS

BBC Enterprises: cover, 99 top, 100 (main picture), 104 bottom BBC Hulton Picture Library: 100 top, centre and bottom, 101 top left, top centre (inset), top right, bottom centre, bottom right, 104 top right BBC Written Archives Centre, Caversham: 8–9 Philip Glassborow: 104 top left Tessa Le Bars: 97, 101 centre L.R.C. Products Ltd: 68 Littlewoods Organisation PLC: 126 Photo Source: 99 bottom, 101 top centre Popperfoto: 98, 101 bottom left, 102 Radio Times: 34, 52, 68, 83, 110, 126, 145, 159 Redring Electric Ltd: 159 Sport and General Press Agency Ltd: 103.

NOTE

Chris Bumstead is retiring from the Presidency of the Tony Hancock Appreciation Society in 1988, but as the new address is not yet available all enquiries should be sent to 10 Devenish Road, Winchester, Hants, SO22 6EX.